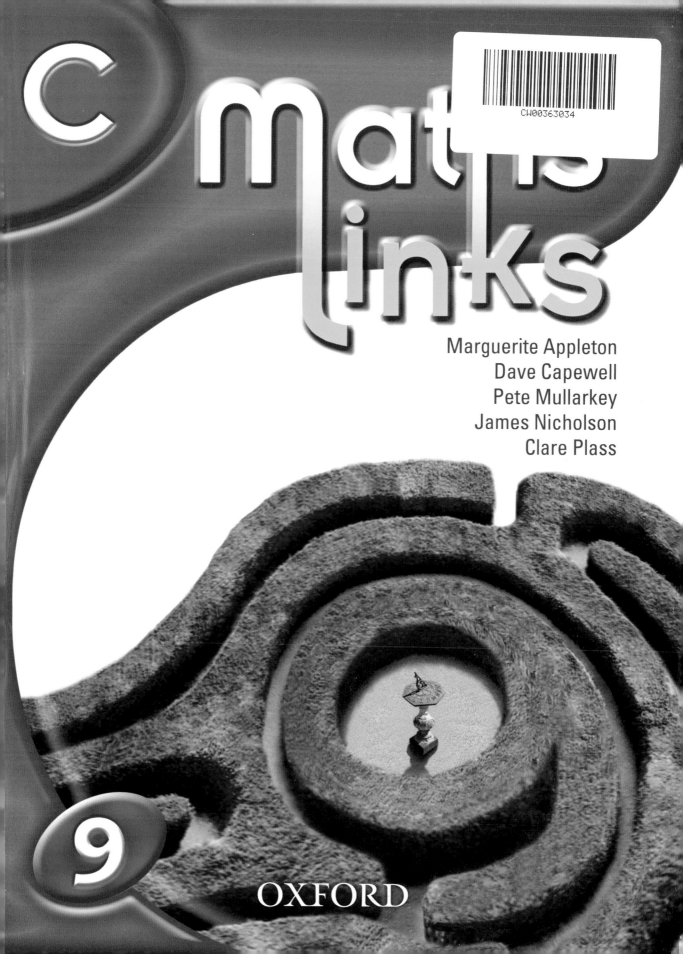

C

Maths links

Marguerite Appleton
Dave Capewell
Pete Mullarkey
James Nicholson
Clare Plass

9

OXFORD

OXFORD
UNIVERSITY PRESS

Great Clarendon Street, Oxford OX2 6DP

Oxford University Press is a department of the University of Oxford.
It furthers the University's objective of excellence in research, scholarship,
and education by publishing worldwide in

Oxford   New York

Auckland   Cape Town   Dar es Salaam   Hong Kong   Karachi
Kuala Lumpur   Madrid   Melbourne   Mexico City   Nairobi
New Delhi   Shanghai   Taipei   Toronto

With offices in

Argentina   Austria   Brazil   Chile   Czech Republic   France   Greece
Guatemala   Hungary   Italy   Japan   South Korea   Poland   Portugal
Singapore   Switzerland   Thailand   Turkey   Ukraine   Vietnam

Oxford is a registered trade mark of Oxford University Press
in the UK and in certain other countries

British Library Cataloguing in Publication Data

Data available

ISBN 9780199153046

10 9 8 7 6 5 4 3 2 1

Printed in Spain by Cayfosa (Impresia Iberica)

Paper used in the production of this book is a natural, recyclable product made from wood grown in sustainable forests.
The manufacturing process conforms to the environmental regulations of the country of origin.

Acknowledgements

The publisher would like to thank Pete Crawford for his work in creating the case studies.

The publisher is grateful for permission to reproduce the following photographs;

P7: Luis Cortes/Dreamstime.com; **P17:** Michael Jung/Shutterstock; **P21:** Janusz B/I-stock; **P23:** Mary Evans Picture Library/Photolibrary; **P29:** SuperlightR/Big Stock; **P33:** Mike Segar/Reuters; **P34t:** Jean Morrison/Shutterstock; **P34b:** NASA; **P35:** OUP/Photodisc/Digital Vision; **P39:** Bridgeman Art Library/Photolibrary; **P47:** Droste Holland; **P59:** AP Photo/Frederick News-Post; **P65:** OUP/Photodisc; **P77:** OUP/Corbis/Digital Stock; **P78l:** Alan Heartfield/Shutterstock; **P78r:** Michaela Stejskalova/Shutterstock; **P79:** Péter Gudella/Shutterstock; **P81:** Franc Podgor_ek/Shutterstock; **P88:** Nagy-Bagoly Arpad/Shutterstock; **P97:** Sebastian Kaulitzki/Dreamstime.com; **P103t:** Megan Paonessa; **P105t:** Steve Skinner/Dreamstime.com; **p105m:** Robert Pratta/Reuters; **P105b:** STR New/Reuters; **P113:** OUP/Photodisc; **P131:** Derek Proctor/Dreamstime.com; **P135:** OUP/Photodisc; **P139:** OUP/Photodisc; **P141:** Shutterstock/Brett Mulcahy; **P143:** Nick Biemans/Shutterstock; **P149:** OUP/Digital Vision; **P150b:** OUP/Photodisc; **P151b:** Hirlesteanu Constantin-Ciprian/Shutterstock; **P151t:** Andres Rodriguez/Dreamstime.com; **P150t:** Jonathan Ross/Dreamstime.com; **P171:** OUP/Image Source; **P174:** Achim Prill/I-stock; **P175:** Gary Ombler/Dorling Kindersley/Getty Images/James R; **P177:** Gallivan, Pomona CA; **P189:** OUP/Photodisc; **P197:** OUP/Photodisc; **P201:** OUP/Photodisc; **P213:** Royal Geographical Society; **P215:** Russell Kightley/Science Photo Library; **P219:** Philip Halling; **P221:** Chrislofoto/Shutterstock; **P225:** Jodie Coston/I-stock; **P227:** Johannes Compaan/Dreamstime.com; **P228t:** OUP/Photodisc; **P228b:** OUP/Photodisc; **P233:** Mazor/Dreamstime.com; **P133:** Reed Daigle/Dreamstime.com; **P153:** OUP/Digital Vision. **CASE STUDY 1: THE GOLDEN RATIO**, Dmitry Kovyazin/Dreamstime.com; Rixie/Dreamstime.com; Feng Yu/Dreamstiem.com; Valentín García/Dreamstime.com; Parfta/Dreamstime.com; John Archer/I-stock; Christophe Testi/Dreamstime.com **CASE STUDY 2: GARDEN DESIGN** Achim Prill/I-stock; Lucian Coman/I-stock; Sierpniowka/Dreamstime.com; Felinda/I-stock; Robyn Mackenzie/Dreamstime.com; Elena Elisseeva/Dreamstime.com; TT/I-stock; Fernando Soares/Dreamstime.com; Jan Rihak/I-stock; Gerald Hng/Dreamstime.com; Hanquan Chen/I-stock; Yakobchuk/Dreamstime.com. **CASE STUDY 3: TELEVISION VIEWING FIGURES** Tony Cordoza/Alamy; Scott Weichert/Dreamstime.com; Applee/Dreamstime.com; Darko Novakovic/Dreamstime.com; Haywiremedia/Dreamstime.com; Lisa Thornberg/I-stock; Sergey Dolgikh/I-stock. **CASE STUDY 4: HOW DO THINGS FALL?** Cláudio Belli/I-stock; Corbis; Swim Ink 2, LLC/Corbis; Walter Lockwood/Corbis.

Figurative artwork is by Geo Parkin

Contents

1 Algebra

Sequences and graphs

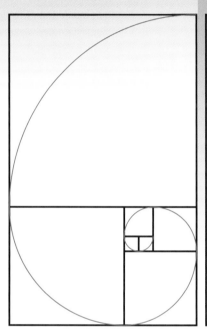

Each term in the Fibonacci sequence is found by adding the two previous terms.

1, 1, 2, 3, 5, 8, 13, 21, 34, 55, 89, 144...

The ratios of successive terms,

$\frac{1}{1} = 1$, $\frac{2}{1} = 2$, $\frac{3}{2} = 1.5$, $\frac{5}{3} = 1.6$, $\frac{8}{5} = 1.666$,

$\frac{13}{8} = 1.625$, $\frac{21}{13} = 1.615$, $\frac{34}{21} = 1.619$, ...

approaches the **golden ratio**, $\phi = 1.618...$, as the sequence approaches infinity.

Rectangles with sides in this ratio are said to be the most pleasing to the eye.

What's the point? The golden ratio is found repeatedly in nature, art and architecture. Maths is an intrinsic part of the world around us.

✓ Check in

Level 5

1 For each of these sequences
   i   write, in words, the term-to-term rule
   ii find the missing numbers.
   a 3, 6, 9, ☐, 15, . . .   b 2, 7, ☐, 17, 22, . . .   c 4, 7, ☐, ☐, 16, . . .
   d 21, ☐, ☐, 9, 5, . . .   e 5, ☐, 21, ☐, 37, . . .   f 50, ☐, 38, ☐, 26, . . .

Level 6

2 Write the equation of each of these lines.

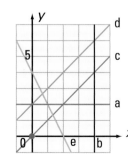

It may help to construct a table of values for each graph.

- Generate terms of a sequence given a position-to-term rule
- Write and justify the position-to-term rule of a sequence

Keywords
Justify   Position-to-
Linear   term
nth term   Sequence

- The **position-to-term** rule of a **sequence** allows you to find any term by substituting into a formula.

This sequence is **linear** because the difference between consecutive terms is a constant, 7.

In the sequence 7, 14, 21, 28, 35, . . .
the position-to-term rule or **nth term** is $T(n) = 7n$.

example

Find the position-to-term rule of the sequence 2, 7, 12, 17, 22

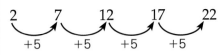

The difference between consecutive terms is 5 so the nth term involves the 5 times table.

Position number, n	1	2	3	4	5	
5 times table	5	10	15	20	25	×5
nth term, $T(n)$	2	7	12	17	22	-3

The nth term is in words 'multiply by 5 and subtract 3'
    as a formula $T(n) = 5n - 3$
Check, $T(1) = 5 \times 1 - 3 = 2$ ✓, $T(2) = 5 \times 2 - 3 = 7$ ✓

The nth term of a linear sequence has the form $T(n) = an + b$ where a is the difference between consecutive terms.

- A pattern of diagrams may contain linear sequences. You can use diagrams to **justify** the form of the nth term.

example

1 Pentagon   2 Pentagons   3 Pentagons   4 Pentagons

The formula that relates the number of pentagons, p, to the number of straws, s, is
    $s = 4p + 1$.
Justify the form of this rule by referring to the diagrams.

These are irregular pentagons. Regular pentagons have all sides the same length and all angles the same size.

The rule works because every new pentagon requires 4 straws plus 1 straw is needed to complete the first pentagon.

Plus 1 straw to complete the first pentagon.

4 straws for the first pentagon.

4 more straws for the second pentagon.

Exercise 1a

1 Generate the first five terms of a sequence whose nth term is given by

a $T(n) = n + 10$ **b** $T(n) = 4n$ **c** $T(n) = n - 5$

d $T(n) = 2n + 3$ **e** $T(n) = 5n - 1$ **f** $T(n) = \frac{1}{2}n + 1$

g $T(n) = 21 - n$ **h** $T(n) = 53 - 3n$

2 Find the nth term of each sequence.

a 6, 12, 18, 24, 30, . . .   **b** 0, 1, 2, 3, 4, . . .

c 4, 7, 10, 13, 16, . . .   **d** 7, 17, 27, 37, 47, . . .

e 36, 42, 48, 54, 60, . . .   **f** -8, -3, 2, 7, 12, . . .

g 1.2, 1.4, 1.6, 1.8, 2.0, . . .   **h** $1\frac{1}{3}, 1\frac{2}{3}, 2, 2\frac{1}{3}, 2\frac{2}{3}, \ldots$

i 49, 48, 47, 46, 45, . . .   **j** 68, 61, 54, 47, 40, . . .

k -3, -8, -13, -18, -23, . . .   **l** $1\frac{1}{2}, 1, \frac{1}{2}, 0, -\frac{1}{2}, \ldots$

3 Using the information given for each sequence

    i find $T(n)$

    ii hence generate the first five terms of the sequence.

    a $T(10) = 29$, $T(11) = 32$ and $T(12) = 35$

    b $T(8) = 42$ and $T(10) = 52$.

> There are two differences between the 8th and 10th terms.

4 Jason makes a pattern of simple fish shapes using lollipop sticks.

| 1 fish | 2 fishes | 3 fishes |

a Find a formula that connects the number of fishes, f, to the number of lollipop sticks, l.

b Explain why this formula works.

c Jason wants to make a wall frieze using 50 fishes. How many lollipop sticks will he need?

investigation

The position-to-term rule of a sequence is $T(n) = 2n + b$, where b is a constant.

> A constant is a fixed value, that is, a number.

a Write the difference between consecutive terms of this sequence.

b Write the value of b if

    i the first term is 0

    ii the sequence consists of the odd numbers, starting from 1.

c Investigate other sequences of the form $T(n) = 3n + b$, $T(n) = 4n + b$, . . . $T(n) = an + b$.

- Generate terms of a quadratic sequence given a position-to-term rule
- Write the position-to-term rule of a quadratic sequence

Keywords
Coefficient   Second
nth term   difference
Quadratic

In the **quadratic** sequence the first difference increases but the **second difference** is constant.

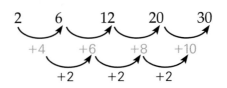

In a quadratic sequence the difference between consecutive terms may increase or decrease.

- A sequence is linear if the first difference is constant and quadratic if the second difference is constant.

- The position-to-term rule of a quadratic sequence is always of the form
  $$T(n) = an^2 + bn + c$$
  where the **coefficients** a, b and c are constants.

A coefficient is a number that multiplies an algebraic term.

The coefficients b and c may be equal to zero.

- The coefficient a is always half the value of the second difference.

---

example

Find the position-to-term rule of the sequence 3, 11, 23, 39, 59, . . .

3   11   23   39   59

+8   +12   +16   +20

+4   +4   +4

The second difference is 4 and so $a = \frac{1}{2} \times 4 = 2$.
The formula will contain $2n^2$.

Position number, n	1	2	3	4	5
Sequence, $T(n)$	3	11	23	39	59
Quadratic term, $2n^2$	2	8	18	32	50
Linear part, $T(n) - 2n^2$	1	3	5	7	9

+2   +2   +2   +2

When $n = 5$,
$2n^2 = 2 \times 5^2 = 50$.

Subtracting the quadratic term from the sequence leaves a linear sequence.

2 times table, $2n$	2	4	6	8	10
Subtract 1, -1	-1	-1	-1	-1	-1
Linear part, $2n - 1$	1	3	5	7	9

The difference is always 2 so the nth term of the linear part involves the 2 times table.

The **nth term** is $T(n) = 2n^2 + 2n - 1$.

Exercise 1b

1 Generate the first five terms of each quadratic sequence if

a $T(n) = n^2$ **b** $T(n) = 3n^2$ **c** $T(n) = 2n^2 - 1$

d $T(n) = n^2 - 5$ **e** $T(n) = 10 - 2n^2$ **f** $T(n) = n^2 + 2n$

g $T(n) = 2n^2 - 3n$ **h** $T(n) = n^2 + 3n - 5$ **i** $T(n) = 4n^2 - 2n + 1$

j $T(n) = \dfrac{n(n-1)}{2}$

2 Complete the differences and nth terms for these quadratic sequences.

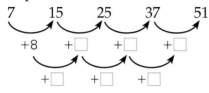

$$n\text{th term} = \square n^2 + 5n + 1$$

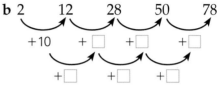

$$n\text{th term} = \square n^2 + \square n - 2$$

3 Find the nth term of each of these quadratic sequences.

a 2, 8, 18, 32, 50, . . .   **b** 5, 20, 45, 80, 125, . . .

c 2, 5, 10, 17, 26, . . .   **d** -1, 2, 7, 14, 23, . . .

e 4, 10, 18, 28, 40, . . .   **f** 7, 18, 33, 52, 75, . . .

g 0, 1, 4, 9, 16, . . .   **h** 6, 15, 28, 45, 66, . . .

4 Aliens from the planet Zorg have a pattern of dots on their chest which relates to how old they are.

a Copy and complete this table of values.

b Find the rule that connects the age of the alien in years, n, to the number of dots on their chest, $T(n)$.

1 year old   2 years old   3 years old

Age of alien in years, n	1	2	3
Number of dots, $T(n)$			

c Work out the number of dots on an alien aged 100 years.

d King Zorgon states that he uses the formula $T(n) = n(n + 1)$. Explain why this formula works and prove that it is equivalent to the formula you found in part **a**.

> Expand the brackets.

A quadratic sequence has the general term $T(n) = an^2 + bn + c$

a Write an expression for $T(1)$ by substituting $n = 1$ into the formula.

b Write expressions for $T(2)$, $T(3)$ and $T(4)$.

c Using your knowledge of algebra, write the differences between consecutive terms in this sequence.

> As the sequence is quadratic the second difference is constant.

d Find the second difference and hence prove that the second difference in a quadratic sequence is always $2a$.

- Explore spatial patterns for triangular and square numbers

Keywords
Square numbers
Triangular numbers

Here are the first four terms in the sequence of **square numbers**.

To square a number you multiply the number by itself.

T(1) = 1   T(2) = 4   T(3) = 9   T(4) = 16

- The general term of the sequence of square numbers is $T(n) = n^2$.

A triangular pattern of dots forms the sequence of **triangular numbers**.

T(1) = 1   T(2) = 3   T(3) = 6   T(4) = 10

- To find the nth triangular number add a row of n dots to the $(n - 1)$th triangle
  $$T(n) = T(n - 1) + n.$$

The $(n - 1)$th triangle is the one before the nth triangle.

| 1 dot |
| 2 dots |
| 3 dots |
| 4 dots |
| 5 dots | $T(5) = 1 + 2 + 3 + 4 + 5 = 15$

To find the 5th triangular number add a row of 5 dots to the 4th triangle

You can find the nth triangular number by evaluating the sum
$$T(n) = 1 + 2 + 3 + \cdots + n.$$
This formula becomes tedious when you want to find the 50th or 100th triangular number.
You can find a general formula using rectangles.

T(1) + T(1)   T(2) + T(2)   T(3) + T(3)   T(4) + T(4)
= 1 × 2   = 2 × 3   = 3 × 4   = 4 × 5

Each rectangle is made of two identical triangles. The number of dots in a rectangle is twice the triangular number.

The number of dots in the nth rectangle is $n(n + 1)$, so $2T(n) = n(n + 1)$.

- The general term of the sequence of triangular numbers is $T(n) = \frac{1}{2}n(n + 1)$.

Exercise 1c

1 The formula for the sum of the whole numbers from 1 to n is
$T(n) = \frac{1}{2}n(n+1)$.

Use this formula to find the sum of the whole numbers from 1 to

a 10   **b** 20   **c** 50   **d** 100   **e** 1000.

2

$T(1) = 1$ $T(2) = 1 + 3$ $T(3) = 1 + 3 + 5$

a Draw the next two diagrams in this sequence.
The nth term for this sequence
is in words 'sum the consecutive odd numbers from
1 to $2n - 1$'
as a formula $T(n) = 1 + 3 + 5 + 7 + \cdots + (2n - 1)$.

b By inspecting the shape of the diagrams find another way
of writing the nth term of this sequence.

c Use your answer to part **b** to find the sum of the
odd numbers from 1 to 49.

> **Did you know?**
>
> Since Pythagoras
> people have been
> fascinated by num-
> bers arising from pat-
> terns of objects. The
> square based pyramid
> gives the sequence
> 1, 5, 14, 30, 51, 91, ...
> $\frac{1}{6}n(n + 1)(2n + 1)$.

3

   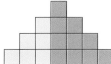

> Hint: Move the lightly
> shaded bricks in order to
> create a new shape.

Write a formula that relate the height of the pile, h, to the
number of bricks, b.

4 Lynda asks her Dad for some pocket money and is offered two choices.
Option 1 1 penny on the first day, 2 pennies on the second day,
3 pennies on the third day for one whole year.
Option 2 £20 per month for one whole year.
Advise Lynda on which option to choose, showing the total
amount of pocket money that she receives for each choice.

2 lines
1 crossing

3 lines
3 crossings

From the diagram you can see that the *maximum* number
of times that two straight-lines can cross is once. The *maximum*
number of times that three straight-lines can cross is three.

a Draw diagrams for four and five straight lines and construct a table of results.

b Predict how the sequence continues and draw diagrams to check.

c Explain why the sequence continues in this way.

investigation

- Generate points and plot graphs of linear functions
- Recognise that equations of the form $y = mx + c$ correspond to straight line graphs
- Given values for m and c, find the gradient of lines given by equations of the form $y = mx + c$

Keywords
Equation   Linear function
Explicit   Straight line
Implicit   graph

 p. 134

- The **equation** of a **straight line graph** can be expressed in the form
  $y = mx + c$, where m is the gradient and c is the y-intercept.

The gradient, m, is a measure of the steepness of the line.

---

example

A straight line has equation $6x - 2y = 1$.
Write   **a** the gradient
            b the coordinates of the y-intercept.

The y-intercept is the point at which the line cuts the y-axis. The coordinates of this point are $(0, c)$.

· ·

The equation $6x - 2y = 1$ is in **implicit** form.

Rearranging gives $6x = 1 + 2y$ Add $2y$ to both sides.

$\qquad\qquad\quad 6x - 1 = 2y$ Subtract 1 from both sides.

$\qquad\qquad\quad 3x - \frac{1}{2} = y$ Divide both sides by 2.

When y is the subject, an equation is in explicit form. When y is not the subject, an equation is in implicit form.

In **explicit** form the equation is
$$y = 3x - \frac{1}{2}.$$ Compare this equation with $y = mx + c$.

a Gradient, 3   **b** Intercept, $(0, -\frac{1}{2})$

- To plot the graph of a **linear function**, construct a table of values. A linear function will always produce a straight line graph.

A linear function does not contain variables with powers.
$y = 5x + 2$ is a linear function.
$y = x^2 + x - 12$ is not a linear function.

example

a Plot the graph of $y = 5 - 3x$ on a pair of coordinate axes.
b Without plotting, explain how you know that the graphs $y = 5 - 3x$ and $y = 2 - 3x$ do not intersect.

· ·

a

x	0	1	2
y	5	2	-1

b $y = 5 - 3x$ and $y = 2 - 3x$
both have gradient = -3
and hence are parallel.
Parallel lines do not intersect.

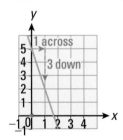

A gradient of -3 means that for every 1 unit across you move 3 units *down*.
A gradient of +3 means that for every 1 unit across you move 3 units *up*.

Exercise 1d

1 Match each graph with its equation.

a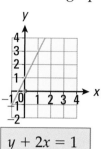

b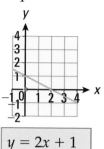

c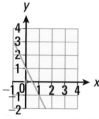

A $y + 2x = 1$

B $y = 2x + 1$

C $y = 1 - \frac{1}{2}x$

2 a Copy and complete the table of values for the equation $y = 4 - 3x$.

x	0	1	2
y		1	

b Plot these values on a set of coordinate axes.

c Write the equation of a line that is parallel to $y = 4 - 3x$.

3 Construct a table of values for each of these equations and hence plot their graphs.

a $y = 3$ **b** $x = -1$ **c** $y = 5x + 1$ **d** $2y = x + 2$ **e** $2x + y = 10$

4 Are these statements true or false?

a The point (2, 5) lies on the line $y = 4x - 3$.

b The lines $2y = 6x + 1$ and $y - 3x = 1$ do not intersect.

c The lines $x = 2$ and $y = -3$ are perpendicular.

5 Write the equations of these straight lines.

a The line has a gradient of 3 and passes through (0, 5).

b The line has a gradient of 2 and passes through (3, 5).

c The line passes through (0, 1) and (1, 5).

6

A $y = 2x - 1$ B $y = x + 2$ C $x + y = 5$ D $y - 2x = 3$ E $y = 2(1 - x)$

Make a sketch of these graphs to find the pair of perpendicular lines.

Choosing from the equations above, find

a a pair of parallel lines.

b a pair of lines with the same y-intercept.

c a pair of perpendicular lines.

challenge

Write the equations of the four straight lines that make up the sides of this parallelogram.

What do you notice about the equations?

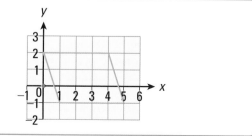

- Draw mapping diagrams for simple functions
- Find the inverse of a linear function
- Plot the graph of a linear function and its inverse

Keywords
Function
Inverse
Linear

• A **function** is a rule that maps every input to a unique output.

A linear function is a function that produces a straight line graph.

The **linear** function $x \rightarrow 3x - 2$ can be represented by a mapping diagram.

In words $x \rightarrow 3x - 2$ reads 'multiply by 3 and subtract 2'.

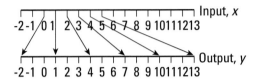

• Every linear function has an **inverse** function that reverses the direction of the mapping.

The inverse mapping diagram is the 'reversal' of the mapping diagram for the function $x \rightarrow 3x - 2$.

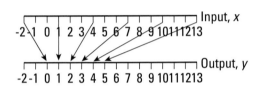

The inverse function is $x \rightarrow \dfrac{x + 2}{3}$.

The operation that was performed last is 'subtract 2' so this is undone first.

Addition and subtraction are inverse operations
Multiplication and division are inverse operations.

---

example

a Plot the linear function $y = 2x + 5$ and its inverse on the same graph.
b Write the line of symmetry.

∙∙

a Read the function $y = 2x + 5$ as 'multiply by 2 and add 5'.
The reverse is 'subtract 5 and divide by 2'.
The inverse function is $y = \dfrac{2x - 5}{3}$.
Constructing tables of values gives

x	0	1	2
$y = 2x + 5$	5	7	9

x	5	7	9
$y = \dfrac{x - 5}{2}$	0	1	2

b The line of symmetry is $y = x$.

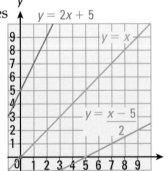

A function can be written as a mapping $x \rightarrow 3x - 2$ or an equation $y = 3x - 2$.

Notice that the x and y values are simply reversed in the two tables.

• A function and its inverse are reflections in the line $y = x$.

Exercise 1e

1 The identity function $x \rightarrow x$ maps any number onto itself.
Draw a mapping diagram to represent the identity function.

2 a Copy and complete this mapping
diagram for $x \rightarrow 3(x - 1)$.
Use values of x from 0 to 5.

b Draw the inverse mapping diagram
for $x \rightarrow 3(x - 1)$.

c Find the inverse of $x \rightarrow 3(x - 1)$.

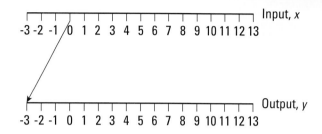

3 Find the inverse of each of these functions.

a $x \rightarrow x + 5$ **b** $x \rightarrow 7x$ **c** $x \rightarrow 4x + 3$

d $x \rightarrow 2x - 9$ **e** $x \rightarrow 5(x + 1)$ **f** $x \rightarrow \dfrac{x - 1}{4}$

g $x \rightarrow \dfrac{1}{2}x + 10$ **h** $x \rightarrow x^2$ **i** $x \rightarrow \dfrac{1}{x}$

4 For each table, find the function that maps the x-values onto
the y-values.

a

x	y
1	3
2	6
3	9
4	12

b

x	y
2	0
3	1
4	2
5	3

c

x	y
0	3
1	5
2	7
3	9

> If the inverse of a function
> is the same as the function
> then the function is self-
> inverse.

5 a Copy and complete this mapping diagram for $x \rightarrow 5 - x$.
Use values of x from 0 to 5.

b Draw the inverse mapping diagram for $x \rightarrow 5 - x$.

c By inspecting the diagrams, write the inverse of $x \rightarrow 5 - x$.

d Write the inverse function of $x \rightarrow c - x$ where c is a constant.

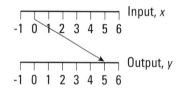

6 For each of the following
  i copy the graph and draw the
    inverse function on the same diagram
  ii write the equation of the
    graph and its inverse.

a

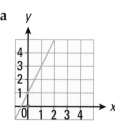

b

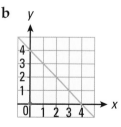

> You can use the fact that a function and its inverse are reflections in the line $y = x$
> in order to draw the graphs of more complex functions.
> **a** Plot the graph of $y = x^2$ and hence sketch the graph of $y = \sqrt{x}$.
> **b** Plot the graph of $y = x^3$ and hence sketch the graph of $y = \sqrt[3]{x}$.

- Know properties of quadratic functions
- Generate points and plot graphs of simple quadratic functions

Keywords
Parabola
Quadratic function

p. 138

- A **quadratic function** has an x^2 term as its highest power of x
  - examples are, $y = x^2$, $y = 3x^2 - 1$, $y = 3 - 2x - x^2$.

- The curved graph produced by a quadratic function is called a **parabola**.

A linear function produces a straight line graph.

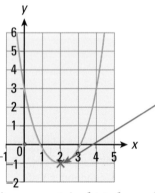

The parabolas have a line of symmetry that passes through the minimum or maximum point.

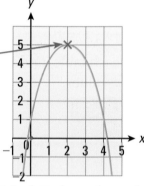

A symmetrical ∪ shaped graph is produced by positive x^2 terms.

A symmetrical ∩ shaped graph is produced by negative x^2 terms.

example

a Plot the graph of the function $y = x^2 - 2x - 3$.
b Write the equation of the line of symmetry of the curve.
c Write the coordinates of the minimum point of the curve.

. . . .

a Construct a table of values.

x	-2	-1	0	1	2	3	4
x^2	4	1	0	1	4	9	16
$-2x$	4	2	0	-2	-4	-6	-8
-3	-3	-3	-3	-3	-3	-3	-3
y	5	0	-3	-4	-3	0	5

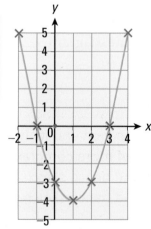

This curve will be a ∪ shaped parabola as the x^2 term is positive.

Plot the coordinate pairs
(-2, 5), (-1, 0), (0, -3), (1, -4), (2, -3), (3, 0) and (4, 5).
b The line of symmetry is $x = 1$.
c The minimum point is (1, -4).

Exercise 1f

Grade C

1 a Copy and complete the table of values for the function $y = x^2 - x$.

x	-3	-2	-1	0	1	2	3	4
x^2		4					9	
-x		2					-3	
y		6					6	

The equation of the line of symmetry is $x = c$, but in this instance the constant c is not an integer.

b Plot the graph of $y = x^2 - x$.

c Write the equation of the line of symmetry of the curve.

2 a Copy and complete the table of values for the function $y = x^2 + x - 2$.

x	-4	-3	-2	-1	0	1	2	3
x^2		9					4	
x		-3					2	
-2		-2					-2	
y		4					4	

The coordinates of the minimum point cannot be read from the table. It must be read from the graph.

b Plot the graph of $y = x^2 + x - 2$.

c Write the coordinates of the minimum point of the curve.

3 a Plot the graph of $y = x^2 - 4x + 3$ for values of x from -1 to 5.

b Write the equation of the line of symmetry of the curve.

c Write the coordinates of the y-intercept of the curve.

d Write the coordinates of the points where the curve crosses the x-axis.

4 This is the graph of $y = x^2 - x - 6$.

a Make an accurate copy of this graph on squared paper.

b On the same diagram, plot the graph of the linear function $y = x - 3$

c Write the coordinates of the points of intersection of these two graphs.

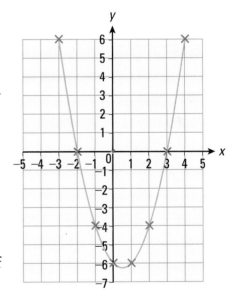

investigation

A cubic function has an x^3 term as its highest power of x. By plotting simple functions, determine the general shape of a cubic graph. Look at what happens to the shape for positive and negative x^3 terms.

Begin by drawing $y = x^3$.

1a

1 For sequences with the following nth terms, find

    i T(10)   **ii** T(100)

    a $T(n) = n + 5$ **b** $T(n) = 5n + 3$

    c $T(n) = 2n - 9$ **d** $T(n) = 10 - 2n$

2 The position-to-term rule of a sequence is $T(n) = an + b$,
where a and b are constants.

    a Write the value of a if the sequence is increasing in steps of 5.

    b What can you say about a if the sequence is decreasing in equal steps?

3 Find the nth term of each of these sequences.

    a 3, 8, 13, 18, 23, . . .   **b** -5, -2, 1, 4, 7, . . .

    c 29, 28, 27, 26, 25, . . .   **d** $2\frac{2}{3}, 2\frac{1}{3}, 2, 1\frac{2}{3}, 1\frac{1}{3}, \ldots$

1b

4 Find the nth term of each of these quadratic sequences.

    a 3, 12, 27, 48, 75, . . .   **b** 3, 6, 11, 18, 27, . . .

    c 5, 12, 21, 32, 45, . . .   **d** 1, 6, 15, 28, 45, . . .

5 Each dress has an embroidered
pattern of squares which relates
to its size.

  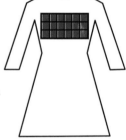

Age 1 year   Age 2 years   Age 3 years

    a Copy and complete this table
of values.

Dress size (age in years), n	1	2	3
Number of squares, T(n)			

    b Find the rule that connects the dress size, n, to the number
of embroidered squares, T(n).

    c The manufacturer of this dress state that they use the formula
$T(n) = n(n + 3)$. Explain why this formula works and prove that it
is equivalent to the formula you found in part **b**.

1c

6

Hint: Move the lightly
shaded tins in order to
create a rectangle.

Mr Stewart stacks tins in the formations above. Find a
formula that connects the height of each stack, h, to the
number of tins, t, in the stack

7 The sum of two consecutive triangular numbers is always a square number.

   a Use diagrams to test this statement for particular cases.

   b Copy and complete this statement:

     '$T(n-1) + T(n) = \square$ where $T(n)$ is the nth triangular number.'

8 **a** Write the equation $4x = 2y + 1$ in explicit form.

   b Copy and complete the table of values for the equation
$4x = 2y + 1$

x	0	1	2
y			

   c Plot these values on a pair of coordinate axes and join them with a straight line.

   d Write the coordinates of the point where the line $4x = 2y + 1$ intercepts the y-axis.

9 Find the inverse of each of these functions.

   a $x \rightarrow x - 3$ **b** $x \rightarrow \frac{x}{2}$ **c** $x \rightarrow 10x$

   d $x \rightarrow 5x - 2$ **e** $x \rightarrow 3(x + 4)$ **f** $x \rightarrow \dfrac{x + 7}{3}$

10 **a** Copy this graph and label the line with its equation.

    b On the same diagram draw the inverse of this graph and label it with its equation.

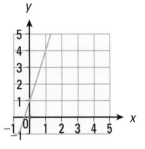

11 **a** Copy and complete the table of values for the function
$y = x^2 - 2x - 3$.

    b Plot the graph of $y = x^2 - 2x - 3$.

    c Write the equation of the line of symmetry of the curve.

    d Write the coordinates of the minimum point of the curve.

x	-2	-1	0	1	2	3	4
x^2	4			1			
$-2x$	4			-2			
-3	-3			-3			
y	5			-4			

1 Summary

Assessment criteria
- Plot graphs of simple quadratic functions **Level 7**
- Find the next term of quadratic sequences and functions **Level 7**

Level 7

1 Plot the graph of
$y = 2x^2 - 10$ for $-3 \leq x \leq 3$

Marisa's answer ✔

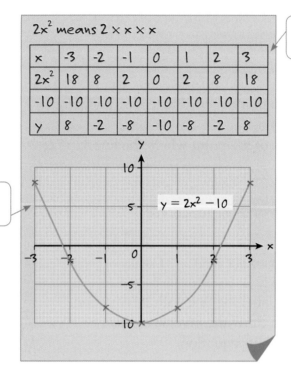

$2x^2$ means $2 \times x \times x$

x	-3	-2	-1	0	1	2	3
$2x^2$	18	8	2	0	2	8	18
-10	-10	-10	-10	-10	-10	-10	-10
y	8	-2	-8	-10	-8	-2	8

Marisa constructs a table of values.

She expects a U shaped curve.

$y = 2x^2 - 10$

Level 7

2 a The nth term of a sequence is $3n + 4$
What is the 8th term of the sequence?

b The nth term of a different sequence is $\dfrac{n - 2}{n^2}$.
Write down the first three terms of this sequence.

KS3 2005 6–8 Paper 2

Proportional reasoning

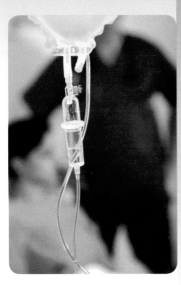

Doctors and nurses must be able to calculate accurately doses of medicines. The patient needs

75 mg of drug A which comes in a solution containing 5 mg/ml

0.5 litres of drug B to be delivered over 12 hours via an intravenous drip for which 20 drops = 1 ml.

How many 5 ml spoonfuls of liquid should you give? How many drops/minute should you set the IV machine to?

What's the point? Proportional reasoning is needed to calculate each of these drug doses. The fact that an error could be life threatening means you must also be able to check the answers.

 **Check in**

Level 5

1 Round each of these numbers to the nearest
 i 10 **ii** 1 dp **iii** 3 dp
 a 12.9725 **b** 342.91378

Level 6

2 Evaluate each of these expressions, giving your answer as a fraction in its simplest form.
 a $\frac{2}{7} + \frac{1}{3}$ **b** $\frac{4}{7} - \frac{2}{5}$ **c** $\frac{2}{3} \times \frac{4}{5}$ **d** $\frac{2}{3} \div \frac{4}{5}$

3 Calculate
 a $\frac{3}{7}$ of £84 **b** $\frac{3}{5}$ of 28 kg **c** Increase £60 by 8% **d** Decrease £350 by 3.5%

4 Write each of these ratios in their simplest form.
 a 18 : 24 **b** 169 : 65 **c** 350 g : 1.5 kg

5 **a** 3 kg of beef costs 840p. What is the cost of 2 kg of beef?
 b A recipe for eight people uses 440 g of potato.
 How much potato do you need for three people?

2a Significant figures

- Round to a given number of significant figures
- Use rounding to make estimates

Keywords
Estimate   Significant
Place value   figure
Rounding

The position of a digit in a number is called its **place value**.

- The first non-zero digit in a number is called the first **significant figure** because it has the greatest value.

First significant figure is 2;   Third significant figure is 4;
it has the value 2 tens = 20. → 23.456   it has the value 4 tenths = 0.4

Second significant figure is 3;
it has the value 3 units = 3.

- You can use significant figures to **round** numbers.

example

Round the number 1234.5678 to
a 1 sf   **b** 3 sf   **c** 5 sf.

· ·

Work out the degree of rounding required for each answer.
a The first significant figure is in the thousands column.
       1234.5678 = 1000 (1 sf)   round to the nearest 1000.

b The third significant figure is in the tens column.
       12**3**4.5678 = 1230 (3 sf)   round to the nearest 10.

c The fifth significant figure is in the tenths column (first
   decimal place).
       1234.**5**678 = 1234.6 (5 sf)   round to 1 decimal place.

When you round a number
you always look at the next
digit
– if it is 5 or more then the
  number is rounded up
– if it is less than 5 then the
  number stays the same
  (rounded down).

- You can use significant figures to round numbers of
  different sizes.

example

Estimate $\dfrac{23 \times 189}{3.9}$

· ·

Round each number in the calculation to 1 significant figure.

$$\approx \frac{20 \times 200}{4} \approx \frac{4000}{4} \approx 1000$$

23 is rounded to the
nearest 10.
189 is rounded to the
nearest 100.
3.9 is rounded to the
nearest unit.

Exercise 2a

1 Round each of these numbers to
  i 1 sf   **ii** 2 sf   **iii** 3 sf
  a 4219   **b** 6788   **c** 1954   **d** 4003   **e** 24 286
  f 37 405   **g** 4698.7   **h** 2854.495 **i** 569 867 **j** 32 678 235

2 Round each of these numbers to
  i 1 sf   **ii** 2 sf   **iii** 3 sf
  a 5.467   **b** 7.394   **c** 8.307   **d** 8.194
  e 4.5146   **f** 28.5251 **g** 217.3474 **h** 0.8917
  i 0.034 57   **j** 0.007 394 **k** 2.000 367 **l** 0.000 489 1

3 Use a calculator to work out each of these calculations and
then round your answer to 3 sf.
  a 123.54 × 11.89   **b** 2 ÷ 3   **c** 2.457 ÷ 145.89

4 Estimate the answer to each of these calculations by rounding
each of the numbers to 1 sf.
  a $\dfrac{54 \times 3.7}{17.3}$ **b** $\dfrac{16.78 \times 1.9}{8.27}$ **c** $\dfrac{2334 \times 9.8}{376.2}$
  d $\dfrac{2.8 \times 47}{4.967}$ **e** $\dfrac{28 \times 2.4}{0.57}$ **f** $\dfrac{20.99 \times 0.04}{1.78}$

5 For each of these calculations work out
  i the exact answer to 2 sf
  ii the answer if you round the intermediate numbers to 2 sf
    after each step of the calculation.
  a Boris buys 14 packets of fun-size sweets at £1.89 per packet. Altogether
    he has 209 sweets. How much does each sweet cost in pence?
  b Sarah drives 14 178 km each month. She notices that her van
    travels 9.2 km for each litre of petrol. A litre of petrol costs 94.9p.
    How much does Sarah spend in pounds on petrol each year?
  c Axel the cat eats 325 g of tinned food each day. She also eats
    230 g of biscuits each week. A 400 g tin of cat food costs 55p.
    A 1.5 kg bag of biscuits costs £7.89. How much does Axel cost
    to feed in a year?

challenge

Hector and Giles are rounding the answer to a calculation.
Hector rounds the answer to 2 sf and gets an answer of 1.4.
Giles rounds the answer to 3 sf and gets an answer of 1.40.
Hector says that both answers are the same.
Giles thinks that the answers are different.
Explain and justify.

- Add and subtract fractions
- Multiply and divide fractions

Keywords
Denominator
Equivalent fraction
Reciprocal

- You can add or subtract fractions with different **denominators** by first writing them as **equivalent fractions** with the same denominator.

---

example

Calculate $\quad 3\frac{3}{4} + 1\frac{5}{6}$

Rewrite both fractions as improper fractions.

$$3\frac{3}{4} = \frac{15}{4} \qquad 1\frac{5}{6} = \frac{11}{6}$$

$$\frac{15}{4} \xrightarrow{\times 3} = \frac{45}{12} \qquad \frac{11}{6} \xrightarrow{\times 2} = \frac{22}{12}$$

Rewrite both fractions as equivalent fractions with the same denominator.

$$\frac{45}{12} + \frac{22}{12} = \frac{45 + 22}{12} = \frac{67}{12} = 5\frac{7}{12}$$

Only add the numerators.

The lowest common denominator (LCM) of 4 and 6 is 12.

- You can multiply fractions by integers or by other fractions.

When you multiply a pair of fractions, both the numerators and denominators are multiplied together.

---

example

Calculate $\quad 2\frac{2}{5} \times 1\frac{1}{9}$

Rewrite both fractions as improper fractions.

$$2\frac{2}{5} = \frac{12}{5} \qquad\qquad 1\frac{1}{9} = \frac{10}{9}$$

$$\frac{12}{5} \times \frac{10}{9} = \frac{\overset{4}{\cancel{12}}}{\underset{1}{\cancel{5}}} \times \frac{\overset{2}{\cancel{10}}}{\underset{3}{\cancel{9}}} = \frac{4 \times 2}{1 \times 3} = \frac{8}{3} = \frac{8}{3} = 2\frac{2}{3}$$

Cancel any common factors.

- You can divide fractions by integers or by other fractions using the **reciprocal**.

To divide by a fraction you multiply by the reciprocal of the fraction.

---

example

Calculate $\quad 1\frac{3}{5} \div \frac{4}{7}$

Change the divisor to its reciprocal.
Change the division into a multiplication.

$$\frac{8}{5} \div \frac{4}{7} = \frac{8}{5} \times \frac{7}{4} = \frac{56}{20} = \frac{14}{5} = 2\frac{4}{5}$$

The reciprocal of $\frac{4}{7}$ is $\frac{7}{4}$.

You find the reciprocal of a number or fraction by inverting it. For example the reciprocal of 4 is $\frac{1}{4}$ the reciprocal of $\frac{2}{3}$ is $\frac{3}{2}$.

Exercise 2b

1 Work out the following leaving your answers as a fractions in their simplest form.

a $\frac{5}{8} + \frac{3}{4}$ **b** $\frac{2}{3} - \frac{3}{8}$ **c** $1\frac{3}{5} + 1\frac{1}{6}$ **d** $2\frac{7}{10} - 1\frac{6}{7}$

e $2\frac{5}{7} + 3\frac{7}{8}$ **f** $1\frac{4}{9} + 2\frac{5}{6}$ **g** $2\frac{1}{5} - 1\frac{5}{7}$ **h** $2\frac{7}{12} + 3\frac{5}{8}$

2 a A picture frame in the shape of a rectangle has a length of $8\frac{7}{16}$ inches and a width of $5\frac{3}{4}$ inches.
Calculate the perimeter of the picture frame.

b Declan takes a train journey from Kwale to Horsel.
The total distance is 30 km.
How far is it from Gornt to Horsel?

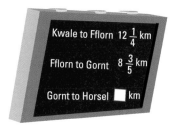

Kwale to Fflorn $12\frac{1}{4}$ km

Fflorn to Gornt $8\frac{3}{5}$ km

Gornt to Horsel   ▢ km

3 Calculate each of the following, using cancellation where appropriate.

a $8 \times \frac{3}{4}$ **b** $12 \times 1\frac{7}{10}$ **c** $24 \times 2\frac{5}{18}$ **d** $\frac{5}{9} \times \frac{6}{11}$

e $1\frac{3}{8} \times \frac{6}{11}$ **f** $2\frac{4}{7} \times 1\frac{13}{15}$ **g** $1\frac{3}{25} \times 1\frac{4}{21}$ **h** $2\frac{13}{16} \times 2\frac{2}{27}$

4 a A book cover is $6\frac{3}{5}$ inches wide and $12\frac{4}{7}$ inches long.
What is the area of the book cover?

b A bag of peanuts weighs $\frac{3}{5}$ of a kg. During October Kirsty eats $3\frac{1}{2}$ bags of peanuts. How many kilograms is that?

5 a How many sixths are there in $3\frac{1}{3}$?

b How many quarters are there in $2\frac{1}{5}$?

6 Calculate each of the following, leaving your answer in its simplest form.

a $3 \div \frac{3}{7}$ **b** $12 \div \frac{6}{11}$ **c** $8 \div 1\frac{3}{5}$ **d** $1\frac{3}{8} \div \frac{5}{6}$

e $2\frac{4}{9} \div \frac{2}{3}$ **f** $2\frac{2}{5} \div 1\frac{1}{8}$ **g** $3\frac{5}{9} \div 1\frac{3}{5}$ **h** $2\frac{3}{16} \div 2\frac{11}{12}$

Did you know?

$\frac{1}{2} + \frac{1}{4} + \frac{1}{8} + \frac{1}{16} \ldots = \square$

The Greek philosopher Zeno of Elea was famous for his paradoxes. Consider a door closing. First it closes half way and then half of the remaining distance and then half the distance again, repeating forever. How does it ever get closed?

---

investigation

a Here is a sequence of fractions: $\frac{1}{2}, \frac{2}{3}, \frac{3}{4}, \frac{4}{5}, \frac{5}{6}, \ldots$

Multiply the fractions in the sequence.
$\frac{1}{2} \times \frac{2}{3}, \frac{1}{2} \times \frac{2}{3} \times \frac{3}{4}, \ldots$
Write down what you notice.

b Investigate what happens when you multiply or add other fraction sequences. For example,
$\frac{1}{2} \times \frac{3}{4} \times \frac{5}{6} \times \frac{7}{8} \ldots$ or $\frac{1}{2} + \frac{1}{8} + \frac{1}{32} + \frac{1}{128} \ldots$ or $\frac{1}{2} \times \frac{3}{4} \times \frac{5}{8} \times \frac{7}{16} \ldots$

- Describe a proportion using fraction notation
- Calculate a fractional change

Keywords
Fraction
Proportion

- You can use **fraction** notation to describe a **proportion** of a shape.

> **example**
>
> What proportion of the rectangle is shaded?
>
>
>
> The area of the rectangle = 12 square units
> Divide the shaded shape into two triangles.
>
> Area of triangle = $\frac{1}{2}$ × base × height
>
> Area of A = $\frac{1}{2}$ × 2 × 3 = 3
>
> Area of B = $\frac{1}{2}$ × 2 × 2 = 2
>
> The area of A + B = 5 square units
> Proportion shaded = $\frac{5}{12}$.
>
> Write the proportion as a
> fraction = $\dfrac{\text{Area shaded}}{\text{Total area}}$.

- You can find a fraction of a number or quantity using multiplication.

> **example**
>
> Calculate $\frac{7}{15}$ of 40 km.
>
> $\frac{7}{15}$ of 40 = $\frac{7}{3\,\cancel{15}}$ × $\cancel{40}^{8}$ = $\frac{56}{3}$ = $18\frac{2}{3}$ km
>
> Cancel to simplify the product.
> Give your final answer as a
> mixed number.

- You can calculate a fractional increase or decrease in a single calculation using multiplication.

> **example**
>
> **a** Decrease £235 by $\frac{1}{5}$.　　　**b** Increase £235 by $\frac{1}{5}$.
>
> **a** The price has decreased by $\frac{1}{5}$
>   New price
>   = $(1 - \frac{1}{5})$ of the old price
>   = $\frac{4}{5}$ of the old price
>   = $\frac{4}{5}$ × 235
>   = £188
>
> **b** The price has increased by $\frac{1}{5}$
>   New price
>   = $(1 + \frac{1}{5})$ of the old price
>   = $\frac{6}{5}$ of the old price
>   = $\frac{6}{5}$ × 235
>   = £282
>
> Decrease　　Increase
> by $\frac{1}{5}$　　　by $\frac{1}{5}$
>
> $\frac{4}{5}$　1　$1\frac{1}{5}$
>
> The whole amount (=1) is
> increased or decreased by $\frac{1}{5}$.
>
> Re-write as an improper
> fraction $1\frac{1}{5} = \frac{6}{5}$.

Exercise 2c

1 Express the shaded shape in each diagram as a fraction of the square.

a   **b**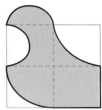

2 Here are two shapes.

    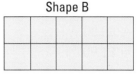

Shape A   Shape B

   a What fraction of shape B is shape A?
   b What fraction of shape A is shape B?

3 Calculate the following leaving your answers as mixed numbers where appropriate.

   a $\frac{5}{9}$ of 12 feet   **b** $\frac{8}{15}$ of 50 m   **c** $\frac{3}{7}$ of 21 m

   d $\frac{7}{12}$ of 42 sec   **e** $1\frac{7}{16}$ of 44 km   **f** $2\frac{3}{5}$ of 8 miles

   g $1\frac{4}{9}$ of 75 g   **h** $3\frac{8}{15}$ of $\frac{3}{4}$ hr

4 Calculate these fractional changes leaving your answer as a mixed number where appropriate.

   a Increase £40 by $\frac{2}{5}$ **b** Decrease £20 by $\frac{3}{5}$

   c Increase 12 kg by $\frac{1}{5}$ **d** Decrease 50 kg by $\frac{1}{3}$

   e Increase 25 miles by $\frac{2}{7}$ **f** Decrease 120 miles by $\frac{2}{9}$

   g Increase $3\frac{1}{2}$ km by $\frac{1}{4}$ **h** Decrease $45\frac{1}{4}$ kg by $\frac{1}{5}$

5 a Gina weighs 64 kg. Twelve months later her weight has increased by $\frac{1}{12}$. What is Gina's new weight?
   b In a sale all prices are reduced by $\frac{1}{3}$. A CD costs £14 before the sale. What is the sale price of the CD?

Did you know?

Thomas Malthus was an economist and demographer. He noticed that populations tend to grow by a constant factor, 1, 2, 4, 8, 16,..., whilst food supplies only grow by a constant amount:, 1, 2, 3, 4, 5,..., thereby restricting population growth.

problem solving

Boris buys a company for £2 million pounds. Each year he wants to increase the size of his company by $\frac{1}{5}$.
   a How big will the company be in two years time?
   b How big will the company be in five years time?
   c How big will the company be in ten years time?
   d Investigate by how much the company will grow for different numbers of years.

- Calculate a percentage increase or decrease
- Express a proportional change as a percentage

Keywords
Equivalent
Percentage decrease
Percentage increase
Proportion

You can calculate a percentage of an amount using mental, written and calculator methods.

example

Calculate 5% of £38.

. . . .

Using a mental method.
 10% of £38 = £3.80
so 5% of £38 = £1.90

10% is a tenth: £38 ÷ 10 = £3.80

5% is half of 10%: £3.80 ÷ 2 = £1.90

Using an equivalent fraction.
$5\% \text{ of } £38 = \dfrac{5 \times 38}{100} = \dfrac{190}{100} = £1.90$

Change the % into a fraction and multiply.

Using the decimal equivalent.
$5\% \text{ of } £38 = 5 \div 100 \times 38$
$= 0.05 \times 38 = £1.90$

Change the % into a decimal and multiply.
$5\% = \frac{5}{100} = 5 \div 100 = 0.05$

- You can calculate a **percentage increase** or **decrease** in a single calculation using an **equivalent** decimal.

example

a Increase £70 by 12%
b Decrease 250 g by 12%

. . . .

a New price
 = (100 + 12)% of the old price
 = 112% of £70
 = 1.12 × £70
 = £78.40

b New weight
 = (100 − 12)% of the old weight
 = 88% of 250 g
 = 0.88 × 250
 = 220 g

Decrease   Increase
by 12%   by 12%

88% 100% 112%

- You can express a **proportional** change as a percentage of the original amount.

example

A chocolate bar is decreased in weight from 250 g to 220 g. What is the percentage decrease in weight?

. . . .

Decrease in weight = 250 g − 220 g = 30 g
Proportional decrease = $\frac{30}{250}$
Percentage decrease = (30 ÷ 250) × 100% = 12%

Proportional decrease
$= \dfrac{\text{Decrease}}{\text{Original weight}}$

Exercise 2d

1 Calculate these percentages using a suitable method.

    a 15% of £35   **b** 95% of 180 kg   **c** 11% of 85 km.   **d** 6% of £37

    e 99% of 2.5 m **f** 17.5% of £2450   **g** 3.5% of £28 000 **h** 0.5% of 55 kg

2 a Out of every 800 tins of beans tins made in a factory, 11 are
    rejected. What proportion of tins are rejected?

   b Nadeem scores 53 out of 60 in his Maths exam.
    What proportion of the test did he answer incorrectly?

3 Use an appropriate method to work out the following.

    a Increase £75 by 15%   **b** Decrease £142 by 15%

    c Increase 12.5 km by 11%   **d** Increase 1.2 million by 4.5%

    e Decrease 30 cm by 78%   **f** Decrease 2900 kJ by 13.5%

4 Match each of these statements with the correct mathematical calculation.

A Increase £75 by 30%	B 30% of £75
C Decrease £75 by 30%	D Increase £75 by 3%
E 3% of £75	F Decrease £75 by 3%
G Increase £75 by 0.3%	H 0.3% of £75

a 0.03×75	b 1.03×75
c 0.3×75	d 1.3×75
e 1.003×75	f 0.97×75
g $0.003 \times £75$	h 0.7×75

5 a A DVD costs £19. In a sale the price is reduced to £12.
    What is the percentage reduction?

   b A skirt normally costs £25. In a sale the price is reduced by 35%.
    What is the sale price of the skirt?

   c Hector's weekly wage is increased from £320 to
    £329.60.
    What is the percentage increase in Hector's wage?

6 These are the prices of four items in 1982 and in 2007.
Which item has increased in price by
the greatest proportion?
Explain and justify your answer.

	1982	2007
Cinema ticket	£1.65	£6.50
Pint of milk	20p	36p
Weekly food bill	£32.20	£84.82
Chocolate bar	16p	41p

Geoff went out for a meal. At the end of the meal
the waiter added 17.5% for VAT and an 8% service
charge. Geoff asked the waiter to add the service charge
first and then the VAT. Was Geoff correct? Explain and
justify your answer.

2e Percentage change

LEVEL 8

- Calculate a percentage increase or decrease
- Use percentage change to solve problems

Keywords
Percentage change

p. 226

- You can use **percentage changes** to solve problems.

---

example

In a sale a tennis racket is reduced in price by 35%. The racket now costs £18.85. What was the original price of the racket?

. . . .

In the sale the price decreases by 35%.
Sale price of racket = (100 − 35)% of the original price
                     = 65% of original price

To work out 65% of the original price you multiply by 0.65

$$\times 0.65$$
$$\times 65\%$$

Original price   decrease by 35% →   Sale price
                ← $\div 0.65$

The inverse of multiplying by 0.65 is dividing by 0.65

Original price of racket = Sale price ÷ 0.65
                         = £18.85 ÷ 0.65
                         = £29

- You can check your answer to a percentage change calculation by working out the percentage increase/decrease of your answer.

---

example

Check the answer to the previous example.

. . . .

Use the answer to work out the sale price.
        Sale price = (100 − 35)% of the original price.
                   = 65% of £29
                   = 0.65 × £29
                   = £18.85
Check this answer with the price (£18.85) given in the question.
The calculation is correct.

Exercise 2e

1 a In a sale, a DVD is reduced in price by 25%. The sale price of the DVD is £18. What was the original price of the DVD?

b A chocolate bar is increased in price by 15%. The price of the chocolate bar is now 69p. What was the original price?

c A coat is on sale at £48.40. If this is 88% of the original price, what was the original price?

2 Match each of these questions with the correct mathematical calculation.

> a A pair of trainers costs £30. The price is increased by 20%. Calculate the new price.
>
> b In a sale all prices are reduced by 20%. A pair of trousers costs £30 in a sale. Calculate the old price of the trainers.
>
> c A pair of shoes costs £30. The price is reduced by 20%. Calculate the new price.
>
> d In a shop all prices are increased by 20%. A pair of slippers now costs £30. What was the old price of the slippers?

> A $30 \div 0.8$
> B $30 \div 1.2$
> C 30×0.8
> D 30×1.2

3 a Felippe bought a computer in a sale and saved £49. The label said that it was a 20% reduction. What was the original price of the computer?

b A packet of sweets is increased in size by 23%. The new packet weighs 184.5 g. What was the weight of the original packet?

4 A company advertises its new packet of sweets claiming that it is 27% bigger. The new packet contains 19 sweets. How many sweets were there in the original packet? Comment on your answer.

investigation

Mr P. Centage owns a shop. He always puts up his prices by 5% on the 1st April each year. In 2009 the price of a chocolate bar in his shop was 80p.

a How much will the chocolate bar cost in two years' time?

b What did the chocolate bar cost last year?

c What did the chocolate bar cost two years ago?

d Investigate the price of the chocolate bar in different years.

- Calculate a repeated percentage increase or decrease
- Use percentage change to solve problems

Keywords

Decimal   Percentage
    multiplier Repeated
Interest

- You can calculate a **repeated percentage** increase using a **decimal multiplier**.

example

Victor invests £3000 in a bank with an annual **interest** rate of 4%.
How much money will he have after 3 years?

Each year the money grows by 4%

£3000 →(×1.04)→ £3120 →(×1.04)→ £3244.80 →(×1.04)→ £3374.592
      Increase by 4%   Increase by 4%   Increase by 4%

At the end of each year
the bank works out
4% of the money in
the account, called the
interest, and adds this on.

After three years he will have £3374.59 (2 dp)

You can also perform the same
calculation in one step
    £3000 $\times (1.04)^3$ = £3374.59

Multiply by the single
multiplier to the power of
3 (the number of years).

- You can calculate a repeated percentage decrease using a decimal multiplier.

example

Violet buys a new van for £20 000. Each year the value of
the van depreciates by 12%. What will be the value of the
van in two years' time?

Most cars go down in value
each year. This is called
depreciation.

Each year the value of the van decreases by 12%.

£20 000 →(×0.88)→ £17 600 →(×0.88)→ £15 488
      Decrease by 12%   Decrease by 12%

At the end of each year the
decrease is subtracted from
the current value of the van.

After two years the van is worth £15 488.

You can also perform the same
calculation in one step
    £20 000 $\times (0.88)^2$ = £15 488

Multiply by the single multiplier to the power
of 2 (the number of years).

Exercise 2f

1 a Ruby puts £8000 into a bank account. Each year the bank pays interest at 7%. Work out the amount of money in Ruby's bank account after two years.

 b Shahid buys a new car for £12000. Each year his car depreciates in value by 15%. What will be the value of Shahid's car in three years' time?

2 Work out the value of each of these items after the number of years stated.

Item	Cost (£)	Time (years)	Percentage change each year
Car	24500	3	Decrease 7%
House	125000	2	Increase 8%
TV	250	5	Decrease 12.5%
Savings	15000	4	Increase 3.29%

3 a Teresa invests £85000 in a bank account. The bank pays 6% interest a year. How many years will it take for Teresa's money to be worth more than a million pounds?

 b Bertie owes £1800 on his credit card. Each month the credit card company adds 2.6% interest on his outstanding balance to his bill. Bertie manages to pay £80 a month to the credit card company. How long will it take him to pay off the whole bill?

---

investigation

Beatrice borrows £90000 from a bank to buy a house. The bank charges 6% a year interest. She wants to know how much money she will have to pay back after 25 years. She uses a spreadsheet to help her investigate the problem.

 a Set up a spreadsheet to investigate the problem.

 b How much money will Beatrice owe in 25 years?

 c Plot a graph of time in years against the money owed. Write down what you notice.

 d Investigate changing the interest rate.

 e Investigate what happens if Beatrice starts to pay back some money at the end of each year. Find how much she has to pay back each year so that at the end of the 25 years she owes the bank no money?

	A	B	C	D
			Percentage	New
1	Year	Amount	change	amount
2	1	90000	1.06	95400
3	2	95400	1.06	101124
4	3	101124	1.06	107191
5	4	107191	1.06	113623
6	5	113623	1.06	120440
7	6	120440		

• Understand the relationship between ratio and proportion
• Solve problems involving ratio and proportion

Keywords
Proportion
Ratio

• You can solve problems using **ratios**.

---

example

Brass is made from zinc and copper. Johann mixes 3 kg of zinc with 4.5 kg of copper.
a How much copper does Johann need to mix with 25 kg of zinc?
b How much zinc does Johann need to mix with 50 kg of copper?

Simplify the ratio   zinc : copper

$$3 : 4.5$$
$$\times 2 \quad \quad \times 2$$
$$6 : 9$$
$$\div 3 \quad \quad \div 3$$
$$2 : 3$$

> You simplify a ratio by dividing or multiplying all parts of the ratio by the same number.

a Amount of copper $= \frac{3}{2} \times$ amount of zinc
$$= \frac{3}{2} \times 25 \, \text{kg} = 37.5 \, \text{kg}$$

$\times \frac{3}{2}$
Zinc : Copper
$\times \frac{2}{3}$

> The ratio tells you how many times bigger each part is compared to the other part.

b Amount of zinc $= \frac{2}{3} \times$ amount of copper
$$= \frac{2}{3} \times 50 \, \text{kg} = 33\frac{1}{3} \, \text{kg}$$

• You can compare ratios by expressing them in the form 1 : *n*.

---

example

Simeon is investigating the ratio of potato to other ingredients in two pies. The ratio is 7 : 20 for cottage pie and 9 : 25 for shepherd's pie. Which pie contains more potato as a **proportion**?

Express both ratios in the form 1 : *n*

Cottage pie
potato : other
$$7 : 20$$
$$\div 7 \quad \quad \div 7$$
$$1 : 2.86 \ (2 \, \text{dp})$$

Shepherd's pie
potato : other
$$9 : 25$$
$$\div 9 \quad \quad \div 9$$
$$1 : 2.78 \ (2 \, \text{dp})$$

> The ratio tells you how many times more other ingredients there are compared to potato.

Shepherd's pie has the greater proportion of potato.

Exercise 2g

1 Write each ratio in its simplest form.

    a $0.4 : 3$ **b** $0.5 : 2$ **c** $1.6 : 2.4$ **d** $2.1 : 3.5 : 4.2$

    e $2 : 2.4 : 3$ **f** $1.2\,\text{m} : 200\,\text{cm}$ **g** $4.5\,\text{kg} : 2000\,\text{g}$ **h** £3.60 : 80p

2 Express each of these ratios in the form $1 : n$.

    a $2 : 8$ **b** $4 : 10$ **c** $3 : 20$ **d** $5 : 75$

    e $4 : 11$ **f** $3 : 22$ **g** $22 : 3$ **h** $11 : 4$

3 a The ratio of nylon to other materials in two T-shirts are $4 : 7$
    and $9 : 16$. Which T-shirt has the greater proportion of nylon?

   b The ratio of teachers to pupils in Appleby School is $3 : 40$,
    compared to Plumley Academy where the ratio is $4 : 51$.
    Which school has the higher proportion of teachers?

4 a John and Kaseem divide £21 in the ratio $3 : 7$.
    How much money does Kaseem receive?
    What proportion of the money does John receive?

   b A wall covers $70\,\text{m}^2$. The wall is painted blue, white and yellow
    in the ratio $5 : 4 : 5$. What area of the wall is painted blue? What
    proportion of the wall is painted yellow?

   c In a sports club the ratio of men to women is $7 : 9$.

    i If there are 272 members, how many are women.

    ii If there are 91 men, how many women are there?

5 a In a running club, $\frac{5}{8}$ of the members are men.
    What is the ratio of men to women?

   b Hector plays basketball. He scores a 'basket' $\frac{11}{12}$ of the time he shoots.
    What is Hector's ratio of successful baskets to shots taken?

   c Sarah is 1.6 m tall. Keenan is 15% taller than Sarah.
    What is the ratio of Sarah's height to Keenan's height?

   d Orange paint is made using 2 parts of red paint mixed with 3 parts of
    yellow paint. Aleshia has 450 ml of red paint and 700 ml of yellow paint.
    What is the maximum volume of orange paint she can make?

challenge

The ratio of area C to area B is $1 : 2$.
Find the area of A.

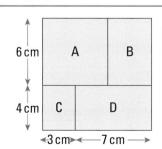

The diagram is not drawn to scale.

- Understand direct proportion
- Solve problems involving direct proportion

Keywords
Direct Proportion
Ratio

- When two quantities are in **direct proportion** the **ratio** between the quantities is fixed.

example

The table shows the number of inches and the corresponding number of centimetres.

Inches	3	5	6	10	15	50
Centimetres	7.5	12.5	15	25	37.7	125

What is the ratio of inches to centimetres?
Are inches and centimetres in direct proportion?

Inches : centimetres

3 : 7.5
6 : 15
2 : 5
1 : 2.5

$\times 2.5$
$\times \frac{5}{2}$

Inches : Centimetres
2 : 5

$\times \frac{2}{5}$
$\times 0.4$

You can write the ratios as fractions using division
$\frac{7.5}{3} = 7.5 \div 3 = 2.5$

Inches and centimetres are directly proportional because all the ratios are equal.

$$\frac{\text{Centimetres}}{\text{Inches}} = \frac{7.5}{3} = \frac{12.5}{5} = \frac{15}{6} = \frac{25}{10} = 2.5$$

Number of centimetres = 2.5 × number of inches

- You can use fractions to solve direct proportion problems.

example

Brown paint is made by mixing 7 parts of red paint with 4 parts of green paint. How many litres of red paint should you mix with 23 litres of green paint?

Express the ratios in fractional form

$$\frac{\text{Red}}{\text{Green}} = \frac{7}{4} = \frac{\square}{23}$$

Amount of red $= \dfrac{7 \times 23}{4} = \dfrac{161}{4} = 40\frac{1}{4}$ litres

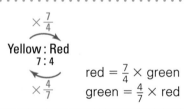

$\times \frac{7}{4}$

Yellow : Red
7 : 4

$\times \frac{4}{7}$

red $= \frac{7}{4} \times$ green
green $= \frac{4}{7} \times$ red

LEVEL 7

Exercise 2h

Grade D

1 Identify which of these sets of data are in direct proportion.
Explain and justify your answers.

a

Weight (kg)	2	3	6	10	15	50
Cost (£)	2.50	3.75	7.50	12.50	18.75	62.50

b

x	1	3	6	10	15	50
y	6.5	19	37	61	90	275

c

x	3	5	7	9	11	13
y	3.6	6	8.4	10.8	13.2	15.6

2 Solve each of these problems.

a 3 kg of carrots cost 75p. What is the cost of 8 kg of carrots?

b A recipe for four people uses 600 g of potato. How much potato do you need for seven people?

3 Solve each of these problems.

> Try to use the fractional method.

a To make green paint, 6 parts of yellow paint are mixed with 5 parts of blue paint. How many litres of blue paint should you mix with 40 litres of yellow paint?

b Travis knows that 8 kilometres is the same distance as 5 miles. How far in miles is 25 km?

c Jackson changed £350 into €385. At the same exchange rate how many pounds will Jackson get for €200?

d In a sale all the prices in the shop are reduced by the same percentage. A coat is reduced in price from £95 to £66.50. A pair of shoes normally costs £108. What is the sale price of the shoes?

e A model of a plane is 1.2 m long. The plane is 9 m long in real life. If the wingspan of the real plane is 13 m, what is the wingspan of the model?

Did you know?

Suprabha Beckjord is the only woman to have finished the self-transcendence 3100 mile race. Her fastest time is 49 days 14.5 hours.

4 Gina reads a newspaper that says a man can run 1 km in 3 minutes. She works out that he can run 40 km in 2 hours. Explain why this might not be correct.

investigation

Gavin draws some circles with different radii. For each one he works out the area and records his answers in a spreadsheet. Investigate to see if the area of a circle is directly proportional to the radius of the circle.

	A	B	C	D	E	F
1	Radius	2	3	5	10	20
2	Area	12.572	28.27	78.54	314.16	1256.64

- Use and interpret maps and scale drawings
- Solve problems involving direct proportion and scale factors

Keywords
Direct Proportion
Ratio
Scale factor

- When a photograph or shape is enlarged by a **scale factor**, the **ratio** of the length and width stays the same.

example

Calculate the length of the enlarged photograph.

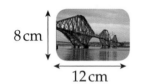

8 cm
12 cm

14 cm
☐

$$\frac{\text{length}}{\text{width}} = \frac{12}{8} = \frac{\square}{14} = 1.5$$

or

$$\frac{\text{enlarged width}}{\text{original width}} = \frac{14}{8} = \frac{\square}{12} = 1.75$$

length = 1.5 × width

scale factor = 1.75

enlarged length $= \frac{12}{8} \times 14 = 1.5 \times 14$
$= 21 \text{ cm}$

enlarged length $= \frac{14}{8} \times 12 = 1.75 \times 12$
$= 21 \text{ cm}$

- You can use **direct proportion** to solve problems involving maps and scale drawings.

example

A map is drawn on a scale of 2 cm to represent 7 km.
The real distance between two towns on the map is 30 km.

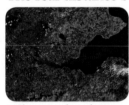

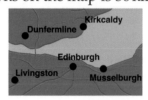

Kirkcaldy
Dunfermline
Edinburgh
Livingston
Musselburgh

What is the distance on the map between the towns?

The scale of the map is
2 cm : 7 km
= 2 : 700 000
= 1 : 350 000

$$\text{Map scale} = \frac{\text{Map measurement}}{\text{Real measurement}} = \frac{2 \text{ cm}}{7 \text{ km}} = \frac{\square}{30 \text{ km}}$$

$$\text{Distance on map} = \frac{2 \text{ cm} \times 30 \text{ km}}{7 \text{ km}} = \frac{60 \text{ cm}}{7} = 8\tfrac{4}{7} \text{ cm} = 8.6 \text{ cm (1 dp)}$$

Exercise 2i

1 Each pair of photographs shows the original photo and its enlargement. Calculate the missing length in each pair.

Give answers to 1dp.

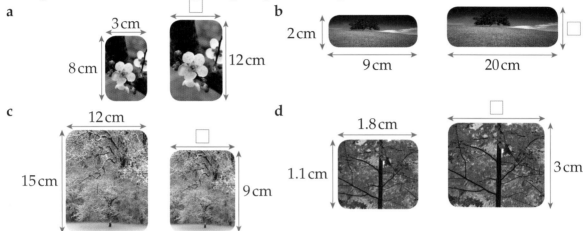

a 3 cm · 8 cm · □ · 12 cm

b 2 cm · 9 cm · 20 cm · □

c 12 cm · 15 cm · □ · 9 cm

d 1.8 cm · 1.1 cm · □ · 3 cm

2 **a** A map has a scale of 1 : 25 000.

  i What distance does 3.8 cm on the map represent in real life?

  ii What distance on the map represents a real-life measurement of 8 km?

  b A model of a plane is built to a scale of 1 : 24. The wingspan of the real plane is 12.8 m. How long is the wingspan of the model?

3 A map scale uses 3 cm to represent 20 km.
  The real distance between two towns is 13 km.

  a What is the distance on the map between the towns?

  b Write the scale of the map as a ratio in the form 1 : n.

4 The distance on a map between Plydale and Harrop is 7 cm. In real life the distance is 1.75 km.

  a Write the scale of the map as a ratio in the form 1 : n.

  b The distance on the map between Harrop and Gizdell is 12.4 cm. How far apart are the towns in real life?

---

investigation

Mohinder draws a rectangle, and works out its area.

He enlarges his rectangle by different scale factors and he records the areas of the new rectangles in a spreadsheet.

	Original	Enlargement A	Enlargement B	Enlargement C	Enlargement D	Enlargement E
Length	6 cm	12 cm	18 cm	9 cm	4.8 cm	7.5 cm
Width	4 cm	8 cm	12 cm	6 cm	3.2 cm	
Area						

a Copy and complete the spreadsheet.

b Write down the scale factor Mohinder used for each enlargement.

c Investigate how the area of the rectangle changes after each enlargement.

2a

1 Round each of these numbers to
   i 1 sf   **ii** 2 sf   **iii** 3 sf.
   a 3729   **b** 1.295 64   **c** 0.370 04   **d** 0.000 285 44

2 Estimate the answer to each of these calculations by rounding each number to 1 significant figure.

   a $\dfrac{73 \times 2.7}{32.3}$ **b** $\dfrac{8.38 \times 5.6}{3.97}$ **c** $\dfrac{243 \times 18.8}{0.2}$

2b

3 Do these calculations leaving your answers as fractions in their simplest form.

   a $1\frac{5}{6} + 2\frac{1}{8}$ **b** $3\frac{7}{9} - 1\frac{7}{8}$ **c** $2\frac{1}{5} \times 1\frac{5}{7}$ **d** $4\frac{7}{12} \div 1\frac{3}{8}$

2c

4 Calculate these quantities leaving your answers as mixed numbers where appropriate.

   a $\frac{3}{5}$ of 45 m   **b** $\frac{7}{15}$ of 20 km   **c** $1\frac{3}{7}$ of £42   **d** $2\frac{5}{8}$ of 30 kg

5 Calculate these fractional changes leaving your answers as mixed numbers where appropriate.

   a Increase £80 by $\frac{7}{16}$ **b** Decrease £50 by $\frac{3}{10}$

2d

6 Use an appropriate method of calculation to work out the following.
   a Increase £35 by 35%   **b** Decrease £250 by 17.5%
   c Increase 24.6 kg by 21%   **d** Decrease 176 km by 8.5%

7 **a** A CD costs £12.50. In a sale the price is reduced to £10.
     What is the percentage reduction?
   b A shirt normally costs £45. In a sale the price is reduced by 12%.
     What is the sale price of the shirt?

2e

8 **a** In a sale, a DVD is reduced in price by 15%. The sale price is £15.30.
     What was the original price of the DVD?
   b A cereal bar is increased in price by 8%. The new price is 81p.
     What was the original price of the bar?

9 **a** Heidi bought a TV in a sale and saved £30. The label said that it was
     a 12% reduction. What was the original price of the TV?

b At the start of December Keiley bought a pack of Xmas bells for £3.50. On Christmas Eve she bought another pack but paid £1.40 less. What was the percentage decrease in the price of the bells?

10 Work out the value of each item after the number of years stated.

Item	Cost	Time	Percentage change each year
Car	£12800	4 years	Decrease 12%
House	£220000	3 years	Increase 4%
Savings	£1.5 million	5 years	2.49%

11 The ratio of Lycra to other materials in two gym suits are 3 : 8 and 5 : 13. Which gym suit has the greater proportion of Lycra?

12 a Sebastian and Belle divide £38 in the ratio 3 : 5.
   i How much money does Sebastian receive?
   ii What proportion of the money does Belle receive?
b In a running club the ratio of men to women is 5 : 4. There are 196 women members. How many men are there in the club?

13 Solve these problems.
   a 5 kg of apples cost £1.85. What is the cost of 11 kg of apples?
   b A recipe for 6 people needs 500 ml of stock. How much stock do you need for 9 people?

14 Solve these problems.
   a To make pink paint mix 5 parts of white paint with 7 parts of red paint. How many litres of red paint should you mix with 12 litres of white paint?
   b Jenny changed £480 into $744 when she went to America. On her return she had $310 left. If the exchange rate stayed the same, how many pounds did she get back?

15 The distance on a map between Kerso and Larroz is 4.5 cm. In real-life the distance is 1.35 km.
   a Write the scale of the map as a ratio in the form 1 : n.
   b The distance on the map between Larroz and Horten is 18.2 cm. How far apart are the towns in real life?

2 Summary

Assessment criteria

- Use a calculator efficiently and appropriately, knowing not to round during intermediate steps of a calculation **Level 7**
- Calculate the original quantity given the result of a proportional change **Level 8**

Level 8

1 In 2005 there was a survey of red kites in Scotland.
In 2008 the survey was repeated.
There was a 60% increase in breeding pairs.

Year	Approximate number of breeding pairs of red kites
2005	x
2008	122

The number of breeding pairs seen in 2005 was x.
Work out the value of x.

Joe's answer ✔

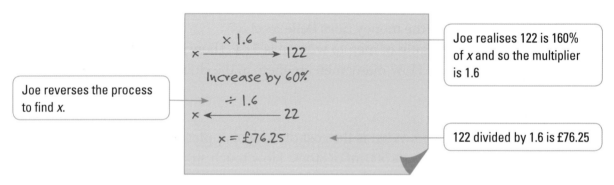

Joe reverses the process to find x.

Joe realises 122 is 160% of x and so the multiplier is 1.6

122 divided by 1.6 is £76.25

$$\times 1.6$$
$$x \longrightarrow 122$$
Increase by 60%
$$\div 1.6$$
$$x \longleftarrow 22$$
$$x = £76.25$$

Level 7

2 A teacher said to a pupil

> To the nearest per cent, $\frac{1}{6}$ is 17%.

The pupil said

> So, to the nearest per cent, $\frac{2}{6}$ must be 34%.

Show that the pupil is wrong.

KS3 2005 6–8 Paper 1

3 Geometry

Geometrical reasoning and constructions

Pythagoras of Samos was a Greek philosopher and mathematician, who was born about 570 BC. A famous theorem is named after him, although there is evidence that it may have been known by earlier civilisations.

What's the point? Despite being at least two thousand years old Pythagoras' theorem is still widely used today to calculate distances.

✔ Check in

Level 5

1 Calculate the value of the unknown angles.

a 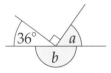 **b**  **c**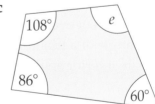

2 Indicate the shapes that are congruent.

A   B   C   D

3 Write down the coordinates of the points A, B, C, D and E.

39

- Distinguish between a practical demonstration and a proof
- Understand proofs about angle properties of a triangle and a quadrilateral

Keywords

Demonstration   Proof
Exterior   Prove
Interior   Show

- A practical **demonstration** only **shows** a property (fact) is true in one particular situation.

   The four interior angles fit together at a point.

This shows that the **interior** angles of this particular quadrilateral add to 360°.

- A **proof** is a logical argument which **proves** a property for every situation.

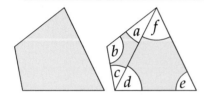

$a + b + c = 180°$ in one triangle
$d + e + f = 180°$ in the other triangle
$a + b + c + d + e + f$
$\qquad = 360°$ adding the equations

a, b, c, d, e and *f* can take any values.

This proves that the interior angles of every quadrilateral add to 360°.

example

Use the diagram to prove the following statements.
a The interior angles of every triangle add to 180°.
b The **exterior** angle of a triangle is equal to the sum of the opposite interior angles.

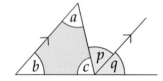

a
$\qquad p = a$ Alternate angles – the Z shape.
$\qquad q = b$ Corresponding angles – the F shape.
$\quad c + p + q = 180°$ Angles on a straight line add to 180°.
So $c + a + b = 180°$

b
$\qquad p = a$ Alternate angles – the Z shape.
$\qquad q = b$ Corresponding angles – the F shape.
So $a + b = p + q$

Exercise 3a

1 Calculate the unknown interior angles and state the type of triangle.

a 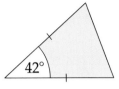 **b** 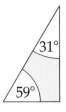 **c**

2 Calculate the values of the unknown angles.

a 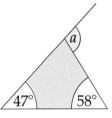 **b** 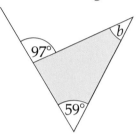 **c**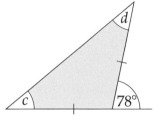

3 Calculate the angles marked with letters.

a 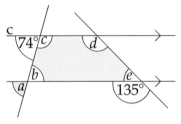 **b** 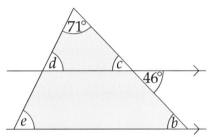 **c**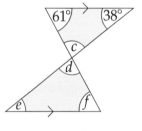

4 Prove that the opposite angles of a parallelogram are equal.

5 A triangle is drawn between two parallel lines.

   a Explain why
$$p + b + q = 180°.$$

   b Prove
$$a + b + c = 180°.$$

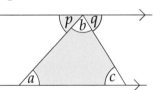

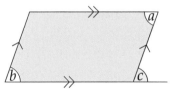

Draw a quadrilateral and colour the angles.

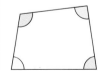

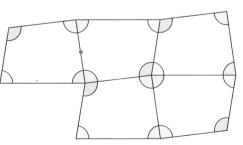

Rotate the quadrilateral about the midpoint of
each side to create a tessellation.
Show that the interior angles of a quadrilateral add to 360°.

- Calculate and use the angle properties of regular and irregular polygons

Keywords

Exterior	Regular
Interior	Symmetry
Polygon	Tessellation

- The exterior angles of any **polygon** add to 360°.
- At each vertex, the exterior and the interior angles add to 180°.

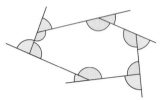

You can split
…a quadrilateral into two triangles.
Sum of interior angles = 2 × 180° = 360°

…a pentagon into three triangles.
Sum of interior angles = 3 × 180° = 540°
…a polygon with n sides into (n − 2) triangles.

The green angles are the **interior** angles.
The pink angles are the **exterior** angles.

- The interior angles of a polygon with n sides sum to (n − 2) × 180°.

example

A polygon has 14 sides.
Calculate **a** the sum of the exterior angles   **b** the sum of the interior angles.
···
       a 360°   **b** (14 − 2) × 180° = 2160°

- A **regular** polygon has equal sides and equal angles.

The side lengths and angles are not equal in irregular polygons.

- A regular polygon with n sides has n lines of reflection **symmetry** and rotation symmetry of order n.

- A **tessellation** is a tiling pattern with no gaps.

example

A regular polygon has six lines of symmetry.
Explain why this polygon tessellates.
···
A regular hexagon has six lines of symmetry.
Sum of the interior angles of a hexagon = (6 − 2) × 180°
                                               = 720°
                one interior angle = 720° ÷ 6
                                = 120°

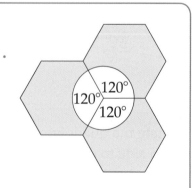

3 × 120° = 360°
Angles at a point add to 360°.

Exercise 3b

1 Eight kites fit together to form a regular octagon.
Calculate
  a the four interior angles of the kite
  b the interior angle of a regular octagon.

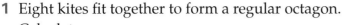

2 Calculate the exterior and interior angle of
  a a regular pentagon   **b** a regular decagon
  c a regular 20-sided polygon   **d** a regular 30-sided polygon
  e a regular heptagon   **f** a regular 17-sided polygon.

3 The exterior angle of a regular polygon is 15°.
Calculate
  a the number of sides
  b the value of one interior angle
  c the sum of the interior angles
  d the number of lines of symmetry
  e the order of rotation symmetry of the polygon.

Did you know?

When he was only 19,
Carl Friedrich Gauss
showed that it was
possible to construct a
regular 17-sided polygon
using just compasses
and a straight edge. The
first such new construc-
tion for over 2000 years!

4 Calculate the unknown angles.

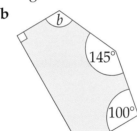
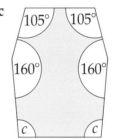

5 A triangle, a regular hexagon and a regular dodecagon
(12 sides) fit together as shown.
  a Use the angle properties of polygons
    to find each angle in the triangle and
    state its mathematical name.
  b Draw a diagram to illustrate the tessellation of these
    triangles, regular hexagons and regular dodecagons.

challenge

A polygon with *n* sides can be divided into $n - 2$ triangles.
Each triangle has an angle sum of 180°.
  a Write an expression, in terms of *n*, for the sum of the interior angles.
  b What is the sum of the exterior angles?
  c Add your answers to find the sum of all the exterior and interior angles in a polygon.
  d Explain this answer.

- Know the vocabulary of parts of a circle
- Use the properties of a circle

Keywords

Chord	Inscribed
Circle	Tangent
Circumcircle	
Circumscribed	

A **circle** is a set of points equidistant from its centre O.

A **chord** is a straight line across the inside of a circle.

A **tangent** is a line that touches the outside of a circle.

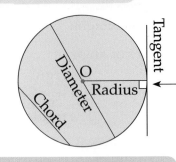

Symmetry tells you the angle is 90°.

- The tangent is perpendicular to the radius at the point of contact.

- A circle that passes through all the vertices of a polygon is called a **circumscribed** circle or a **circumcircle**.

- An **inscribed** circle is the largest circle that fits inside a polygon and touches each side of the polygon.

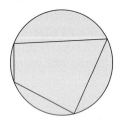

'Circumscribe' from the Latin 'to draw a line around'.

'Inscribe' from the Latin 'to write in or upon'.

You can construct a regular polygon using a circumscribed circle.

Divide 360° by the number of sides of the polygon.

The chords and radii form isosceles triangles to create the polygon.

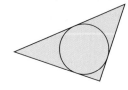

$360° \div 5 = 72°$

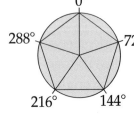

This is an inscribed pentagon.

---

example

ABC is a triangle with a circumscribed circle, centre O. Calculate the values of angles a, b, c and d.

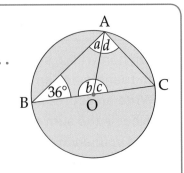

. . . .

$a = 36°$ AOB is an isosceles triangle as OB = OA = radius of the circle.

$b = 108°$ Angle sum of a triangle.

$c = 72°$ Angle sum on a straight line.

$d = 108° \div 2 = 54°$ AOC is an isosceles triangle as OA = OC = radius of the circle.

Exercise 3c

1 O is the centre of the circle and AB is the tangent at Q.
  a State the value of angle OQA.
  b Explain why triangle OPQ is isosceles.
  c Calculate the values of angles a and b.

2 A circumscribed circle of a square
  has a radius of 10 cm.
  Calculate the area of the square.

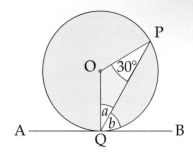

3 a Construct an inscribed regular decagon, using a circle
      of radius 5 cm.
  b Measure the interior angle of the decagon.
  c Calculate the sum of the interior angles.
  d Check your answer using the formula:
      sum of the interior angles of a polygon $= (n - 2) \times 180°$
      where n is the number of sides.

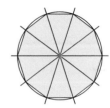

4 BC is the diameter of a circle with centre O.
  A is any point on the circumference.
  a Explain why angle ABO $= b$.
  b Explain why angle ACO $= c$.
  c Find the angle sum of triangle ABC in terms of b and c.
  d Find the value of $b + c$.
  e What is the value of angle BAC?

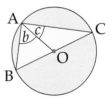

activity

  a Use the circumscribed circle of a
      regular pentagon to draw a 5-point star.
  b Calculate
      i the angle at a point of the star
      ii the sum of the angles at all 5 points.
  c Repeat for a 6-point and an 8-point star.

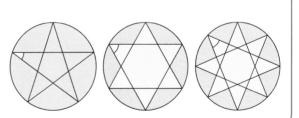

- Understand and use Pythagoras' theorem to calculate lengths

Keywords
Hypotenuse   Square
Pythagoras   Square root
Right-angled
   triangle

The longest side of a **right-angled triangle** is called the **hypotenuse**.

You can draw **squares** on each side of a right-angled triangle.

The yellow area + the blue area = the green area

 + =

- **Pythagoras'** theorem states for a right-angled triangle,
  the area of the square = sum of the areas of the
  on the hypotenuse   squares on the other two sides.
  $c^2 = a^2 + b^2$ where c is the hypotenuse.

example

a Calculate the value of c.

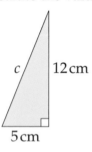

b Calculate the value of a.

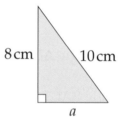

. . . .

a c is larger than 12 cm and 5 cm.

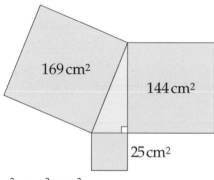

$c^2 = 12^2 + 5^2$ You add the areas.

$= 144 + 25$

$= 169$

$c = \sqrt{169}$ $\sqrt{}$ means **square root**.

$= 13$ cm

b a is smaller than 10 cm.

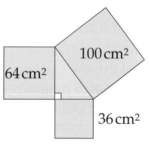

$a^2 = 10^2 - 8^2$ You subtract the areas.

$= 100 - 64$

$= 36$

$a = \sqrt{36}$

$= 6$ cm

Exercise 3d

1 Calculate the length of the hypotenuse in each triangle.
State the units of your answer.

a

4 cm
3 cm

b
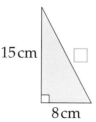
15 cm
8 cm

c

24 m
7 m

Did you know?

Pythagoras' theorem has appeared on several stamps. This one is from Suriname in South America.

2 Calculate the unknown lengths in these right-angled triangles.

a
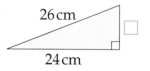
26 cm
24 cm

b

16 m   20 m

c
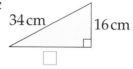
34 cm   16 cm

3 Calculate the unknown lengths in these triangles.

Each answer is an integer.

a
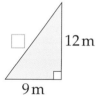
12 m
9 m

b
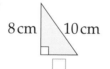
8 cm   10 cm

c
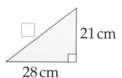
21 cm
28 cm

d

40 cm
9 cm

e

2.5 m
1.5 m

f
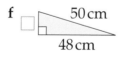
50 cm
48 cm

activity

Draw a 3 cm, 4 cm, 5 cm right-angled triangle with a square on each side.

Cut out another 3 cm by 3 cm square.

Cut out another 4 cm by 4 cm square and cut it into 4 pieces exactly as shown.

Use these five pieces to fit in the 5 cm by 5 cm square to demonstrate Pythagoras' theorem.

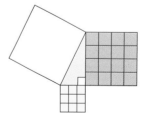

• Use Pythagoras' theorem to calculate lengths in a variety of contexts

Keywords
Pythagoras
Pythagorean triple
Right-angled triangle

You can use **Pythagoras'** theorem to calculate the length of a side in a **right-angled triangle**.

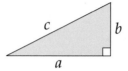

• $c^2 = a^2 + b^2$ where c is the hypotenuse.

It must be a right-angled triangle.

example

Calculate the distance between the points (-3, 6) and (5, 2).

· ·

First draw the right-angled triangle.
The hypotenuse is c.
$$c^2 = 4^2 + 8^2$$
$$= 16 + 64$$
$$= 80$$
$$c = \sqrt{80} = 8.9 \text{ units (1 dp)}$$

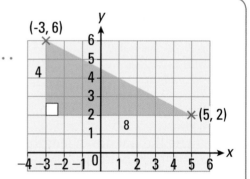

example

Calculate the area of the equilateral triangle.

· ·

Use Pythagoras' theorem in the right-angled triangle.
$$h^2 = 10^2 - 5^2$$
$$= 100 - 25$$
$$= 75$$
$$h = \sqrt{75} = 8.660254 \ldots \text{cm} \quad \text{Do not round the value of } h.$$

Area of the equilateral triangle
$$= \frac{1}{2} \times 10 \times 8.660254 \ldots$$
$$= 43.30127 \ldots$$
$$= 43.3 \text{ cm}^2 \text{(1 dp)} \qquad \text{Now round the answer.}$$

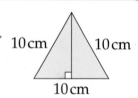

p. 214

A **Pythagorean triple** consists of three integers that could be the lengths of the sides of a right-angled triangle, that is, a, b, c where $a^2 + b^2 = c^2$

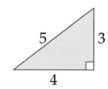

The most well-known triple is 3, 4, 5.

Exercise 3e

1 Use Pythagoras' theorem to decide if these triangles are right-angled.

a

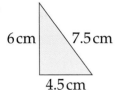

6 cm   7.5 cm

4.5 cm

b

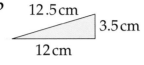

12.5 cm

3.5 cm

12 cm

c

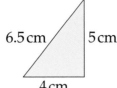

6.5 cm   5 cm

4 cm

d

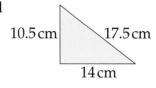

10.5 cm   17.5 cm

14 cm

2 Calculate the distances between these pairs of points.

  a (1, 2) and (4, 6) **b** (2, -1) and (3, 2) **c** (-2, 5) and (2, 1) **d** (-1, -2) and (1, 0)

3 A 4 metre ladder leans against a wall with its base 1.5 metres from the wall.
How far up the wall does the ladder reach?

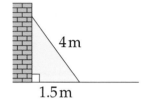

4 m

1.5 m

4 Draw a rectangle measuring 4 cm by 6 cm.
  a Draw and measure the diagonal of the rectangle.
  b Use Pythagoras' theorem to check your answer.

5 Two isosceles triangles have sides of length 24 cm, 20 cm, 20 cm and 32 cm, 20 cm, 20 cm.
For each triangle calculate its
  i perpendicular height   **ii** area.

a

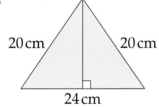

20 cm   20 cm

24 cm

b

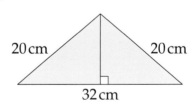

20 cm   20 cm

32 cm

The famous mathematician Euclid generated Pythagorean triples (a, b, c) using the formulae

  $a = 2pq$ $b = p^2 - q^2$ $c = p^2 + q^2$

where p and q are integers and $p > q$.
a Check that a, b and c are a Pythagorean triple when
  i $p = 2$ and $q = 1$ **ii** $p = 3$ and $q = 2$ **iii** $p = 4$ and $q = 3$
b Investigate Pythagorean triples if p and q are
  i both even   **ii** both odd   **iii** have a common
                                            factor greater than 1.

3f Constructing a triangle

- Use a ruler, compasses and protractor to construct 2-D shapes

Keywords
Construct
Hypotenuse

You can always **construct** a unique triangle if you are given

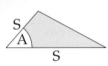

Two sides and the included angle (SAS)

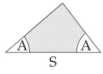

Two angles and the included side (ASA)

> A triangle is unique if it is the only one that can be drawn using the information given.

> Included means 'in between'.

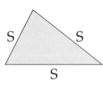

Three sides (SSS)

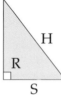

A right angle, **hypotenuse** and side (RHS)

> The hypotenuse is the longest side in a right-angled triangle.

You cannot construct a unique triangle if you are given

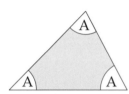

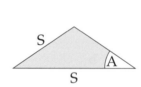

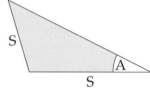

Three angles (AAA)

Two sides and the non-included angle (ASS)

> Many similar triangles can be constructed from the same information.

> Two different triangles may be constructed from the same information.

a Construct a triangle PQR where PQ = 7.5 cm, PR = 4 cm and angle Q = 25°.

b Can you draw more than one triangle with this information?

> The information you are given in this example is ASS.

a First draw a sketch   then a construction.

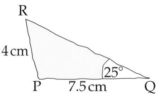

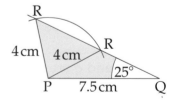

b Two possible triangles can be constructed with this information. There are two possible positions for the vertex R.

50 **Geometry** Geometrical reasoning and constructions

Exercise 3f

1 State whether the information given in each triangle is SAS,
ASA, SSS or RHS.
Construct each triangle using ruler, protractor and compasses.

a
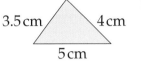
3.5 cm   4 cm
5 cm

b
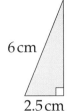
6 cm
2.5 cm

c
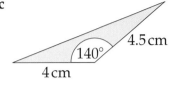
4.5 cm
140°
4 cm

d
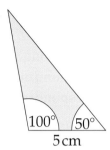
100° 50°
5 cm

2 Repeat the construction of the RHS triangle in question
1 using only a ruler and compasses.

3 Construct these quadrilaterals.
Measure the length of the diagonals in each quadrilateral.

a

3 cm   3 cm
5 cm
4 cm   4 cm

b
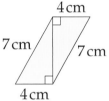
4 cm
7 cm   7 cm
4 cm

c
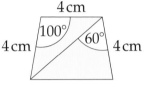
4 cm
100° 60°
4 cm   4 cm

4 You are asked to construct a triangle ABC, where angle
A = 70° and angle B = 60°.
What one extra piece of information do you need to ensure
you construct a unique triangle?

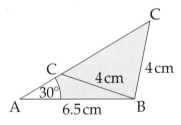
C
70° 60°
A   B

5 a Construct the two different triangles that are possible for
this information
AB = 6.5 cm, BC = 4 cm, angle A = 30°.
b Measure AC for each of your triangles.

C
4 cm
C   4 cm
30°
A   6.5 cm   B

Angle C is either a right angle, an acute or an obtuse angle in these triangles.

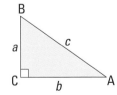
B
a c
C b A

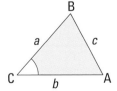
B
a c
C b A

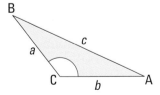
B
a c
C b A

If angle C = 90°, then Pythagoras' theorem states $c^2 = a^2 + b^2$.
Construct triangles to investigate the relationship between c^2 and
$a^2 + b^2$ if angle C is acute or if it is obtuse.

investigation

- Recognise congruent shapes
- Understand and use congruence

Keywords
Congruence
Congruent
Corresponding angles
Corresponding sides

- **Congruent** objects are exactly the same shape and size.

If shapes are congruent, then
- **corresponding angles** are equal
- **corresponding sides** are equal.

Two triangles are congruent if they satisfy
one of these four sets of conditions
- two sides and the included angle are equal (SAS)
- two angles and the included side are equal (ASA)
- three sides are equal (SSS)
- a right angle, hypotenuse and side are equal (RHS).

These are the same
conditions required to
construct a unique triangle.

These two triangles are congruent.

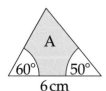 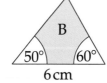

Reflect triangle B and then
the triangle will fit exactly on
top of each other.

The two angles and the included side are equal (ASA) so the
triangles are congruent.

- You can use **congruence** to prove mathematical
  properties of shapes.

---

example

ABC is a triangle with AB = AC.
AX is perpendicular to BC.
Prove angle ABX = angle ACX and BX = CX.

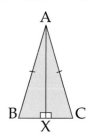

. . . .

AB = AC   and   angle BXA = angle CXA = 90°   given
AX = AX   it is the same line
Therefore triangles ABX and ACX are congruent by RHS.
This means the corresponding angles ABX and ACX are equal.
The base angles of an isosceles triangle are equal.
This means the corresponding sides BX and CX are equal.
The foot of the perpendicular bisects the base of an isosceles triangle.

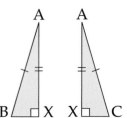

Exercise 3g

1 Match the congruent triangles.
Use SAS, ASA, SSS or RHS to help you decide.

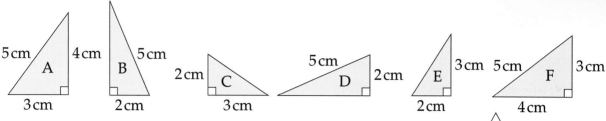

2 Name the two congruent triangles.
Explain your answer using SAS,
ASA, SSS or RHS.

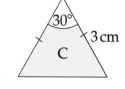

3 Explain why these two triangles are congruent.
Hence find x and y.

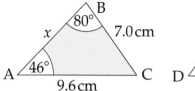
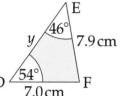

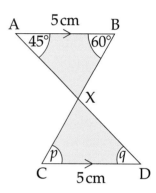

4 AB and CD are two parallel lines. AB = CD = 5 cm.
  a Find the values of angles p and q.
  b Explain why triangles ABX and DCX are congruent.

challenge

Copy the two diagrams which show constructions for the angle
bisector of angle ABC and perpendicular bisector of line PQ.

a

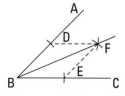

b

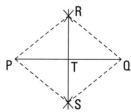

i Explain why BD = BE and DF = EF.
ii What shape is BDFE?
iii Show that triangles BDF and BEF are
    congruent; hence deduce that angle
    DBF = angle EBF.

i Show that triangles PRS and QRS
    are congruent and identify all pairs
    of equal angles.
ii Show that triangles PRT and QRT
    are congruent; hence deduce that
    PT = QT and angle PTR = angle
    QTR = 90°.

- Find the locus of a point that moves according to a rule
- Devise instructions for a computer to generate shapes

Keywords
Hemisphere
Locus
Perpendicular bisector

The **locus** of an object is its path.

- A point that moves according to a rule forms a locus.

The plural of locus is loci.

The rule could be a set of instructions.

```
REPEAT 2
[FORWARD 5 TURN RIGHT 60°
 FORWARD 5 TURN RIGHT 120°]
```

The locus is a rhombus.

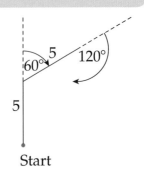

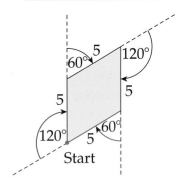

---

example

Find the three loci of points which are the same distance from A and B, from B and C and from C and A.

. . . .

The set of points equidistant from A and B lie on the **perpendicular bisector** of the line segment AB.
Likewise for BC and CA.

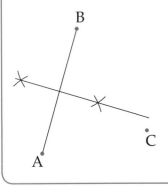

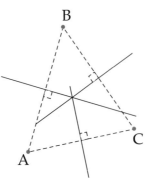

The common point, which is equidistant from A, B and C is the centre of the circumcircle of triangle ABC.

---

example

A conger eel lives in a hole in an underwater cliff face. If a diver's finger comes within 50 cm of the hole it will be bitten. Describe the locus of the finger's closest safe approach.

. . . .

The locus of points of closest safe approach form a **hemisphere** of radius 50 cm centred on the hole.

Exercise 3h

1 For the following sets of instructions
  i construct the shape using a suitable scale
  ii give the mathematical name of the shape produced.

  a REPEAT 3
   [FORWARD 6 TURN LEFT 120°]

  b FORWARD 8, RIGHT 120°
   REPEAT 3
   [FORWARD 4 TURN LEFT 60°]

2 Write a set of instructions for drawing
  a a regular pentagon   **b** a letter 'W'.

3 Three friends stand at the corners of a triangular field.
Each friend walks towards the centre of the field being careful
to stay an equal distance from the two edges of the field nearest
them. By drawing your own triangle (about 8 cm across) and
constructing the friends' paths, show that the they will all pass
through the same point.

The common point is the
centre of the inscribed circle.

4 A goat is tethered 3 m from the end of an 8 m long wall.
On a scale drawing show the area that the goat can reach
if the rope is
  a 2 m long   **b** 5 m long   **c** 6 m long

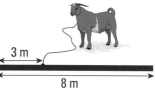

5 A Van de Graaff generator puts a large electrical charge on a
metal sphere of diameter 20 cm. If your finger comes closer than
30 cm you receive an electric shock. Describe the locus of points
that are just at a safe distance.

6 A man stands 2 m from the top of a 6 m ladder which suddenly
starts to slide down the wall. By making a scale drawing find
the locus of the man's feet.

activity

Mark two points A and B approximately 6 cm apart.
Place a sheet of paper so that the edges pass
through points A and B.
Mark the position X, where angle AXB = 90°.
Move the sheet of paper to different positions,
each time marking the position of X,
where angle AXB = 90°.

Describe the locus of the point X.

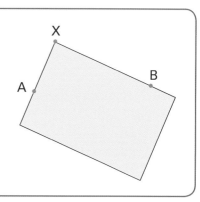

1 Calculate the values of the marked angles.

a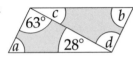

parallelogram

b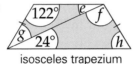

arrowhead

c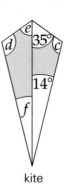

kite

d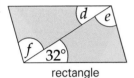

rectangle

e isosceles trapezium

2 **a** Construct a regular nonagon (9 sides).
  b Draw the lines of reflection symmetry.
  c State the order of rotation symmetry.
  d Measure an interior angle of the nonagon.
  e Explain why the regular nonagon will
    not tessellate.

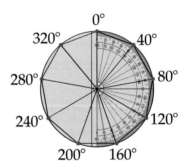

3 You can draw a circumscribed circle for a square.
  If possible, draw a circumscribed circle for
  a a rectangle   **b** a kite   **c** a rhombus
  d a parallelogram   **e** an isosceles trapezium.

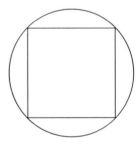

4 Use Pythagoras' theorem to calculate the unknown lengths.

a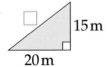
15 m
20 m

b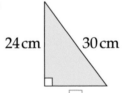
24 cm   30 cm

c
8.5 cm
7.5 cm

Each answer is an integer.

5 A square is drawn inside a 4 by 4 square. Calculate
  a the length c
  b the area of the shaded square.

6 There are two right-angled triangles in
  the diagram.
  Calculate the value of p and q.

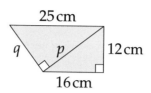

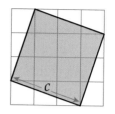

7 Using the information given below
  i draw a sketch of each triangle
  ii state whether the information you are given is
    SAS, ASA, SSS, RHS, AAA or ASS.
  iii Does the information given result in a unique triangle?

  a
  | angle A = 80° |
  | angle B = 70° |
  | angle C = 30° |

  b
  | QR = 10 cm |
  | PQ = 8 cm |
  | PR = 9 cm |

  c
  | angle D = 30° |
  | angle E = 40° |
  | DE = 5 cm |

  d
  | JK = 8 cm |
  | LK = 7.5 cm |
  | angle K = 40° |

  e
  | angle S = 90° |
  | ST = 3 cm |
  | UT = 8 cm |

  f
  | YZ = 6 cm |
  | XZ = 4 cm |
  | angle Y = 35° |

8 a Find the value of a.
  b Explain why the two triangles are congruent using
    SSS, SAS, ASA or RHS.

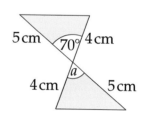

9 For the following sets of instructions
  i construct the shape using a suitable scale
  ii give the mathematical name of the shape produced.
    a REPEAT 2
      [FORWARD 8 TURN RIGHT 90°
      FORWARD 5 TURN RIGHT 90°]
    b REPEAT 2
      [FORWARD 5 TURN RIGHT 45°
      FORWARD 3 TURN RIGHT 135°]

10 Two lines AB and CD intersect at X.
  a Construct the locus of a point equidistant
    i from XA and XD   **ii** from XD and XB.
  b What is the angle between these loci?

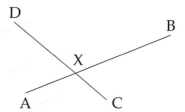

3 Summary

Assessment criteria

- Understand and apply Pythagoras' theorem when solving problems in 2-D **Level 7**
- Understand and use congruence **Level 8**

1 ABC is a right-angled triangle.
Calculate
a the length a
b the area of the triangle.

Vicki's answer ✔

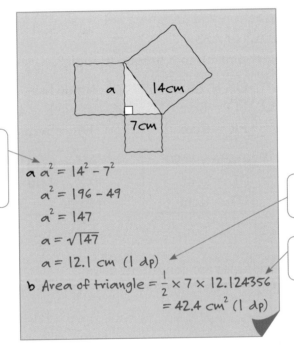

Vicki knows the unknown length is less than 14 cm and so she subtracts the areas.

a $a^2 = 14^2 - 7^2$

$a^2 = 196 - 49$

$a^2 = 147$

$a = \sqrt{147}$

$a = 12.1$ cm (1 dp)

b Area of triangle $= \frac{1}{2} \times 7 \times 12.124356$

$= 42.4$ cm^2 (1 dp)

She rounds to a suitable degree of accuracy.

She uses 12.124356 at this stage of the calculation.

2 Two pupils each drew a triangle with one side 5 cm, one angle of 20° and one angle of 60°.
Must their triangles be congruent?

☐ Yes   ☐ No

Explain your answer.

KS3 2007 6–8 Paper 1

4 Algebra

Equations

The first electronic computer was built around 1942 by John Vincent Atanasoff with the help of his student Clifford Berry. The Atanasoff-Berry Computer (or ABC) ran with the aid of electronic valves.

What's the point? This computer was built purely to solve simultaneous equations more quickly than by pencil and paper methods.

Check in

1 Expand and simplify
   a $12(2x + 10)$ **b** $3(4a + 1) + 8(a + 3)$
   c $5x(x - 4)$ **d** $3(2y + 5) - 4(5 - y)$

2 Solve these equations
   a $5x + 15 = 30$ **b** $3(2m - 4) = 30$

3 Construct and solve an equation to find the number in the puzzle below.
   "I think of a number, double it, add 7 and treble all of this to get 57"

4 All of these expressions except one have a value of 13 when $x = 2$.
   Which is the odd one out?
   $3x^2 + 1$ $x^3 + 5$ $x^2 + x + 5$ $20 - 2x^2 + 1$

- Solve linear equations involving negative terms, brackets and algebraic fractions

Keywords
Cross-multiply
Linear equation
Solution
Solve
Term

- **Linear equations** with unknowns on both sides are **solved** by subtracting the smallest algebraic **term** from each side.

example

The area of carpet needed to cover two bedrooms in a house are equal.
Find the dimensions of each room.

$8 - x$ [rectangle, width 8]
$x + 1$ [square, width 4]

You may have to construct an equation from given information.

Area of rectangle = length × width

$$8(8 - x) = 4(x + 1)$$
$$64 - 8x = 4x + 4$$
$$64 = 12x + 4$$
$$12x = 60 \qquad \text{so } x = 5$$

-8x is smaller than 4x so subtract -8x from both sides. This is the same as adding 8x to both sides.

Hence, the first room measures 3 m by 8 m and the second room 4 m by 6 m.

- If an equation has only one negative algebraic term simplify it by first adding the inverse of the negative term to both sides.

example

Solve $10 - 5x = 12$

Just as $10 - 3 = 7$ can be rewritten as $10 = 7 + 3$ then $10 - 5x = 12$ can be written as $10 = 12 + 5x$.

$$10 - 5x = 12$$
$$10 = 12 + 5x$$
$$-2 = 5x$$
$$\frac{-2}{5} = x$$

Solutions can be fractions, negatives or both.

 p. 188

- Equations with fractions can often be solved using **cross-multiplication**.

example

Solve $\dfrac{4}{2 - 3x} = \dfrac{5}{6 - 2x}$

Just as $\dfrac{10}{2} \diagup \dfrac{25}{5}$ leads to
$10 \times 5 = 25 \times 2$
then $\dfrac{4}{2 - 3x} \diagup \dfrac{5}{6 - 2x}$ leads to
$4(6 - 2x) = 5(2 - 3x)$.

$$\frac{4}{2 - 3x} = \frac{5}{6 - 2x}$$
$$4(6 - 2x) = 5(2 - 3x)$$
$$24 - 8x = 10 - 15x$$
$$24 + 7x = 10$$
$$7x = -14 \text{ so } x = -2$$

Cross-multiplication only works for equations of the form "fraction = fraction".
For $\dfrac{x}{2} + 1 = 7$
first rewrite as $\dfrac{x}{2} = 6$ or $\dfrac{x}{2} = \dfrac{6}{1}$.

Exercise 4a

1 Solve these equations.

You should find your solution in the list below.

a $5x - 12 = -2$ **b** $12 - 3y = 2$ **c** $2(4x + 1) = 5(3x - 2)$

d $6 - 4y = 10 - 8y$ **e** $100 - a = 56$ **f** $\dfrac{x + 12}{5} + 3 = 5$

g $\dfrac{y + 1}{6} = \dfrac{3y}{5}$ **h** $\dfrac{3}{x + 5} = \dfrac{9}{2x + 1}$

| A 1 | B -2 | C $\frac{5}{13}$ | D 2 | E 44 | F $3\frac{1}{3}$ | G -14 | H $1\frac{5}{7}$ |

Fractions are exact and don't need rounding, unlike many decimals.

2 Amie solved three equations but got them all wrong.

Can you spot and correct her error in each case?

a
$$8y - 1 = 4y + 1$$
$$4y - 1 = 1$$
$$4y = -2$$
$$y = \frac{-1}{2}$$

b
$$18 - 3a = 6 - 9a$$
$$18 = 6 - 2a$$
$$12 = 12a$$
$$a = 1$$

c
$$\frac{x + 6}{2} = \frac{x + 14}{3}$$
$$3x + 6 = 2x + 14$$
$$x + 6 = 14$$
$$x = 8$$

3 In each part, form an equation to represent the given information and solve it to find the unknown.

a I think of a number, multiply it by 8 and add five. This gives me the same answer as when I subtract the number from 50. What is the number?

b If the areas of the triangle and trapezium are equal, find x.

c If the means of the expressions in each box are equal, find y.

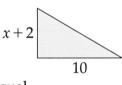

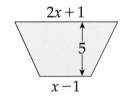

| $y + 3$ | $10 - 4y$ |
| $5y - 3$ | $2(y + 1)$ |

$7y - 3$	
	$6y + 6$
$2 - y$	

4 a Simplify $\dfrac{x + 1}{3} + \dfrac{x}{7}$

b Hence, solve $\dfrac{x + 1}{3} + \dfrac{x}{7} = \dfrac{x - 1}{4}$

Remember how to add fractions

$$\frac{2}{5} + \frac{3}{8} = \frac{2 \times 8 + 3 \times 5}{5 \times 8}$$

challenge

This equation has two solutions. Can you find them both?

$$\frac{25}{x + 2} = x + 2$$

Can you write an equation of your own with no solutions or with two solutions?

4b Introducing simultaneous equations

- Solve a pair of simultaneous linear equations by eliminating one variable

Keywords
*Elimination   Solve
Simultaneous Substitute
     equations   Variable*

- **Simultaneous equations** are equations **solved** at the same time to find the value of more than one **variable**.

---

example

Alex plays a computer game. He scored 31 points by destroying two planets and three satellites and then 45 points by destroying two planets and five satellites.
How many points are scored for destroying a planet and for a satellite?

Simultaneous equations are needed here since we have two unknowns: the number of points scored for destroying a planet and the number of points scored for destroying a satellite.

Let x represent the number of points for a planet and y for a satellite.

$$2x + 3y = 31 \quad (1)$$
$$2x + 5y = 45 \quad (2) \qquad \text{Label the equations.}$$

Subtract (1) from (2) $\qquad 0 + 2y = 14 \qquad x$ has been eliminated.
$$\Rightarrow \qquad y = 7$$

Substitute $y = 7$ into (1) $\quad 2x + 21 = 31$
$$\Rightarrow \qquad 2x = 10 \text{ and } x = 5$$

Check using equation (2)
$2 \times 5 + 5 \times 7 = 10 + 35$
$= 45$ ✔

So 5 points are scored for destroying a planet and 7 points for a satellite.

- You can solve simultaneous equations using **elimination.**

Add or subtract the equations to eliminate one variable. When you eliminate a variable, look at the signs. If the signs are opposite then add. If they are the same then subtract.

Remember
Same Signs Subtract (SSS).

---

example

Solve the following pairs of simultaneous equations
$$3x - 4y = 22 \quad (1)$$
$$x + 4y = 18 \quad (2)$$

Eliminate the y-terms since they have the same coefficients (4).
They have opposite signs so add.
$$(1) + (2) \qquad 4x + 0 = 40$$
$$\Rightarrow \qquad x = 10$$
Substitute $x = 2$ into (2) $\quad 10 + 4y = 18$
$$\Rightarrow \qquad 4y = 8 \text{ and } y = 2$$

Check using (1)
$3 \times 10 - 4 \times 2 = 30 - 8$
$= 22$ ✔

62   **Algebra** Equations

Exercise 4b

1 Solve the following pairs of simultaneous equations by subtracting.

> Remember to check both solutions.

  a $x + 2y = 4$
      $5x + 2y = 16$
  b $2x + y = 10$
      $5x + y = 22$
  c $4x + 5y = 9$
      $4x - 2y = 2$
  d $a + 6b = 31$
      $a + 3b = 16$

2 Solve the following pairs of simultaneous equations by adding.

  a $3x + 2y = 19$
      $8x - 2y = 58$
  b $5x + 2y = 16$
      $3x - 2y = 8$
  c $2a + 3b = 3$
      $7a - 3b = 24$
  d $2m + 3n = 19$
      $-2m + n = 1$

3 Solve the following pairs of simultaneous equations.

  a $x + y = 3$
      $3x - y = 17$
  b $x + y = 9$
      $x + 2y = 16$
  c $2x + 3y = 5$
      $2x - 2y = -10$
  d $a + 3b = 14$
      $-a + 3b = 10$

4 Leah used her mobile phone to send 6 text messages and 8 picture messages and was charged £1.92. When she sent 2 text messages and 8 picture messages she was charged £1.44. Use simultaneous equations to find the cost of each type of message.

> Pence are easier to work with than pounds.

5 Use the equations below to make as many pairs of simultaneous equations as possible. Solve each pair that you make.

   $5x + 2y = 11$ $x + 2y = 3$ $x - 2y = -5$

6 The difference between two numbers is 9 and their sum is 25. Use simultaneous equations to find the two numbers.

---

challenge

Alex plays a computer game where he destroys planets and stars. Destroying two planets and five stars and gaining 30 points could be represented with the equation

   $2x + 5y = 30$.

Explain how Alex's computer game may have led to each of the following equations.

   $7x + 9y = 99$ $5x + 2y = -10$

- Solve a pair of simultaneous linear equations by eliminating one variable

Keywords
Eliminate
Simultaneous equations

Imogen bought a chocolate bar and two cereal bars for 50 pence.

Ava bought three chocolate bars and two cereal bars for 90 pence.

Since Ava spent 40 pence more and got two extra chocolate bars, each chocolate bar must cost 20 pence. Using algebra

$$x + 2y = 50 \quad (1)$$
$$3x + 2y = 90 \quad (2)$$
$$(2) - (1) \quad 2x + 0 = 40$$
$$x = 20$$

Imogen bought a chocolate bar and two cereal bars for 50 pence.

Ava bought two chocolate bars and three cereal bars for 85 pence.

×2

It helps to imagine Imogen buying twice as much as she did.

$$x + 2y = 50 \quad (1) \qquad \times 2 \qquad 2x + 4y = 100 \quad (3)$$
$$2x + 3y = 85 \quad (2) \qquad\qquad\qquad 2x + 3y = 85 \quad (2)$$
$$(3) - (2) \qquad y = 15$$

> This problem is harder because the girls did not buy the same quantity of one of the items.

The cereal bar cost 15 pence so the chocolate bar must be 20 pence.

- To **eliminate** a variable multiply one or both simultaneous equations to make its coefficient the same in both.

Solve the following pairs of simultaneous equations

a $x + 3y = 16 \quad (1)$
$ 2x - y = -3 \quad (2)$

b $5x - 3y = 13 \quad (1)$
$ 3x + 2y = 4 \quad (2)$

. . . .

a Eliminate the x-terms
$2 \times (1) \quad 2x + 6y = 32 \quad (3)$
All terms have been doubled.
$ 2x - y = -3 \quad (2)$
$(3) - (2) \qquad 7y = 35$
$\Rightarrow \qquad y = 5$
$ \text{and } x = 1$

b Eliminate the y-terms
$2 \times (1) \quad 10x - 6y = 26 \quad (3)$

$3 \times (2) \quad 9x + 6y = 12 \quad (4)$
$(3) + (4) \qquad 19x = 38$
$\Rightarrow \qquad x = 2$
$ \text{and } y = -1$

> Alternatively for **b**
> $5 \times (2) - 3 \times (1)$
> would eliminate x and allow y to be found.

Exercise 4c

1 Solve the following pairs of simultaneous equations by first multiplying one of the equations.

a $x + y = 5$
$2x + 3y = 14$

b $2x + y = 7$
$4x + 3y = 20$

c $2x - y = 9$
$3x + 2y = 17$

d $5a - b = 12$
$7a - 3b = 20$

2 Solve the following pairs of simultaneous equations by first multiplying both of the equations.

> Don't be put off by the number zero.

a $2x + 3y = 12$
$3x + 2y = 13$

b $2x - 3y = 19$
$7x + 4y = 23$

c $5a - 2b = 11$
$3a + 3b = -6$

d $6m - 3n = 0$
$5m + 4n = 13$

3 Use simultaneous equations to work out the value of each symbol in this puzzle.

 + + + = 69

 + + + = 66

4 Write a pair of simultaneous equations with solutions $x = 3$ and $y = 4$.
Repeat for $m = -3$ and $n = \frac{1}{2}$.

5 Simran has two folders on her computer. One contains three songs and two photos and is 570 KB in size. The second contains four songs and five photos and is 900 KB in size. Assuming each song and each photo are equal in size, how big is each type of file?

Did you know?

Companies use systems of simultaneous equations to work out how to make the most profit or cause the least pollution.

6 Write a problem that could be represented by the simultaneous equations
$2x + 5y = 10$ and $7x + 6y = 58$.
Solve these equations. Does the solution make sense for the problem you have written? Explain.

7 Try solving these simultaneous equations and explain what goes wrong and why this happens. How many solutions are possible?
$x + 5y = 1$ and $2x + 10y = 2$

---

challenge

Use graphs to explain why these simultaneous equations have no solution.

$y = 2x + 4$ $\qquad$ $y = 2x + 6$

4d Constructing simultaneous equations — LEVEL 7

- Solve a pair of simultaneous linear equations by eliminating one variable
- Represent problems in algebraic form

p. 132

Keywords
Construct
Interpret

- Simultaneous equations can be **constructed** in order to solve problems in which there are two unknowns.

example

One week Claire earns £6.78 for delivering 18 magazines and 43 newspapers.
The next week she earns the same amount for delivering 6 magazines and 52 newspapers.
How much does she earn for delivering each item?

Let x be the money earned for delivering a magazine.
Let y be the money earned for delivering a newspaper.

$$18x + 43y = 678 \quad (1)$$
$$6x + 52y = 678 \quad (2)$$

$3 \times (2)$ $\quad 18x + 156y = 2034 \quad (3)$ — Multiply equation (2) by 3.
$\qquad\qquad\; 18x + 43y = 678 \quad (1)$

$(3) - (1) \quad 0 + 113y = 1356$ — Subtract equation (1) from equation (3).
$\qquad\qquad\qquad\quad y = 12$

> Check the solution using (2):
> LHS $= 6 \times 9 + 52 \times 12$
> $\quad = 54 + 624$
> $\quad = 678 =$ RHS ✔

Substitute $y = 12$ into (1)

$$18x + 516 = 678$$
$$18x = 162$$
$$x = 9$$

> **Interpret** the solution in terms of the problem. Don't just quote $x = 9$ and $y = 12$.

Claire earns 9p for each magazine and 12p for each newspaper delivered.

example

The perimeter of this triangle is 70 cm.
How long is each side?

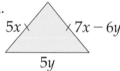

$5x$, $7x - 6y$, $5y$

> It may not always be obvious that simultaneous equations are required and you may need to use other mathematical knowledge.

Isosceles triangle $\quad 5x = 7x - 6y \qquad\qquad\qquad \Rightarrow \qquad 2x - 6y = 0 \quad (1)$
Perimeter = 70 $\quad 5x + 5y + 7x - 6y = 70 \qquad \Rightarrow \qquad 12x - y = 70 \quad (2)$
$\qquad\qquad\qquad\qquad\qquad\qquad\qquad 6 \times (2) \qquad 72x - 6y = 420 \quad (3)$
$\qquad\qquad\qquad\qquad\qquad\qquad\qquad (3) - (1) \qquad 70x = 420$
$\qquad\qquad\qquad\qquad\qquad\qquad\qquad\qquad\qquad x = 6, y = 2$

First side $5 \times 6 = 30$ cm, second side 30 cm and base $5 \times 2 = 10$ cm.

Exercise 4d

1 Match the problem with the pair of simultaneous equations
  that represent it and with their solution.
  Interpret each solution in terms of the problem given.

A Two coffees and two teas cost £1. Four coffees and a tea cost £1.40.	a $2x + 2y = 100$ $x - y = 20$	α $x = 35, y = 15$
B One angle is 20 degrees more than another and their sum is 100.	b $2x + 2y = 100$ $4x + 2y = 180$	β $x = 60, y = 40$
C The sum of double two numbers is 100. Their difference is 20.	c $x + y = 100$ $x - y = 20$	γ $x = 30, y = 20$
D Hitting two planets and two satellites in a computer game scores 100 points. Hitting four planets and a two satellites scores 180 points.	d $2x + 2y = 100$ $4x + y = 140$	δ $x = 40, y = 10$

2 Set up a pair of simultaneous equations and solve them to
  find the solution to each problem.

> A solution can be tested by substitution.

  a The sum of two numbers is 34 and their difference is 6.
    What is their product?
  b Grace told her mum that the sum of their ages is half
    a century and the difference between them is two dozen.
    Is Grace a teenager?
  c A theatre takes £700 in ticket sales for a show where
    80 children and 30 adults are in the audience and
    £950 for a show where 30 children and 80 adults are
    in the audience.
    What is the price of a child's ticket?
  d The perimeter of this square is 80 cm.
    Find x and y.

$x + 3y$ □ $7y$

3 a Invent a problem that could be represented by
        $x + 4y = 16$
        $3x + y = 16$.
  b Solve and interpret your solution.

> **challenge**
>
> The line $y = mx + c$ passes through the points (1, 4) and (3, 14).
> Use simultaneous equations to find the equation of the line.

- Solve linear inequalities in one variable
- Represent the solution set on a number line

Keywords
Inequality   Solution set
Integer   Solve

- **Inequalities** are mathematical statements containing one or more of the symbols $<$, $\leq$, $>$ or $\geq$.

$<$ less than
$\leq$ less than or equal to
$>$ greater than
$\geq$ greater than or equal to

Since an inequality can have more than one solution, the **solution set** is represented on a number line.

| Under 3s travel for free | Bridge not suitable for lorries over 3m | You must be over 1.5m to ride this roller coaster | You must be at least 15 years old to enter **Y Factor** |

$A < 3$ | $h \leq 3$ | $h > 1.5$ | $A \geq 15$

0 1 2 3 4 | 0 1 2 3 4 | −1 0 1 2 3 4 | 14 15 16 17 18 19

The solid circle shows that the end number is part of the solution set and the hollow circle shows that it is not.

You can **solve** an inequality in a similar way to solving an equation since most operations can be applied to each side.

$3 < 10 \Rightarrow$

$7 < 14$ Add 4 to both sides.
$-1 < 6$ Subtract 4 from both sides.
$12 < 40$ Multiply both sides by $+4$.

$3 < 10$ could also be written as $10 > 3$.

- However if you multiply or divide an inequality by a negative number the inequality sign must be reversed.

$3 > 10$ $-6 < -20$ FALSE   Multiply both sides by -2.
$\Rightarrow$ $-6 > -20$ TRUE   Reverse the inequality sign.

example

a Solve these inequalities and represent the solutions on a number line.

i $5x + 5 > 2x + 1$ **ii** $-5y \geq -20$

b Find the **integers** that satisfy
$10 < 2x \leq 17$.

. . . .

i $5x + 5 > 2x - 1$ $- 2x$
$3x + 5 > -1$ $- 5$
$3x > -6$ $\div 3$
$x > -2$

−3 −2 −1 0 1 2

ii $-5y \geq -20$ $\div(-5)$ and reverse
$y \leq 4$ the inequality.

0 1 2 3 4 5

b $10 < 2x \leq 17$ $\div 2$
$5 < x \leq 8\frac{1}{2}$
The integers are
6, 7 and 8.

You can think of
$10 < 2x \leq 17$ as two
separate inequalities
$2x < 10$ and $2x \leq 17$.

Exercise 4e

1 Decide, with a reason, if each of these inequalities is true or false.

   a $3^2 > 2^3$ **b** 10% of 450 $\geq$ 20% of 225

   c $\frac{-1}{3} > \frac{-1}{2}$ **d** $\sqrt{25} \leq 30 < \sqrt[3]{8000}$

2 Use inequalities to write these real-life statements.

  a 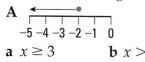   **b** Have you got talent? Contestants over 16 needed   **c** 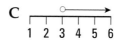 Dresses to fit ladies 155 to 175cm   **d** Free Entry for children under 3 and over 60s

    Use *S* for speed.   Use *A* for age.   Use *h* for height.   Use *A* for age.

3 Match the three number lines to one of the given inequalities.
For the remaining inequalities, draw their number lines.

  A (number line: −5 −4 −3 −2 −1 0, arrow left from −3)
  B (number line: 1 2 3 4 5 6, arrow right from 3)
  C (number line: 1 2 3 4 5 6, open circle at 2, arrow right)

  a $x \geq 3$ **b** $x > 3$ **c** $x < 2$ **d** $x \leq 0$

  e $x > -4$ **f** $x \leq -2$ **g** $2 < x \leq 5$

4 Solve these inequalities and illustrate your solutions
on a number line.

  a $3x - 5 < 16$ **b** $5y + 2 \leq 3y + 8$ **c** $4z - 3 \geq 3(z - 5)$ **d** $6 > 3x$

  e $-5a \leq 30$ **f** $10 - 2x < 3$ **g** $\dfrac{x + 7}{2} \leq \dfrac{x - 1}{5}$ **h** $36 < 6m \leq 72$

5 **a** Find all the integers that satisfy $2x \geq 10$ and $3x - 2 < 31$.

   b Explain why there are no integers such that $y \geq 10$ and $2y < 8$.

> An integer is a whole number:
> . . . -3, -2, -1, 0, 1, 2, . . .

6 The number of square centimetres in the area of this
rectangle is greater than the number of centimetres in
its perimeter. Write an inequality to represent this
information and solve it to find the range of values of x.

    (rectangle, width labelled $x - 1$, height labelled 6)

7 If the mean of the first set of expressions is less
than the mean of the second set, write and solve
an inequality to find the possible values for x.

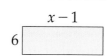

    $2x$ 10 $3x$ 4 x

    $7x$ 2 $-x$ 5 $8x$

---

investigation

Investigate the $x!$ button on your calculator.

Can you work out what it does?

Find the smallest value of x such that $x! > 1\,000\,000$.

> Be systematic in your investigation. Make a table of results for 1!, 2!, 3!, . . .

- Find approximate solutions to equations using trial and improvement
- Construct equations from given information

Keywords
Equation
Formula
Solution
Trial-and-improvement

Linear **equations** can be solved using algebraic methods but with more difficult equations you sometimes need to use **trial-and-improvement** to find a **solution**.

example

Use trial-and-improvement to solve $x^2 + x = 48$, giving your answer to one decimal place.

	A	B	C	D
	x	x^2	$x^2 + x$	Result
1				
2	6	36	42	low
3	7	49	58	high
4	6.4	40.96	47.36	low
5	6.5	42.25	48.75	high
6	6.45	41.6025	48.0525	high

$6.4 < x < 6.45$ so $x = 6.4$ (1 dp)

The full answer is
6.42820323 . . .
Therefore 6.4 is correct to
1 dp.

Organise trials to sandwich the solution.

Do not choose 6.4 because it is 'closer' than 6.5. Choose 6.4 because the answer lies between 6.40 and 6.45, which both equal 6.4 (1 dp).

Always work to one more decimal place than asked for.

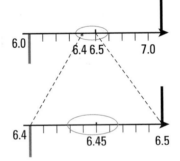

You may need to construct an equation, perhaps using **formulae** from other areas of mathematics.

example

The volume of this cuboid is $392\,\text{cm}^3$.
How long is each side?

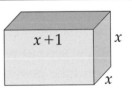

Volume of cuboid $= lwh$
So, $x \times x \times (x + 1) = 392$ $\Rightarrow$ $x^2(x + 1) = 392$

x	x^2	$x + 1$	$x^2(x + 1)$	Result
5	25	6	150	low
6	36	7	252	low
7	49	8	392	exact

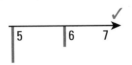

Brackets are required due to BIDMAS,
$x \times x \times x + 1$ is not the same as $x \times x \times (x + 1)$.

$x = 7$ so the width and height are both 7 cm and the length is 8 cm.

Exercise 4f

1 Select three equations that you need trial-and-improvement to solve.

   a $x^2 - 2x = 40$ **b** $5x + 4 = 2 - x$ **c** $x^3 + x = 68$

   d $x(x + 2) = 10$ **e** $x^2 = 25$

2 Find the exact solutions of the following equations using trial-and-improvement.

   a $x^2 - 2x = 255$ **b** $3x^3 + x = 1544$

   c $y(y + 5) = 644$ **d** $2^x = 33554432$

3 Construct an equation and solve it, using trial-and-improvement, to find the exact solution in each case.

   a The product of three consecutive numbers is 32 736.

   b The sum of the square of a number and its square root is 4104.

4 Two students used trial-and-improvement to solve $x^2 + 3x = 60$ to 1 dp. List all of the mistakes that each student has made.

x	x^2	$3x$	$x^2 + 3x$
6	36	18	54
6.8	46.24	20.4	66.64
6.2	38.44	18.6	57.04
6.4	40.96	19.2	60.16

     $x = 60.16$

x	x^2	$3x$	$x^2 + 3x$
6	36	18	54
7	49	21	70
6.3	39.69	18.9	58.59
6.4	40.96	19.2	60.16
6.35	40.3225	19.05	59.3725
6.36	40.4496	19.08	59.5296
6.37	40.5769	19.11	59.6869
6.38	40.7044	19.14	59.8444
6.39	40.8321	19.17	60.0021

     $x = 6.4$

5 Use trial-and-improvement to solve these equations to 1 dp.

   a $x^2 + 4x = 100$ **b** $x^3 - x = 700$

   c $5x^2 + 3x = 90$ **d** $y(y - 2) = 220$

6 Use trial-and-improvement to solve these equations to the given number of decimal places.

   a $3x^2 - x = 280$ (2 dp)   **b** $3^x = 42$ (2 dp)

   c $\sqrt{x} + x = 90$ (3 dp)   **d** $x^4 + 2x = 630$ (3 dp)

7 The volume of this cuboid is 780 cm³.

   Find x.

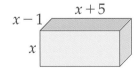

---

task

Many equations on this page are quadratic equations. What is a quadratic equation and do you really need trial-and-improvement to solve them?

1 Solve the following equations.

   a $5a + 11 = 3a - 2$ **b** $10 - 5x = 2(3 - 2x)$

   c $15 - 2y = 25$ **d** $\dfrac{5}{2x - 1} = \dfrac{2}{x + 3}$

2 The means of the numbers in each box are equal. By first using an equation to find x, find this mean.

10	x	-6
$5x$	2	$4x$

7	$4x$	-1
$-12x$	15	

3 Solve the following pairs of simultaneous equations.

   a $5x + 2y = 6$ **b** $3a + b = 14$
      $7x + 2y = 8$ $3a + 6b = 9$
   c $5m + 3n = 16$ **d** $4x - y = 13$
      $3m - 3n = -3$ $8x - y = 21$

4 Solve the following pairs of simultaneous equations.

   a $5x + y = 7$ **b** $2a + 7b = -15$
      $3x + 2y = 7$ $4a - 5b = 27$
   c $5m + 3n = 17$ **d** $3x - 8y = 10$
      $3m - 5n = -17$ $2x - 6y = 7$

5 Construct and solve a pair of simultaneous equations to find the solution to each problem.

   a If two compact discs and four DVDs cost £60 and five compact discs and three DVDs cost £66, how much is a DVD?

   b If the perimeter of this rectangle is 22 cm, what are its dimensions?

$x - 2y$ $2x + 7y$
      8

   c At half term two groups of pupils and teachers set off on school trips. 71 people on the year 9 trip just fill three minibuses and five cars, whilst 33 people on the sixth form trip fill one minibus and four cars. How many people can each type of vehicle hold?

6 For each inequality given below
   i draw a number line to represent the inequality
   ii state at least three integers that satisfy the inequality.
   a $x > 3$
   b $y \leq -2$
   c $m < 8$
   d $5 < x \leq 8$
   e $7 > p$

7 Solve the following inequalities and show the solution set on a number line.
   a $4x + 8 > 2x + 20$
   b $6(2 - 3y) \leq 3(3 - 3y)$
   c $-5x < 20$
   d $10 - 7x < 3$

8 The product of two consecutive integers is 1056.
   a Write an equation to represent this information.
   b Solve this equation using trial-and-improvement to find the consecutive integers.

9 Solve the following equations, to the required number of decimal places, using trial-and-improvement.
   a $x^2 + x = 80$ (1 dp)
   b $x(x + 2) = 194$ (2 dp)

10 A rectangle's length exceeds its width by 3 cm.
   a Write an expression for the length of the rectangle if the width is x.
   b If the area of the rectangle is $100 \, \text{cm}^2$, form an equation in x.
   c Use trial-and-improvement to find the dimensions of the rectangle to one decimal place.

Maths life

Garden design

Sensory gardens are designed to stimulate the senses - sight, sound, smell, touch and even taste - and are thought to have a beneficial effect on people who visit them. Whilst they must be designed for all users, this case study considers their accessibility for wheelchair users.

Raised flowerbeds are easier to reach for a person in a wheelchair.

Cross section of a raised bed

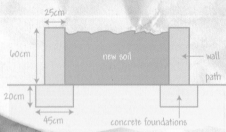

25cm

60cm

new soil

wall

path

20cm

45cm

concrete foundations

PLAN FOR A SENSORY CORNER

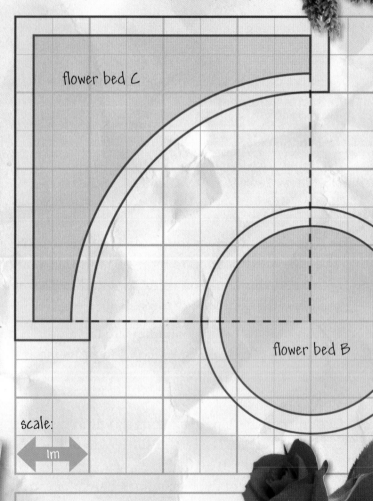

flower bed C

flower bed B

scale:

1m

Widths for paths

1.8m : 2 wheelchairs or 2 people side by side.
1.2m : wheelchair with pedestrian alongside.
0.9m : wheelchair on its own no room alongside.

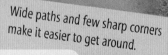

Wide paths and few sharp corners make it easier to get around.

What volume of soil will be needed to fill each flowerbed to 5cm below the top of the wall?

- What volume of concrete will be needed for the foundations of flowerbeds A and B?

- What volume of concrete would be needed to make the walls of flowerbeds C and D?

Plants have different feels, different scents and make different sounds as the wind blows. They also attract insects which add to the sounds.

GRADIENT OF PATHS

Gradients should be no steeper than 1:12

Gradients of 1:20 are preferred where possible

Slopes are needed to access different levels.

flower bed D

Which gradient gives the longer slope?

- What is the shortest slope that would give a 30cm rise?
- How long would the less steep slope be?
- What volume of concrete would be needed to make each slope for a path that is 1.2m wide?

flower bed A

All walls are 0.25m wide and 0.6m high

Water features add sound and touch to a garden.

The area surrounding the flowerbeds will need to be paved or concreted. What area of paving or concrete is needed?

Designs can add texture to walls and surfaces.

- Design your own sensory garden. Make sure that it is accessible to all.
- Work out the quantities of materials that would be needed to build the flowerbeds and pathways
- You could add other features such as water and textures to increase the range of experiences for a visitor to your garden.

You could decide which plants to use to give different scents, sounds and feel.

75

4 Summary

Assessment criteria

- Solve inequalities in one variable and represent the solution set on a number line **Level 7**
- Use algebraic methods to solve simultaneous equations in two variables **Level 7**

1 Solve the inequality
$4x + 14 < 10$.
Show your solution on the number line.

Christopher's answer ✔

He divides both sides of the equation by 4.

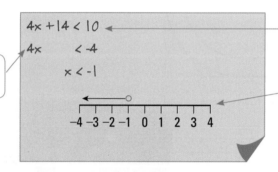

Chris subtracts 14 from both sides of the equation.

He shows x is less than -1 by using the symbol ○ at $x = $ -1.

2 Solve these simultaneous equations using an algebraic method.
$4x + 3y = 21$
$2x + y = 8$
You must show your working.
$x = $ _____ $y = $ _____

KS3 2005 6–8 Paper 1

Surveys

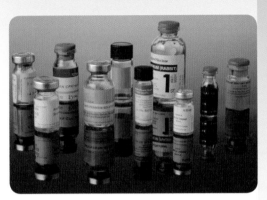

Regulatory bodies insist that new drugs are tested, in experiments called clinical trials, to verify that they are effective and safe.

On a random basis a group of patients is given the new drug or an existing (or a dummy – placebo) drug and differences looked for. Often neither patients nor researchers know who received which drug until the end – the trial is double blind. These trials may be refined and repeated several times.

What's the point? The data handling cycle helps you to carefully design and analyse clinical trials.

 **Check in**

1   The table shows the number of cars owned by the families of children in Mrs Hamilton's Year 9 class.

Numbers of cars	0	1	2	3
Frequency	8	12	6	3

Calculate the mean number of cars per family in the class.

2   The table shows the resting pulse rates of a number of Year 8 students.
Construct a bar chart to show this data.

Pulse rate, p (beats per min.)	$60 \leq p < 65$	$65 \leq p < 70$	$70 \leq p < 75$	$75 \leq p < 80$	$80 \leq p < 85$
Frequency	6	14	35	22	8

Level 6

- Suggest a problem to explore, frame questions and raise hypotheses
- Identify possible primary and secondary data sources

Keywords
Hypothesis
Primary data
Secondary data

People discuss many questions but how often do they look at evidence?

Who is the best band ever?

Are genetically modified crops safe?

Evidence is not always available but when it is statistics can help you answer such questions. First, you must refine your question into a statement that can be tested using data; this is called the **hypothesis**. Your hypothesis might be

The Beatles are the best band ever.

Second, you must obtain data to test your hypothesis against.

- **Primary data** is data you collect yourself.

- **Secondary data** is data someone else has collected.

> To make a comparison with the past, you might be able to collect primary data about the present but you might have to rely on secondary data for the past.

To investigate the Beatles popularity you could
– Carry out a survey.

– Look at the number of music downloads/cds sold or the time spent and highest position reached in the charts.

---

example

Do boys or girls do better in GCSE Maths exams?
a What do you think? – write a hypothesis.
b Identify **i** primary data and
       ii secondary data you could use to investigate your hypothesis.

. . . .

a Possible hypotheses are
`Boys do better than girls in GCSE Maths exams'
`There is no difference between boys and girls in GCSE Maths exams'
b i You could survey people who have taken the exams at your school.
  ii Your school may provide anonymised data for previous years exam results or you could use published national or regional data.

> For each hypothesis it is possible to find evidence to test it against.

> If you do not attend a co-educational school you may have to collect data from two schools. However interpreting any differences between data from two schools will be more difficult.

Exercise 5a

1 For each of the following questions
  i say what you think.
  ii write a hypothesis.

  a Are boys or girls absent from school more often?

  b Do pupils have more homework in Year 11 than in Year 10?

  c Does more rain fall in your area now than in the past?

  d Are trains or airplanes more punctual nowadays?

  e Do people who live near nuclear power stations suffer more from cancer?

  f Will there be a change of goverment at the next general election?

2 For the six iss.ues raised in question 1 identify sources of
  i primary
  ii secondary
    data that you could use to investigate your hypothesis.

> **discussion**
>
> Look back at the data you have identified in question **2**. How easy would it be to get this data? Which is easier to get, primary or secondary data?

- Understand the difference between a survey and an experiment
- Use explanatory and response variables
- Use primary and secondary data

Keywords

Control group
Experiment
Experimental group

Explanatory variable
Response variable
Survey

Data to investigate statistical questions can be collected by a **survey** or an **experiment**.

> Surveys include using questionnaires to seek opinions but also taking measurements, for example, to investigate whether boys or girls are taller at age 14.

> In an experiment one of the variables (the **explanatory variable**) will be controlled while its effect on the **response variable** is observed.

example

Do people's reaction times increase after exercise?

a Should you use an experiment or a survey to investigate this question?

b Describe how you would carry out the investigation.

> Exercise is the explanatory variable and the reaction time is the response variable.

a An experiment is appropriate to investigate the effect of exercise on reaction times.

b Take a number of different people and record their normal reaction times and their reaction times after different amounts of exercise.

example

Does a new drug give better results than an old drug for a given medical condition?

a Describe how you could carry out an experiment to investigate this.

b The performance of the drug is affected by the severity of the condition and the patient's age, weight and gender. Modify the design of your experiment to take account of this.

a The explanatory variable is the drug the person is given. The response variable is the measurement of any improvement in their condition. Ideally, people will be assigned randomly to the two treatments.

b Match patients up in pairs as far as possible in terms of the severity of their condition, age, weight and gender and then randomly assign one to the existing and the other to the new drug. For each pair, then take the difference in outcome between the two patients.

> The group taking the existing treatment is called the **control group** and those taking the new drug are the **experimental group**.

> Pairing patients removes a source of variability making it easier to test for a difference between the drugs.

Exercise 5b

1 For each of the following
   i explain whether you should investigate it using an experiment or a survey
   ii describe how you would do the experiment or decide who to survey.

   a Does practice improve people's performance on Sudoku puzzles?

   b How often do people go to the cinema?

   c Are you more likely to see at least one 6 when you throw two fair dice or at least 6 heads when you toss 10 fair coins?

   d What is the most popular holiday destination?

   e Do a majority of teenagers download music from the internet illegally?

   f Do people react more quickly with their left or with their right hand?

2 For the six investigations in question **1**, how long would it take you to collect the data?

> You should always take time to plan data collection carefully. It is usually much harder to obtain information that was initially missed out.

Did you know?

Sudoku was invented in 1979 by the American architect Howard Garns and by 2005 had swept the world. Up to symmetries, there are 5.472 billion possible Sudoku grids.

investigation

News agencies often commission surveys to try to measure the popularity of political parties. What methods do polling agencies use and how reliable do you think their results are?

- Know how to design surveys and experiments to minimise bias

Keywords
Bias
Population
Sample

example

A survey is done to find out the proportions of people unemployed, in part time work or in full time work.

a Explain why asking people in a town centre at 11 am on Tuesday morning is not a good idea.

b How could you improve the survey?

a People in full time employment are likely to be at work and therefore under-represented in the **sample**. Housewives and the unemployed are likely to be over-represented. Since these groups are not fairly represented the sampling method is **biased**.

b Doing the survey at the weekend when more people who have a job are not at work would be better. Also carry out the survey in more than one location.

- If the proportions of types of people in a sample are not the same as those in the whole **population** then the sample is biased.

Possible cause of bias include

– Only surveying people in one place at one time.

– Not matching the sample to the population.
   For example, in a survey about the reliability of mobile phones if you only included phones less than six months old.

– Asking sensitive questions without ensuring confidentiality.
   For example, 'have you ever taken drugs?'

– Poor response rates to surveys.
   You don't know if the people who don't respond are similar to those who do respond.

– Asking leading questions
   For example, 'do you agree that all children should learn to swim?'

Radio phone-in surveys are almost completely worthless because of the self-selecting bias of the participants.

Exercise 5c

1 A school wants to know how many books pupils read. The Deputy Head asks the librarian to find out, so she surveys the next 40 pupils who visit the library.

   a Explain why this will give a biased sample and whether it is likely to over or under estimate the number of books pupils read.

   b Suggest a better way for the librarian to take her sample.

2 Carole wanted to investigate whether wealthy people holiday abroad more often than less well-off people. She sent out a survey to 100 people but did not supply an envelope or stamp.

   a Give two reasons why this sample is likely to be biased.

   b Suggest how Carole could improve the survey.

3 A town wants to know how far people in the town travel to work. They asked Keith to investigate. The next day, he asked all the people on the bus that he takes to work.

   a Explain why this will give a biased sample and whether it is likely to over or under estimate the distance people travel.

   b Suggest a better way for Keith to take his sample.

4 A council wants to do a survey on gender roles in local households. It decides to select a property at random and to take the first named person on the council tax register at that property.

   a Explain why this is not a good way to take the sample.

   b Could you give any way to improve the survey?

Carole's Holidays Survey

Name: _____

Age: _____

Salary: _____

In the last two years how often have you been abroad on holiday?

_____

Please post your reply to the address supplied.

---

investigation

Most households get junk mail including surveys which companies send out. If you can get hold of some of these, decide if any of them have any sources of possible bias. Do the companies offer any incentives (such as entry into a prize draw) to encourage people to take part?

- Construct a frequency polygon
- Find the modal class and estimated range for grouped frequency data

Keywords
Estimated range
Frequency polygon
Modal class

Bar charts and **frequency polygons** are types of frequency diagrams.

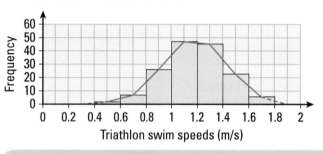

Frequency polygons make it easy to compare the shapes of several distributions at once.

> A frequency polygon joins up the midpoints of the tops of the bars.

> To show the shape of the full distribution, join the midpoints of the tops of the first and last bars to points on the x-axis where the next bars would appear.

- The **modal class** is the interval with the highest point in the frequency polygon.

> The modal class is 1.0 to 1.2 m/s.
> The estimated range is $1.8 - 0.4 = 1.4$ m/s.

- The **estimated range** is the largest possible data value minus the lowest possible data value.
  – The estimated range equals the largest possible range.

A frequency polygon can be drawn without first drawing a bar chart.

Draw a frequency polygon to illustrate the distances (in metres) which a young golfer hit some practice shots with a wedge.

Distance d	$60 \leqslant d < 65$	$65 \leqslant d < 70$	$70 \leqslant d < 75$	$75 \leqslant d < 80$	$80 \leqslant d < 85$
Frequency	6	14	35	22	8

For the main frequency polygon, plot (62.5, 6), (67.5, 14), (72.5, 35), (77.5, 22) and (82.5, 8). To complete the diagram, add (57.5, 0) and (87.5, 0).

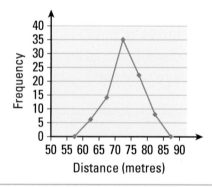

Exercise 5d

1 a Draw a bar chart and frequency polygon for the data on the
ages of members of a choral society.

Age x years	$20 \leq x < 25$	$25 \leq x < 30$	$30 \leq x < 35$	$35 \leq x < 40$	$40 \leq x < 45$
Frequency	3	8	12	9	2

  b What is the modal class for ages in the choral society?

2 a Draw a frequency polygon for the data on the times taken
to get to school by a group of pupils.

Time t min	$0 \leq t < 10$	$10 \leq t < 20$	$20 \leq t < 30$	$30 \leq x < 40$	$40 \leq t < 50$
Frequency	27	18	6	4	1

  b Estimate the range of times pupils take to get to school.
  c What is the modal class for the time taken to get to school?

3 a Draw a frequency polygon for the data on the times taken for
the 104 runners who completed the mens' 2008 USA Olympic
marathon trial.

Time t min	$120 \leq t < 130$	$130 \leq t < 140$	$140 \leq t < 150$	$150 \leq t < 160$	$160 \leq t < 170$
Frequency	1	38	49	15	1

  b What is the modal class for the time taken in the trial?
  c A number of runners did not complete the course. If they
had, and their times were included in the graph, what
differences would you expect to see?

discussion

In question **2**, there was only one pupil who took at least
40 minutes to get to school. Looking at the shape of the
distribution, do you think it is equally likely that the pupil
took 40–45 minutes or 45–50 minutes?
Can you devise a better rule for estimating range for a set
of data than using the maximum possible?

- Draw and use a line of best fit for a scatter graph
- Recognise when fitting a straight line is not appropriate

Keywords
Line of best fit
Non-linear relationship
Predict

example

p. 200

The scatter graph shows the maximum distances at which a number of people could read a motorway sign and their ages.

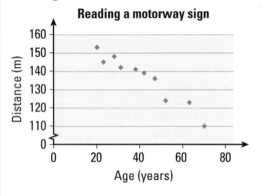

a Draw a **line of best fit** for this data.
b Use your line to **predict** the maximum distance at which someone aged 50 could read a motorway sign.

The ⭫ symbol indicates a 'broken scale', that is, one that does not start at zero.

If the correlation is strong, a line of best fit can be drawn by eye.

If the correlation is only moderate it may help to imagine an oval round the data.

a

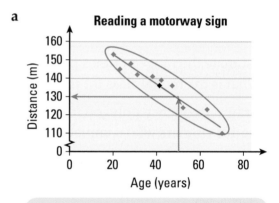

The line of best fit passes through the point defined by the mean x and mean y values.

b 130 metres for someone aged 50.

It is safer to make predictions for values within the range of data (interpolation) than outside (extrapolation).

Data that appears to lie on a curve shows a **non-linear relationship**. In this case you should not draw a (straight) line of best fit, though you still may be able to make a prediction confidently.
The distance a car takes to stop at 55 mph can be predicted to be 65 m.

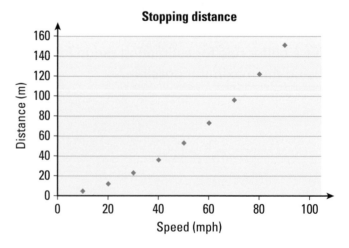

Exercise 5e

1 The scatter graph shows the age at marriage of a number of couples.

Use the line of best fit shown to estimate

  a the age of the wife of a man aged 33

  b the age of the husband of a woman aged 27.

Age at marriage

2 The scatter graph shows the prices of a number of cars of the same model and their ages.

  a Explain why you should not draw a line of best fit.

  b Could you predict what a 5-year-old car of this model would cost?

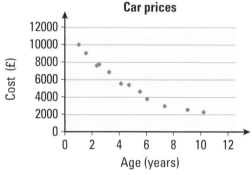

Car prices

3 The table shows the numbers of text messages sent and received by some of the girls in class 9A over one weekend.

  a Draw a scatter graph for this data and add a line of best fit.

  b Another girl in the class sent 22 texts over the weekend.

  Estimate how many texts she received.

Sent	25	32	14	28	31	42	17	19	6	53
Received	29	28	17	25	24	35	22	15	8	46

4 The table shows the cover prices and the discount price from an online bookseller, for hardback books on a fiction long list.

Cover price	£12.99	£12.00	£16.00	£25.00	£12.99	£16.00	£17.99	£17.99	£12.99	£11.99
Discount price	£11.99	£7.79	£11.89	£12.49	£7.79	£8.49	£10.79	£13.49	£6.49	£7.99

  a Draw a scatter graph for this data and add a line of best fit.

  b A different hardback book on the list has a cover price of £15.00.
     How much would you expect to have to pay the online bookseller for it?

  c Another hardback book on the list costs £7.39 online.
     What would you expect its cover price to be?

challenge

  a Why would it not make sense to use the scatter graph in question **1** to predict the age of the wife of a man aged 14?

  b Using your scatter graph from question **4**, can you reasonably estimate the discount prices of the following items?
     Explain your reasoning.

     i A hardback book on the list which has a cover price of £35.00.

     ii A book on the list published in paperback with a cover price of £8.99.

     iii A DVD with a cover price of £13.50.

• Identify trends in time series data

Keywords
Seasonal variation
Time series
Trend

• A graph of repeated measurements of a quantity against time is called a **time series**.

Many time series show both regular short term patterns as well as underlying long term patterns.

example

Describe the long term trend and any other patterns you see in the index data for retail food sales.

The food sales index gives the sales in each quarter as a percentage of the average sales in the whole of the year 2000.

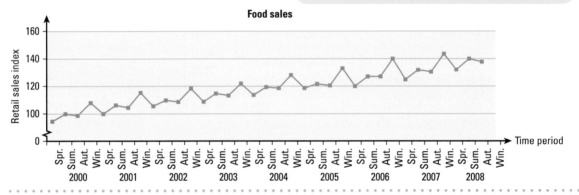

The long term trend is steadily upward (inflation). Each year, there is a peak in the Winter, which includes Christmas, and a slight dip in the Spring.

A trend describes how the 'average' data value changes.

• A pattern which repeats each year is called a **seasonal variation**.
• A longer term pattern is called a **trend**.

example

The graph shows three time series for the carbon dioxide emissions from industry, domestic use and transport since 1970. Describe the trends in the data.

Do not give detailed descriptions of fluctuations. Instead try to describe overall patterns in the data

Transport emissions have increased steadily, and doubled in the period shown. Domestic use has varied quite a lot during the period but there is a slight general downward trend. Industry has reduced its CO_2 emissions by about half over the 35 year period, though it has not been a steady rate of decrease.

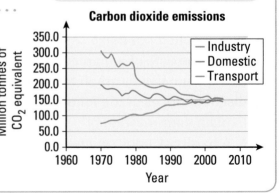

Exercise 5f

1 The average daily numbers of deaths or serious injuries in road traffic accidents, for each hour, on weekdays in 2002 is shown in the graph.

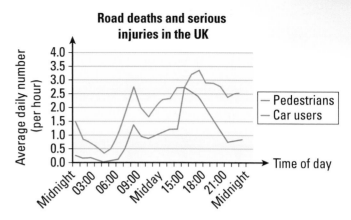

Road deaths and serious injuries in the UK

a What times of the day are there peaks in the number of accidents for both pedestrians and car users?

b Can you suggest why this is?

2 The graph shows the number of new cars (in thousands) registered each month during 1994–1996.

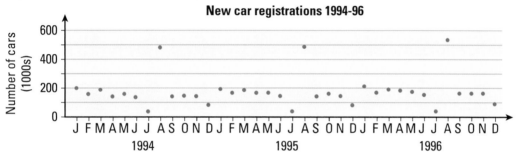

New car registrations 1994-96

a Describe the long term trend for the data.

b There were about two million new cars registered each year in this period. Approximately what fraction of them were registered in August?

c After August, what was the second most popular month for new registrations?

> During this period new cars registration plates changed in August.

challenge

In 2001, the system for number plates was changed, so the time identifier changes twice every year. From the time series of new registrations during 2005–2007, which months do you think the changes occur? Why do you think the change was brought in?

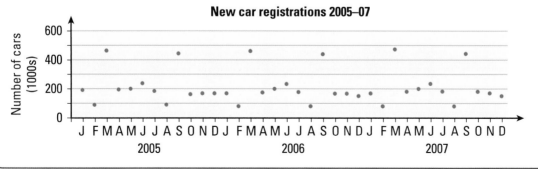

New car registrations 2005–07

- Identify trends in time series data by using moving averages
- Predict future values in a time series

Keywords
Cycle   *Predict*
Moving   *Smooth*
      average   *Trend line*

Consider the index data for retail food sales for the period Spring 2006 to Autumn 2008.

	2006				2007				2008	
Spr.	Sum.	Aut.	Win.	Spr.	Sum.	Aut.	Win.	Spr.	Sum.	Aut.
119.7	127.2	127.0	139.4	124.8	131.9	130.4	143.5	132.3	139.7	138.2

The short term variation repeats in a **cycle** lasting four seasons or one year. To see the long term trend it helps to **smooth** out the peaks and troughs during the cycle using a four-point **moving average**.

The first moving average is $\dfrac{119.7 + 127.2 + 127.0 + 139.4}{4} = \dfrac{513.3}{4} = 128.3$

and it is plotted in the centre of the values used in the average, midway between Summer and Autumn 2006.

A line of best fit for the moving averages gives a **trend line**.

- Using a trend line it is possible to **predict** future values of the moving average and individual data points.

The further into the future you extrapolate the less reliable your predictions become.

example

a Use the trend line to estimate the next moving average.
b Use your estimate to predict the index for Winter 2008.

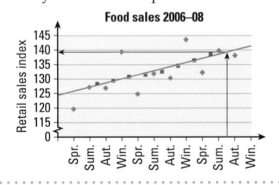

Food sales 2006–08

a The next four-point average occurs midway between Summer and Autumn 2008, reading off from the trend line gives 139.

b If the index in Winter 2008 is x, then

$$\frac{(132.3 + 139.7 + 138.2 + x)}{4} = 139$$

$$410.2 + x = 4 \times 139 \Rightarrow x = 145.8$$

Exercise 5f²

1 The table gives the numbers of orders of wedding cakes at Gina's bakery over a three-year period. The data is given quarterly.

Year	2006				2007				2008			
Quarter	Spr.	Sum.	Aut.	Win.	Spr.	Sum.	Aut.	Win.	Spr.	Sum.	Aut.	Win.
Number of cakes	15	30	22	10	19	35	24	11	20	37	27	14

a Plot the data on a time series graph.
b Calculate four-point moving averages and plot them on the graph.
c Draw a trend line for the moving averages.
d Estimate the number of wedding cakes Gina's bakery will be asked for in Spring 2009.

> The first moving average will be plotted on the horizontal axis midway between Sum. and Aut. of 2006.

2 The table shows the number of units of electricity used by a household over a period of three years.

Year	2006				2007				2008			
Quarter	Spr.	Sum.	Aut.	Win.	Spr.	Sum.	Aut.	Win.	Spr.	Sum.	Aut.	Win.
Number of units	820	543	948	1185	835	527	931	1180	815	530	940	1162

a Plot the data on a time series graph.
b Calculate four-point moving averages and plot them on the graph.
c Draw a trend line for the moving averages.
d Estimate the number of units that will be used in Spring 2009.

3 The table shows the number of workers in a factory who were not at work each day, because of illness or being on leave, over a three-week period.

Day	M	T	W	T	F	M	T	W	T	F	M	T	W	T	F
Number of absentees	12	5	4	3	11	10	4	5	5	12	11	4	2	6	10

a Plot the data on a time series graph.
b Calculate five-point moving averages and plot them on the graph.
c Is there a long term trend?

---

discussion

Why do you think the time series in questions **1** and **2** have the shapes that they do?
In question **2**, if the data had been the cost of electricity in the same period, do you think the graph would have looked the same?
In question **3**, how would you predict the number of workers not at work on the following Monday?

- Find the mean for grouped frequency table
- Use an assumed mean

Keywords
Assumed mean
Estimated mean
Grouped frequency table
Mean

The **mean** is the total of the data values divided by the number of values.
However for a **grouped frequency table**, which does not give the individual data values, you can only find an **estimated mean**.

The grouped frequency table shows the distances (in metres) which a young golfer hit some practice shots with a wedge.

Distance d	$60 \leq d < 65$	$65 \leq d < 70$	$70 \leq d < 75$	$75 \leq d < 80$	$80 \leq d < 85$
Frequency	6	14	35	22	8

In the first interval the six distances will be spread across the interval $60 \leq d < 65$.
Their average should be close to the centre of the interval, 62.5.
Their total can be estimated as $6 \times 62.5 = 375$
Using similar estimates for each interval, the estimated mean

	60.2
	61.3
	61.9
	63.8
	64.1
	62.0
	373.3

$$= \frac{(6 \times 62.5 + 14 \times 67.5 + 35 \times 72.5 + 22 \times 77.5 + 8 \times 82.5)}{(6 + 14 + 35 = 22 + 8)} = \frac{6222.5}{85}$$

$= 73.2058$
$= 73 \, \text{m} \, (2 \, \text{sf})$ It is not sensible to quote more figures since this is an estimate.

Calculating an estimated mean is easier if you use an **assumed mean**. For the golf data assume a mean of 62.5 and subtract this from the mid-interval values. Setting the calculation out in a table.

Distance d	Frequency, f	Mid-interval, m	$x = m - 62.5$	$f \times x$
$60 \leq d < 65$	6	62.5	0	0
$65 \leq d < 70$	14	67.5	5	70
$70 \leq d < 75$	35	72.5	10	350
$75 \leq d < 80$	22	77.5	15	330
$80 \leq d < 85$	8	82.5	20	160
Total =	85		Total =	910

Estimated mean $= 62.5 + \dfrac{910}{85} = 62.5 + 10.7058$
$= 73 \, \text{m} \, (2 \, \text{sf})$

Exercise 5g

1 The table shows the heights of a large sample of boys and girls.

Height h cm	$130 \le h < 140$	$140 \le h < 150$	$150 \le h < 160$	$160 \le h < 170$	$170 \le h < 180$
Number of boys	26	84	312	342	131
Number of girls	23	103	340	311	73

a Without using an assumed mean, estimate separately the mean heights of boys and girls in this sample.

b What would be a sensible assumed mean to choose for this set of data?

2 The lengths of calls made by Naheed on her mobile phone are summarised in the table.

Time t minutes	$0 \le t < 1$	$1 \le t < 3$	$3 \le t < 5$	$5 \le t < 10$	$10 \le t < 20$
Number of calls	15	22	12	35	6

a Without using an assumed mean, estimate the mean length of Naheed's calls.

b Would an assumed mean be helpful for this set of data? Give a reason for your answer.

3 The times taken for a group of Year 9 pupils to complete a set of three sudoku puzzles are recorded in the table.

Time t minutes	$5 \le t < 10$	$10 \le t < 15$	$15 \le t < 20$	$20 \le t < 25$	$25 \le t < 30$
Number of pupils	3	16	15	11	1

Using an assumed mean of 7.5 minutes, estimate the mean time taken to complete the puzzles.

> **discussion**
>
> In question **1**, if the heights had the last interval as $h \ge 170$ instead of $170 \le h < 180$, how could you estimate the mean?

5a

1 Do boys or girls text more?
    a i Say what you think.
       ii Write a hypothesis.
    b i Identify primary data you could use to investigate
         your hypothesis.
      ii Is there any secondary data you could use?

5b

2 For each of the following
    i explain whether you should investigate it using an experiment
      or a survey
    ii describe how you would carry out the investigation
    iii estimate how long it would take you to collect the data?
    a Do girls go to the cinema more often than boys?
    b Does practice improve peoples' performances in being able to estimate
      a minute?

5c

3 A school wants to know how much exercise students take.
    The Deputy Head asks the head of PE to find out, so she surveys the first
    40 students who she sees playing games in the playground at lunchtime.
    a Explain why this will give a biased sample and whether it is likely
       to over or under estimate the amount of exercise students take.
    b Suggest a better way for the head of PE to take her sample.

5d

4 a Draw a bar chart and frequency polygon for the data on the weights
      of bags checked in on a flight.

Weight x kg	$5 \leq x < 8$	$8 \leq x < 11$	$11 \leq x < 14$	$14 \leq x < 17$	$17 \leq x < 20$
Frequency	3	14	19	7	1

    b What is the modal class for this data?
    c Estimate the range of the weights of bags checked in.

5 The table shows the ages on their wedding day of the husband and wife for a sample of marriages at a church.

Husband	24	27	32	24	31	25	37	49	36	29
Wife	22	29	30	25	33	19	31	43	32	29

a Draw a scatter diagram for this data and add a line of best fit.

b The husband in another marriage at the church was 29.
   Use you line of best fit to estimate the age of his wife.

6 The graph shows time series of the stocks of various types of fish in the North Sea since 1963. Describe the trends in the data.

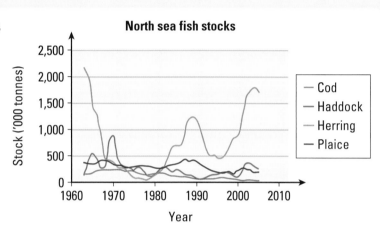

7 The table shows the number of days on which rain fell in a town over a period of three years.

Year	2006				2007				2008			
Quarter	Spr.	Sum.	Aut.	Win.	Spr.	Sum.	Aut.	Win.	Spr.	Sum.	Aut.	Win.
Number of days	33	33	29	32	36	34	28	33	37	35	30	33

a Plot the data on a time series graph.

b Calculate four-point moving averages and plot them on the graph.

c Draw a trend line for the moving averages.

d Estimate the number of days rain fell in the town in Spring 2009.

8 **a** Estimate the mean weight of the bags checked in to the flight in question **4**.

   b Would an assumed mean be helpful for this set of data?
   Give a reason for your answer.

5 Summary

Assessment criteria
- Construct lines of best fit on scatter graphs **Level 7**
- Estimate the mean, median and range of a set of grouped data **Level 7**

1 The table shows the time taken, to the nearest minute, for some people to solve a Sudoku problem.

Time, t, minutes	Number of people
$1 \leq t < 5$	12
$6 \leq t < 10$	8
$11 \leq t < 15$	10
$16 \leq t < 20$	14
$21 \leq t < 25$	6

Work out
a the modal class
b an estimate of the mean.

Zoe's answer ✔

a modal class is $16 \leq t < 20$

b

Time, t, minutes	Number of people, n	Mid-value (MV)	MV × n
$1 \leq t < 5$	12	3	36
$6 \leq t < 10$	8	8	64
$11 \leq t < 15$	10	13	130
$16 \leq t < 20$	14	18	252
$21 \leq t < 25$	6	23	138
Total	50		620

Estimate of the mean = $620 \div 50$
= 12.4

> Most people are in the $16 \leq t < 20$ interval.

> Zoe calculates the total number of people solving the Sudoku problem.

> Zoe knows that this is only an estimate of the mean as the exact values of t are not known.

2 A pupil investigated whether students who study more watch less television.
The scatter graph shows his results.
The line of best fit is also shown.
a What type of correlation does the graph show?
b The pupil says the equation of the line of best fit is $y = x + 40$.
Explain how you can tell this equation is wrong.

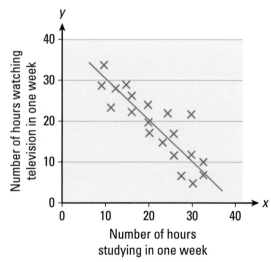

KS3 2006 6–8 Paper 1

Measures

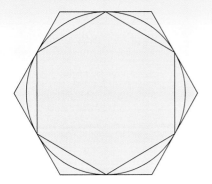

$\pi = 3.14159265358979323846264338327950288...$

For thousands of years, mathematicians have been intrigued by the value of pi (π).

The Greek mathematician Archimedes of Syracuse (287-212 BC) realised that the perimeter of a circle is less than the circumscribed regular polygon, but more than the inscribed regular polygon. Using a 96-sided polygon he showed that $3\frac{1}{7} < \pi < 3\frac{10}{71}$.

What's the point? Today we know millions of digits for π but, for example, we still don't know if there are as many 1s as 9s in the list of digits.

Check in

Level 5

1 Round these numbers to the degree of accuracy given in the brackets.
   a 1434 (nearest 10)   **b** 34.5 (nearest integer)
   c 36.05 (nearest tenth)   **d** 266 (nearest 100)
   e 6200 (nearest 1000)

Level 6

2 The radius of a circle is 6 cm.
   Use $\pi = 3.14$ to calculate
   a the circumference   **b** the area.

6 cm

3 A cuboid measures 5 cm by 6 cm by 8 cm.
   Calculate
   a the surface area   **b** the volume.

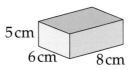
5 cm
6 cm   8 cm

- Convert between metric units
- Know that a measurement can never be exact

Keywords
Area   *Mass*
Capacity   *Measurement*
Degree of   *Metric*
accuracy   *Volume*
Length

You measure quantities using the **metric** system.

Length

millimetre (mm)
centimetre (cm)
metre (m)
kilometre (km)

$$1\,cm = 10\,mm$$
$$1\,m = 100\,cm$$
$$1\,km = 1000\,m$$

Area

square centimetre (cm^2)
square metre (m^2)
hectare (ha)
square kilometre (km^2)

$$1\,cm^2 = 100\,mm^2$$
$$1\,m^2 = 10\,000\,cm^2$$
$$1\,ha = 10\,000\,m^2$$
$$1\,km^2 = 1\,000\,000\,m^2$$

Mass

milligram (mg)
gram (g)
kilogram (kg)
tonne (t)

$$1\,g = 1000\,mg$$
$$1\,kg = 1000\,g$$
$$1\,t = 1000\,kg$$

Capacity/Volume

millilitre (ml)
centilitre (cl)
litre (l)
cubic centimetre (cm^3)
cubic metre (m^3)

$$1\,l = 1000\,ml$$
$$1\,l = 100\,cl$$
$$1\,l = 1000\,cm^3$$
$$1\,m^3 = 1000\,l$$
$$1\,m^3 = 1\,000\,000\,cm^3$$

example

Convert
a $5\,m^2$ to square centimetres
b $60\,000\,cm^3$ to litres.

a
$\times 10\,000$
$1\,m^2 = 10\,000\,cm^2$ $5\,m^2 = 5 \times 10\,000\,cm^2$
$\div 10\,000$ $= 50\,000\,cm^2$

b
$\times 1000$
$1\,l = 1000\,cm^3$ $60\,000\,cm^3$
$\div 1000$ $= 60\,000 \div 1000 = 60\,l$

When you measure a quantity, the **measurement** can never be exact.
You give the measurement to the appropriate **degree of accuracy**.

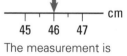

The measurement is given as 46 cm to the nearest 1 cm (1 unit).

- A measurement may be inaccurate by up to one half of the unit in either direction.

example

State the degree of accuracy and the possible range of values for the measurements.
a 46 cm   **b** 16 kg   **c** 16.0 kg

a The measurement is given to the nearest 1 cm.
$1 \div 2 = \frac{1}{2}$
$45\frac{1}{2}$ cm to $46\frac{1}{2}$ cm

b The measurement is given to the nearest 1 kg.
$1 \div 2 = 0.5$
15.5 kg to 16.5 kg

c The measurement is given to the nearest 0.1 kg.
$0.1 \div 2 = 0.05$
15.95 kg to 16.05 kg

Exercise 6a

1 State the degree of accuracy and the possible range of values
for these measurements.

   a 78 m   **b** 4 tonnes   **c** 3.2 kg   **d** 36.0 g   **e** 5.24 km

2 The signpost shows the distances in miles to some villages.

   a State the degree of accuracy for the measurements.

   b Calculate the shortest and longest possible distances
between Rosegreen and Fethard.

$3\frac{1}{2}$ Rosegreen   Fethard $2\frac{1}{2}$

$6\frac{1}{2}$ Cashel

6 New

3 Convert these metric measurements to the units indicated
in brackets.

   a 8.5 km (cm)   **b** 80 cm^2 (mm^2)

   c 5000 m^2 (ha)   **d** 2.5 m^3 (cm^3)

   e 450 kg (tonnes)   **f** 6500 cm^3 (l)

   g 1 million mm (km)   **h** 6000 cm^2 (m^2)

4 The Westfield Shopping Centre in London has
a retail floor space of 150 000 m^2.

A football pitch has an area of 0.6 hectares.

How many football pitches would cover the floor space?

Did you know?

A micrometre µm
(or micron) is a
millionth of a metre.
Bacteria are a few
micrometres in size.

5

Length	Capacity	Mass
1 inch ≈ 2.5 cm	1 gallon ≈ 4.5 litre	1 oz (ounce) ≈ 30 g
1 yard ≈ 1 metre	1 pint ≈ 0.6 litre	1 kg ≈ 2.2 lb (pound)
5 miles ≈ 8 km	1 pint ≈ 600 ml	

Use the metric-imperial equivalents to convert these
measurements to the units indicated in brackets.

   a 8.5 gallons (l)   **b** 3.5 pints (l)   **c** 30 kg (lb)   **d** 6 oz (g)

   e 22.5 feet (m)   **f** 123.2 lb (kg)   **g** 150 ml (pints)   **h** 47.5 miles (km)

investigation

Greengrocers used to weigh vegetables on balance
scales using a set of weights.

a Show that you can obtain every mass from
1 kg to 15 kg using a set of weights containing
1 kg, 2 kg, 4 kg and 8 kg weights.

b Show that you can obtain every mass from
1 kg to 40 kg using a set of weights containing
1 kg, 3 kg, 9 kg and 27 kg weights.

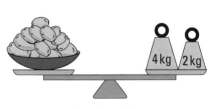

4 kg 2 kg

6 kg of potatoes

- Understand whether a formula represents length, area or volume by considering dimensions

Keywords

Area   Length
Dimension   Volume
Formula

You measure a distance in units of **length**, for example, 1 centimetre (1 cm).

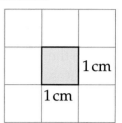

> • A length has one **dimension**: length.

You measure an **area** in squares, for example, 1 square centimetre ($1\,\text{cm}^2$).

> • An area has two dimensions: length × length.

You measure a **volume** in cubes, for example, 1 cubic centimetre ($1\,\text{cm}^3$).

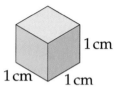

> • A volume has three dimensions: length × length × length.

$\frac{1}{2}, \frac{1}{3}, \frac{4}{3}, 3, \pi, 4$ are examples of numbers with no dimensions.

> • Numbers have no dimension.

example

Decide whether each quantity is a length, an area, a volume or a number.

a 3.141592
b The height of a building
c The surface of a jigsaw piece

a number
b length
c area

You can use dimensions to decide if a **formula** measures length, area or volume.

example

Ameer has to choose a formula for the circumference of a circle. These are his choices.

$C = \pi r^2$ $C = \pi$ $C = 2\pi r$ $C = \pi r^2 d$

Which of these formulae could represent the circumference of a circle?

Circumference is a length.

πr^2	number × length × length	= area	No
π	number	= number	No
$2\pi r$	number × number × length	= length	Yes
$\pi r^2 d$	number × length × length × length	= volume	No

Exercise 6b

1 Decide whether each quantity is a length, an area, a volume or a number.

   a The space inside a car   **b** $10\,\text{cm}^2$

   c The distance to your home   **d** The surface of a carpet

   e The perimeter of a cricket pitch   **f** π

   g The surface of a desk   **h** Your height

   i The perimeter of a rectangle   **j** $9\,\text{mm}$

   k The depth of a lake   **l** The space inside a box

   m The height of a wall   **n** 3

   o The surface of a 3-D shape   **p** $8\,\text{m}^3$

   q The distance from London to Oxford   **r** The width of a car

   s The height of a mountain   **t** The space in a room

2 The formula for the surface area and the volume of a sphere, with radius r, are given by

   surface area $= 4\pi r^2$ volume $= \dfrac{4}{3}\pi r^3$.

   Show that the dimensions of each formula are correct.

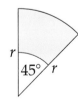

3 State whether the expressions represent a length, an area, a volume or a number.

   a length × width × height   **b** length × width

   c π × diameter   **d** number × length

   e π × radius × radius   **f** length + width + length + width

   g 2 × π × radius   **h** base × perpendicular height

   i π × radius × radius × height   **j** $\dfrac{1}{2}$ × base × perpendicular height

4 A sector of a circle of radius r is shown. Which expression might represent

   a the arc length   **b** the area?

   $\dfrac{1}{8}\pi r^2$ $\dfrac{1}{4}\pi r$ $45\,\pi$ $\dfrac{1}{8}r^3$ $\dfrac{\pi}{4}$

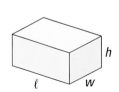

challenge

A cuboid has length ℓ, width w and height h.
Find a formula in terms of ℓ, w and h for

a the total length of all the edges

b the surface area

c the volume of the cuboid.

   Check each formula has the correct dimensions.

- Calculate the area of a 2-D shape
- Calculate the surface area and volume of a prism

Keywords

Area | Perimeter
Circumference | Prism
Cross-section | Volume

You can calculate the **perimeter** and **area** of a 2-D shape using these formulae.

- Perimeter of a rectangle
  $= \ell + w + \ell + w = 2(\ell + w)$.
- Area of a rectangle $= \ell \times w$.

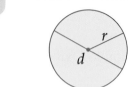

- **Circumference** of a circle $= \pi d = 2\pi r$.
- Area of a circle $= \pi \times r \times r = \pi r^2$.

where d = diameter
r = radius
and $\pi = 3.141592....$
$d = 2r$

- Area of a triangle
  $= \frac{1}{2} \times b \times h$.

- Area of a parallelogram
  $= b \times h$.

- Area of a trapezium
  $= \frac{1}{2} \times (a + b) \times h$.

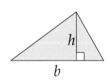

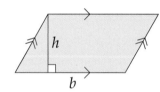

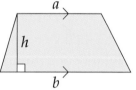

- **Volume** of a prism
  = area of cross-section × length
  $= A \times \ell$.

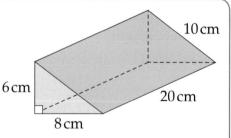

A prism is a 3-D shape that has the same cross-section throughout its length.

example

Calculate
a the surface area
b the volume of the triangular prism.

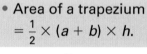

a Area of two triangles $= \frac{1}{2} \times 8 \times 6 + \frac{1}{2} \times 8 \times 6$
$= 24\,\text{cm}^2 + 24\,\text{cm}^2$
Area of three rectangles $= 10 \times 20 + 6 \times 20 + 8 \times 20$
$= 200\,\text{cm}^2 + 120\,\text{cm}^2 + 160\,\text{cm}^2$
Total surface area $= 24\,\text{cm}^2 + 24\,\text{cm}^2 + 200\,\text{cm}^2 + 120\,\text{cm}^2 + 160\,\text{cm}^2$
$= 528\,\text{cm}^2$
b Volume = area of triangular cross-section × length $= 24 \times 20$
$= 480\,\text{cm}^3$

Exercise 6c

1 Calculate the area of cross-section and the volume of each of these prisms.
State the units of each answer.

Use π = 3.14 if required.

a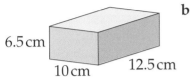
6.5 cm
10 cm   12.5 cm

b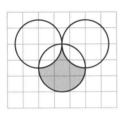
2.5 m
1.5 m
2 m

c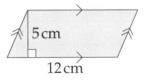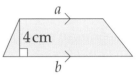
4 mm
2 mm
6 mm
5 mm

2 The areas of the parallelogram and the trapezium are the same.
What is the value of *a* + *b*?

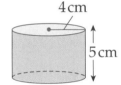
5 cm
12 cm
a
4 cm
b

3 Three circles each of diameter 3 cm are drawn on 1 cm squared paper. Calculate the perimeter and area of the shaded shape.

4 A cylinder has a radius of 4 cm and a height of 5 cm. Calculate the volume of the cylinder.

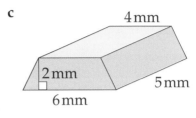
4 cm
5 cm

5 Calculate the circumference and the area of the circumscribed circle of the 2 cm by 4 cm rectangle.

6 In terms of π and *r*, calculate the area of
a the small square
b the circle
c the large square.

r

challenge

The volume of a cuboid is 64 cm³.
All the side lengths are integers.
a Calculate the smallest and largest possible surface areas of the cuboid.
b If the surface area is 136 cm², what are the side lengths of the cuboid?

Volume = 64 cm³

- Calculate an arc length of a circle
- Calculate the area of a sector of a circle

Keywords

Arc	Pi (π)
Area	Radius
Circumference	Sector
Diameter	

You can calculate the **circumference** and **area** of a circle using these formulae.

- Circumference = $\pi \times$ **diameter** $C = \pi d$.
- Circumference = $\pi \times 2 \times$ **radius** $C = 2\pi r$.
- Area of a circle = $\pi \times$ radius $\times$ radius   Area = πr^2.
  - where π = 3.141592...., $d = 2r$

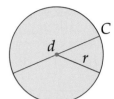

where C = circumference
d = diameter
r = radius

Use π = 3.14

example

The area of a circle is $50\,\text{cm}^2$.
Calculate the radius of the circle.

$$\text{Area} = \pi\, r^2$$
$$50 = \pi\, r^2$$
$$\text{and so } r^2 = 50 \div \pi$$
$$r^2 = 15.92$$
$$r = 3.99$$
$$r = 4.0\,\text{cm (to 1 dp)}$$

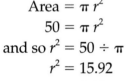

Area = $50\,\text{cm}^2$

The Greek letter θ (theta) is often used for angles.

The length of an **arc** is a fraction of the circumference.
The fraction is proportional to the value of the angle θ.

- Arc length = $\dfrac{\theta}{360°} \times$ circumference
  - where θ is the angle between the two radii.
- Area of **sector** = $\dfrac{\theta}{360°} \times$ area of the circle.

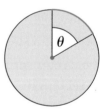

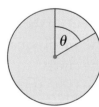

example

Calculate the arc length and area of the sector.

$$\text{Arc length} = \frac{\theta}{360°} \times \text{circumference}$$
$$= \frac{60°}{360°} \times 2 \times \pi \times 10$$
$$= 10.5\,\text{cm (to 1 dp)}$$
$$\text{Area of sector} = \frac{\theta}{360°} \times \text{area of the circle}$$
$$= \frac{60°}{360°} \times \pi \times 10 \times 10$$
$$= 52.3\,\text{cm}^2 \text{ (to 1 dp)}$$

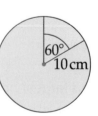

radius = 10 cm

Exercise 6d

1 Calculate the circumference and area of each of these circles.

   a $r = 7.5\,\text{cm}$ **b** $d = 11\,\text{cm}$ **c** $r = 25\,\text{mm}$ **d** $d = 30\,\text{m}$

> d is the diameter
> r is the radius

2 The circumference of a bicycle wheel is 216 cm. Calculate
   a the diameter and radius of the wheel
   b the number of turns of the wheel in a journey of
      one kilometre.

> Use $\pi = 3.14$ for all the
> questions on this page.

3 The area of the top of the the circular pie is $110\,\text{cm}^2$.
Calculate the radius of the pie.

4 Calculate the arc length and area of each pink and
blue sector.

a

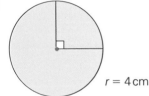

$r = 4\,\text{cm}$

b

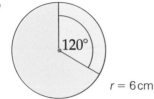

120°

$r = 6\,\text{cm}$

c

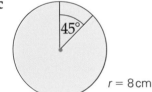

45°

$r = 8\,\text{cm}$

d

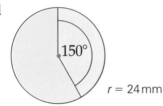

150°

$r = 24\,\text{mm}$

5 The length of the minute hand on a clock
is 10 cm.
The length of the hour hand is 5 cm.
Calculate the distance the tip of each hand
travels in
   a one hour   **b** one day **c** one year.

investigation

A semicircle is drawn on each side of a
3 cm, 4 cm, 5 cm right-angled triangle.
   a Calculate the area of each semicircle.
   b Add the areas of the two smaller semicircles
      and compare the answer with the area of the
      semicircle on the hypotenuse.
   c Repeat this with other right-angled triangles.
   d Use algebra to explain this rule.

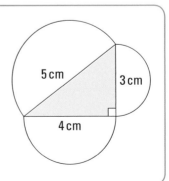

5 cm   3 cm

4 cm

- Understand and use measures of speed, density and pressure

Keywords
Average speed   Pressure
Compound   Rate
Density   Speed

A **compound** measure uses a combination of measurements and units.

A **rate** measures how one quantity changes with another, for example, miles per gallon which is used to compare fuel efficiency.

Speed measures how fast something moves, or how quickly distance changes 'per unit time'.

If the speed is constant,

- Speed (S) = $\dfrac{\text{Distance travelled (D)}}{\text{Time taken (T)}}$

Speed is measured in metres per second (m/s), miles per hour (mph) or kilometres per hour (km/h).

If the speed varies, the same formula gives the **average speed**.

---

example

A cyclist travels 36 km in 1 hour 15 minutes.
Calculate the average speed in
a kilometres per hour
b metres per second.

....

a Speed = $\dfrac{\text{Distance travelled}}{\text{Time taken}} = \dfrac{36}{1.25}$ 15 minutes = 0.25 hours

= 28.8 km/h

b 28.8 km/h = 28.8 × 1000 ÷ 60 ÷ 60 metres per second

= 8 m/s

$D = S \times T$

$S = \dfrac{D}{T}$ $T = \dfrac{D}{S}$

Density measures how heavy something is 'per unit volume'.

- Density (D) = $\dfrac{\text{Mass (M)}}{\text{Volume (V)}}$

Density is measured in grams per cubic centimetre (g/cm³) or kilograms per cubic metre (kg/m³).

$M = D \times V$

$D = \dfrac{M}{V}$ $V = \dfrac{M}{D}$

Pressure measures how force acts 'per unit area'.

- Pressure (P) = $\dfrac{\text{Force (F)}}{\text{Area (A)}}$

A newton (N) is a unit of force. Pressure is measured in newtons per square metre (N/m²).

$F = P \times A$

$P = \dfrac{F}{A}$ $A = \dfrac{F}{P}$

Exercise 6e

1 Kathy ran 100 metres in 25 seconds.
Jayne ran 400 metres in 125 seconds.
   a Calculate their speeds in metres per second.
   b Who ran faster, Kathy or Jayne?

2 A car travels 30 miles in 45 minutes.
Calculate the car's average speed in miles per hour.

3 A 2 centimetre cube of lead has a mass of 90.7 grams.
Calculate the density of lead in g/cm^3.

4 The safety valve on a boiler releases the pressure if the
pressure is greater than 4 million newtons per square metre.
If the force is 1 500 000 newtons and the area is 0.5 square
metres, will the safety valve be activated?

5 In the 2002, the fastest ever lap of a Formula One racing
track was recorded at Monza in Italy. Juan Pablo Montoya
completed one lap of 5783 metres in 80 seconds. Calculate
his average speed in
   a metres per second
   b kilometres per hour.

6 In 1997 Andy Green, an RAF fighter pilot, set the World
Land Speed Record at Black Rock Desert in Nevada, USA,
when he travelled at 768 mph in the ThrustSSC.
   a Calculate his average speed in kilometres per hour.
      At sea level the speed of sound is 1225 km/h.
   b Did Andy Green travel faster than the speed of sound?

7 The density of cork is 0.25 g/cm^3 and the density of water is
1.0 g/cm^3. Calculate the mass of
   a a 10 cm cube of cork
   b a litre of water.

Did you know?

When an aircraft
reaches the speed
of sound, a conical
pressure wave forms
and there is a sonic
boom.

ThrustSSC

investigation

Many singers use the words 'a million miles' in
their lyrics.
   '*It feels like you're a million miles away.*'   Rihanna.
   '*I can't stay a million miles away.*'   Offspring.
   '*I'm still a million miles from you.*'   Bob Dylan.
How many years would it take you to walk
a million miles at a speed of 3 miles per hour?

6a

1 Convert these metric measurements to the units indicated brackets.

Use $\pi = 3.14$ if required

a 7.5t (kg) **b** 480mm (m) **c** 1.5cm² (mm²) **d** 15000cm² (m²)
e 3500m² (ha) **f** 4.8m³ (cm³) **g** 19.6km (cm) **h** 800000mg (kg)
i 0.5m² (cm²) **j** 1.8t (kg)

2 State the degree of accuracy and the possible range for each measurement.
a 32m **b** 480m² **c** 6000m³ **d** 2.4cm
e 5.0g **f** 400m **g** 20000km **h** 10ha

3 Convert these measurements to the units indicated in brackets.
a 9oz (g) **b** 3pints (ml) **c** 60ft (m) **d** 6gallons (l)
e 18l (pints) **f** 45kg (lb) **g** 1.75m (in) **h** 36in (cm)

6b

4 a Which formula could give the curved surface area of a cone? Explain your reasoning.

$A = \pi l$ $A = \pi r l$ $A = \pi r^2 l$ $A = \pi r$ $A = \pi$

b Explain why the formula for the curved surface area of a cone is unlikely to be $A = rl$

5 The plan view of a sports arena is shown.
Which expression could be correct for
a the perimeter **b** the area?

$2l + 2\pi r$ $2rl + \pi r^2$ $\pi r^2 l$ 2π

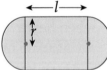

6c

6 Four circles of radius 6cm are placed touching each other.
The centres of the circle are joined to form a square.
Calculate the perimeter and the area of the shaded shape.
State the units of each answer.

7 Calculate the area of the cross-section and the volume of each prism.
State the units of each answer.

a

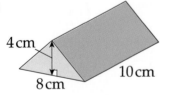
4cm
8cm
10cm

b
12cm
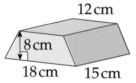
8cm
18cm   15cm

c
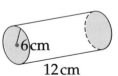
6cm
12cm

8 Calculate the arc lengths and the areas of the shaded sectors.
Round your answers to an appropriate degree of accuracy.

a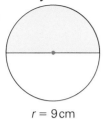

r = 9 cm

b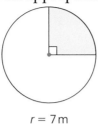

r = 7 m

c

80°

r = 2.5 cm

d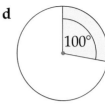

100°

r = 3.5 cm

9 Calculate the shaded area.

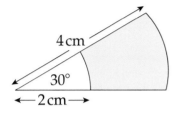

4 cm

30°

←2 cm→

10 The speed limits for vehicles in Ireland are

Motorways	120 km/h
National roads	100 km/h
Other rural roads	80 km/h
Built-up areas	50 km/h

Change these speeds to miles per hour.

50 km/h

11 Copy and complete the table to show the distances, times and speeds for these journeys.

	Distance travelled (km)	Time taken	Speed (km/h)
a	112	5 hours	
b	84	3 hours	
c	15	30 mins	
d	36	4 hours 30 mins	
e		6 hours	25
f		5 hours 30 mins	6
g		1 hour 45 mins	52
h	450		20
i	81		18
j	19		4

6 Summary

Assessment criteria

- Calculate the volume of a prism **Level 7**
- Understand the difference between formula for perimeter, area and volume by considering dimensions **Level 8**

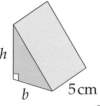

1 The length of the triangular prism is 5 cm.
The volume of the prism is 50 cm^3.
Write down possible values for b and h.

h

b 5 cm

Volume = 50 cm^3

Deepak's answer ✔

Volume of prism = area of
cross-section × length

$50 = \frac{1}{2} \times h \times b \times 5$

$\frac{50 \times 2}{5} = h \times b$

$20 = h \times b$

$h = 5$ cm and $b = 4$ cm

Deepak remembers the formula for the volume of a prism.

She chooses values of h and b that multiply to give 20.

She rearranges the equation.

2 Each expression below represents either a length, an area or a volume.
a, b and c all represent lengths.
For each expression, tick (✓) the correct one.
The first one is done for you.

$2a + c$		
✓ length	☐ area	☐ volume

$3ab$		
☐ length	☐ area	☐ volume

$4a\,(b + c)$		
☐ length	☐ area	☐ volume

a^2b		
☐ length	☐ area	☐ volume

KS3 2008 6–8 Paper 1

7 Number

Calculations

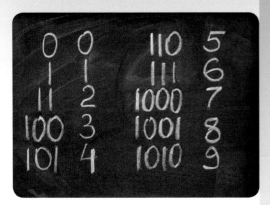

There are many ways of writing numbers. Some can be written as fractions or exact decimals, for example, $\frac{1}{3} = 0.333333\ldots = 0.\dot{3}$, others cannot. Some of these irrational numbers have special names.

$1.414213562373095\ldots = \sqrt{2}$.

$3.141592653589793\ldots = \pi$

Scientists and engineers write very large and very small numbers using powers of 10, for example, $2\,150\,000\,000\,000\,000 = 2.15 \times 10^{15}$. This is called standard form.

What's the point? You need to know the best way of writing a number and how to change between different notations.

Check in

1 Calculate
   a 3.8×0.01 b $2.75 \div 0.1$ c $0.000\,45 \times 100$

2 Write down the value of
   a 3^3 b 2^5 c 10^6 d 5^4

3 Round each of these numbers to two significant figures.
   a 17.475 b 0.7438

4 Calculate these using an appropriate method.
   a 21×32.8 b 3.4×43.7 c $564 \div 24$ d $321.6 \div 7$

5 Copy and complete this table.

Fraction	Decimal
$\frac{11}{13}$	
	1.94
	0.666 ...

6 Write each of these numbers as the product of its prime factors.
   a 100 b 441

7 a Use your calculator to find $\sqrt{20}$ and write your answer to 3 dp.
   b Square your rounded answer, and explain why the answer is not 20.

- Multiply numbers by powers of 10
- Write numbers in standard form

Keywords
Index notation
Power
Standard index form

- The decimal system is based upon **powers** of 10. You can write all powers of ten using **index notation**.

1 million (mega)	= 1 000 000	= 10 × 10 × 10 × 10 × 10 × 10 = 10^6	
1 thousand (kilo)	= 1000	= 10 × 10 × 10	= 10^3
1 hundred	= 100	= 10 × 10	= 10^2
1 ten	= 10	= 10	= 10^1
1 unit	= 1		= 10^0
1 tenth	= $\frac{1}{10}$ = 0.1	= $\frac{1}{10^1}$	= 10^{-1}
1 hundredth (centi)	= $\frac{1}{100}$ = 0.01	= $\frac{1}{10^2}$	= 10^{-2}
1 thousandth (milli)	= $\frac{1}{1000}$ = 0.001	= $\frac{1}{10^3}$	= 10^{-3}

The power is also called the index.

Any number to the power of zero is equal to 1.

- To multiply by a positive power of ten, 10^n, move the digits n places to the left of the decimal point.

example

Write out in full
a 3.3×10^3 **b** 2.75×10^5.
....

a $3.3 \times 10^3 = 3.3 \times 1000$ **b** $2.75 \times 10^5 = 2.75 \times 100\,000$
    $= 3300$ $= 275\,000$

3.3×10^3 and 2.75×10^5 are in **standard index form**.

The digits move to the left of the decimal point.

You use powers of 10 to write very large numbers.

- To write a large number in standard index form, re-write it as a number between 1 and 10 multiplied by a positive power of 10.

example

Write these numbers in standard index form
a 6700   **b** 26 000 000.
....

Divide the number by a power of 10 so that it becomes a decimal between 1 and 10.
a $6700 \div 1000 = 6.7$ **b** $26\,000\,000 \div 10\,000\,000 = 2.6$
    $6700 = 6.7 \times 1000$ $26\,000\,000 = 2.6 \times 10\,000\,000$
        $= 6.7 \times 10^3$ $= 2.6 \times 10^7$

The digits move to the right of the decimal point.

Exercise 7a

1 Each of these numbers is in standard index form. Write out each number in full.

a 3.7×10^2 **b** 4.7×10^3 **c** 1.23×10^6 **d** 4.02×10^7

e 3.01×10^6 **f** 4.9×10^9 **g** 7.37×10^{11} **h** 1.004×10^6

2 Write each of these numbers in standard index form.

a 230 **b** 4870 **c** 340 000 **d** 78 000 000

e 4 100 000 000 **f** 2 380 000 **g** 238.3 **h** 3878.8

3 Write each of these numbers in standard index form.

a The population of Maryport is 35 600.

b The population of the UK in 1990 was 59 million.

c The speed of light is 186 000 miles per second.

d The nearest star is 24 790 000 000 000 miles away.

4 Put these numbers in order from smallest to largest.

a 2.6×10^3, 2.5×10^4, 270, 2.55×10^4, 2.58×10^3

b 3×10^{12}, 2.8×10^{14}, 2.9×10^{13}, 2 980 000 000 000 000

5 Calculate the following, giving your answers in standard form.

> Write out the numbers in full before adding or subtracting.

a $2.4 \times 10^3 + 85$ **b** $3.6 \times 10^4 + 2.2 \times 10^4$

c $3.8 \times 10^4 - 3.3 \times 10^3$ **d** $7.6 \times 10^5 - 3.3 \times 10^3$

6 a Carla flies 3.6×10^3 miles in 6 hours. What is the average speed of the plane?

b Keiley wins €1.3×10^7 in a lottery. She spends €3.85×10^5 on a new house and €32 500 on a new car. How much money does she have left?

7 Write each of these numbers in standard index form.

a 27×10^1 **b** 573×10^2 **c** 0.53×10^4 **d** 34.2×10^3

e 3010×10^4 **f** 0.492×10^6 **g** 0.048×10^5 **h** 0.000378×10^8

8 Round each of these numbers to the nearest thousand. Give your answers in standard form.

a 5.3×10^3 **b** 2.85×10^4 **c** 4.1365×10^5 **d** 3.5072×10^4

---

challenge

Complete these; the first one is done for you.

a $5 \times 10^n = 50 \times 10^\square = 50 \times 10^{n-1}$ **b** $0.5 \times 10^n = 5000 \times 10^\square$

c $500 \times 10^n = 5 \times 10^\square$ **d** $500 000 \times 10^n = 50 \times 10^\square$

- Multiply and divide numbers by powers of 10
- Write small numbers in standard form
- Use a calculator to read and interpret numbers in standard form

Keywords
Index notation
Power
Standard index form

- To multiply or divide by a negative **power** of ten, 10^{-n}, move the digits n places to the right or left of the decimal point.

example

Calculate
a 330×10^{-3} b $27.5 \div 10^{-2}$.

In **index notation**, 10^{-3} is the same as $\frac{1}{10^3} = \frac{1}{1000}$.

Rewrite

a $330 \times 10^{-3} = 330 \times \frac{1}{1000}$
$= 330 \div 1000$
$= 0.33$

b $27.5 \div 10^{-2} = 27.5 \div \frac{1}{100}$
$= 27.5 \times 100$
$= 2750$

Multiplying by $\frac{1}{1000}$ is the same as dividing by 1000.

Dividing by $\frac{1}{100}$ is the same as multiplying by 100.

- To write a small number in **standard index form** write it as a number between 1 and 10 multiplied by a negative power of 10.

example

Write these numbers in standard index form.
a 0.67   b 0.000026

Rewrite the number as a decimal between 1 and 10 divided by a power of 10.

a $0.67 = 6.7 \div 10$
$= 6.7 \div 10^1$

b $0.000026 = 2.6 \div 100000$
$= 2.6 \div 10^5$

Dividing by 10^5 is the same as multiplying by $\frac{1}{10^5} = 10^{-5}$.

Write the number in standard form using a negative power of 10.
$= 6.7 \times \frac{1}{10^1} = 6.7 \times 10^{-1}$ $= 2.6 \times \frac{1}{10^5} = 2.6 \times 10^{-5}$

- You can use a calculator to work with numbers written in standard form by using the exp button.

example

Calculate $(3.2 \times 10^4) \times (2.5 \times 10^3)$.

Enter the numbers on the calculator using the exp button   The calculator display will show

```
3.2ε4x2.5ε3
=8ε7
```

You can interpret this answer as 8×10^7.

Exercise 7b

1 Calculate the following.
   a $47 \div 10^2$ b $2900 \div 10^3$ c $123 \div 10^4$ d $4 \div 10^5$
   e 31.8×10^{-4} f $39\,000 \times 10^{-2}$ g 0.3×10^{-3} h 2.4×10^{-2}

2 Each of these numbers is in standard index form. Write each
   number as a decimal.
   a 2.8×10^{-2} b 3.6×10^{-3} c 9.34×10^{-4} d 5.13×10^{-3}
   e 4.92×10^{-5} f 3.8×10^{-6} g 6.25×10^{-8} h 1.234×10^{-10}

3 Write each of these numbers in standard index form.
   a 0.3   b 0.48   c 0.034   d 0.00078
   e 0.000003   f 0.0067   g 0.00000456   h 0.000000000024

4 Write each of these numbers in standard index form.
   a A millipede is 0.094 inches long.
   b The diameter of a human blood cell is 0.00000068 m.

5 Put these numbers in order from smallest to largest.
   2×10^{-8}, 1.8×10^{-7}, 2.3×10^{-8}, 2.2×10^{-7}

6 Use your calculator to evaluate the following, giving your
   answers in standard form.
   a $(6.5 \times 10^3) \times (2.4 \times 10^5)$ b $(6.5 \times 10^3) + (2.4 \times 10^5)$
   c $(6.5 \times 10^{-3}) \div (2.4 \times 10^{-5})$ d $(6.5 \times 10^{-3}) - (2.4 \times 10^{-5})$

7 Calculate the following, giving your answers in standard form.
   a A light year is 9.43×10^{12} km. A star is 12.4 light years
      from Earth. How far away is the star in km?
   b The population of India is 1.05×10^9 and India has a
      land area of 3.3×10^6 km^2.
      On average how many people live in each square
      kilometre in India?

Did you know?

The most densely populated country on Earth is Monaco with 1.7×10^4 people/km^2. The average population density of Earth is 45 people/km^2.

---

investigation

Here are the probabilities of various events.
i   Winning the national lottery in a week   1 in 14000000
ii Losing your bag at an airport in a year   1 in 138
iii Being struck by lightening in a year   1 in 576000
iv Being bitten by a shark in a year   1 in 300000000

   a Write each probability in standard form.
   b Put the events in order of likelihood.
   c There are 60 million people in Britain. How many people will
      each of these events affect each year?

- Know and use index laws
- Know and use order of operations

p. 178

Keywords
Add   Power
Index form   Subtract
Multiply
Order of operation

- You can multiply and divide numbers written in **index form**.

---

example

Calculate **a** $10^2 \times 10^3$ **b** $10^2 \div 10^4$

a $10^2 \times 10^3 = (10 \times 10) \times (10 \times 10 \times 10) = 10^5$
$\qquad\qquad = 10^{2+3} \qquad\qquad\qquad\qquad = 10^5$

Add the indices when you multiply $x^a \times x^b = x^{a+b}$.

b $10^2 \div 10^4 = \dfrac{(10 \times 10)}{(10 \times 10 \times 10 \times 10)} = \dfrac{1}{10^2} = 10^{-2}$
$\qquad\qquad = 10^{2-4} \qquad\qquad\qquad\qquad = 10^{-2}$

Subtract the indices when you divide $x^a \div x^b = x^{a-b}$.

- You can multiply a number by itself when it is written in index form.

---

example

Calculate **a** $(10^3)^3$ **b** $(10^{-3})^2$

a $(10^3)^3 = 10^3 \times 10^3 \times 10^3 = 10^{3+3+3} = 10^9$
$\qquad\qquad\qquad\qquad = 10^{3 \times 3} \quad = 10^9$

Multiply the indices when you raise an index to a power $(x^a)^b = x^{ab}$.

b $(10^{-3})^2 = 10^{-3} \times 10^{-3} = 10^{-3+-3} = 10^{-6}$
$\qquad\qquad\qquad = 10^{-3 \times 2} = 10^{-6}$

$\dfrac{1}{10^3} \times \dfrac{1}{10^3} = \dfrac{1}{10^6}$.

- When a calculation contains more than one operation, you must do the operations in the correct order. This is called the **order of operations**.

---

example

Calculate $\dfrac{2(3-3^2)^2}{3+\sqrt{4^2-7}}$

$\dfrac{2(3-3^2)^2}{3+\sqrt{(4^2-7)}} = \dfrac{2(-6)^2}{3+\sqrt{9}}$

$\qquad\qquad = \dfrac{2 \times 36}{3+3}$

$\qquad\qquad = (2 \times 36) \div (3+3) = 72 \div 6 = 12$

First, work out the contents of any brackets.

Second, work out any powers or roots.

Rewrite as a division.

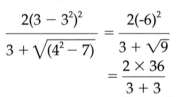

Brackets

Powers

Multiply   Divide

Add   Subtract

Exercise 7c

1 Simplify each of the following leaving your answer as a single power of the number.

a $3^2 \times 3^2$ **b** $4^3 \times 4^4$ **c** $5^2 \times 5^6$ **d** $3^5 \times 3^{-2}$ **e** $7^6 \times 7^{-3}$

f $3^5 \div 3^5$ **g** $4^3 \div 4^5$ **h** $3^5 \div 3^7$ **i** $2^6 \div 2^{-3}$ **j** $3^5 \div 3^{-1}$

2 Calculate the following leaving your answer in index form where possible.

a $4^{-2} \times 4^{-3}$ **b** $4^3 + 4^{-2}$ **c** $5^3 - 5^{-2}$ **d** $4^{-2} \div 4^{-3}$ **e** $4^{-3} \div 4^2$

3 Give four different values for a and b which satisfy this equation.

$a^b = 64$

4 Work out the value of each of the following.

a $2^2 \times 2^2$ **b** $5^4 \times 5^{-2} \times 5^{-2}$ **c** $3^2 \div 3^2$

d $\dfrac{3^4 \times 3^2}{3^8}$ **e** $\dfrac{4^5 \times 4^1}{4^4}$ **f** $10^2 \div 10^7$

5 Simplify each of the following leaving your answer as a single power of the number.

a $2^2 \times 2^4 \times 2$ **b** $3^5 \times 3^2 \times 3^{-3}$ **c** $10^2 \times 10^3 \div 10^6$

d $\dfrac{3^4 \times 3^5}{3^3 \times 3^2}$ **e** $\dfrac{2^2 \times 2 \times 2^3}{2^2 \times 2^8}$ **f** $\dfrac{10^3 \div 10^{-5}}{10^2}$

6 Calculate the following leaving your answer in index form.

a $(4^2)^3$ **b** $(5^3)^2$ **c** $(2^{-2})^3$ **d** $(4^2)^{-2}$ **e** $(10^{-3})^{-2}$

7 Calculate the following giving your answer to 2 dp where appropriate.

a $\dfrac{(5+3)^2}{(5-3)^3}$ **b** $\dfrac{(2^3-1)(7+2)^2}{9-4^2}$ **c** $\dfrac{(3^2)^2 + \sqrt{3^4}}{(10-7)^2}$

d $\dfrac{2.7 \times 11.2}{1.05^2 \times (3.1-2)^2}$ **e** $\dfrac{4 \times \sqrt{1.3^3 + 4^2}}{3.7 - 1.2^2}$ **f** $\dfrac{\sqrt{(3^2+2)}}{2 + \sqrt{(0.4^2+1)}}$

8 George knows that $p^2 = 2$. Use this information to find the value of

a p^4 **b** p^{-2} **c** p^6 **d** $(p^2)^2$.

Work out the following, without using a calculator, giving your answers in standard form.

a $(3 \times 10^3) \times (2 \times 10^5)$ **b** $(6 \times 10^5) \div (2 \times 10^3)$

c $(3 \times 10^{-3}) \times (2 \times 10^5)$ **d** $(6 \times 10^{-3}) \div (2 \times 10^2)$

Use your calculator to check your answers.

Write some rules for multiplying and dividing numbers in standard form without using a calculator.

Use the rules for multiplying and dividing indices to help you.

(7d) Approximation

LEVEL 7

- Round numbers to a given number of significant figures
- Approximate using significant figures
- Understand upper and lower bounds

Keywords
Round
Significant figure
Upper and lower bounds

p. 18
p. 230

- You can use **significant figures** to **round** numbers.

example

Round the number 34.56 to
a 2 sf   **b** 3 sf.

. . . .

a The second significant digit is in the units column, round to the nearest whole number.
34.56 = 35 (2 sf)
b The third significant figure is in the tenths column, round to one decimal place.
34.56 = 34.6 (3 sf)

When you round a number you always look at the next smaller digit, if it is ≥ 5 round up < 5 round down (stays the same).

- If a number has been rounded it is possible to work out the highest and lowest values that the number could be. These are called the **upper and lower bounds**.

example

Find the upper and lower bounds for each quantity.
a The population of Keswick is 6000 people (to the nearest 1000 people).
b The journey from Keswick to Blackburn is 92 miles (to the nearest mile).

. . . .

When a number is rounded to a given amount, for example, the nearest 100, then the number must lie within ± $\frac{1}{2}$ of that amount, that is, ± 50.

a The population lies between 6000 ± 500.

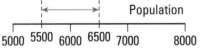
Population
5000 5500 6000 6500 7000   8000

A population is discrete; it only takes whole number values. The upper bound is 6499 as 6500 would be round up to 7000.

b The journey is between 92 ± 0.5 miles.

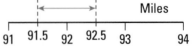
Miles
91 91.5 92 92.5 93   94

A distance is continuous; in principle, it can be given to any number of decimal places. The upper bound is given as 92.5 = 92.4999 . . . even though 92.5 would round up to 93.

The upper and lower bounds are usually written using inequality signs.
5500 ≤ population < 6500   92.5 miles ≤ journey < 93.5 miles

Exercise 7d

1 Round each of these numbers to
   i 1 sf   **ii** 2 sf   **iii** 3sf.
   a 3472   **b** 26 058   **c** 329 154   **d** 6 284 903   **e** 294.3
   f 37.456 **g** 4.7654   **h** 0.254 59   **i** 0.005 987 6   **j** 0.000 002 682 5

2 Round each of these numbers to three significant figures.
   Give your answer in standard form.
   a 4.2381×10^{4} **b** 4.7225×10^{2} **c** 2.0895×10^{-2}

3 Use a calculator to work out these calculations and then
   round your answer to the degree of accuracy stated.
   a $\dfrac{56 + 74}{32 \times 24}$ (3 sf)   **b** $\dfrac{2.98 + 6.78 + 3.29}{4.23}$ (2 sf)
   c $13 \div 7 \times 10^{5}$ (3 sf)   **d** $2 \times 10^{-2} \div 1.3 \times 10^{3}$ (2 sf)

4 Estimate the answer to each calculation by first rounding the
   numbers to one significant figure.
   a $\dfrac{123 \times 9.7}{17.9}$ **b** $\dfrac{6.78 \times 19.4}{0.47}$ **c** $\dfrac{633 \times 2.8}{28.45}$
   d $\dfrac{5.3 \times 36.2}{4.9 \times 11.3}$ **e** $\dfrac{128 \times 8.4}{0.27}$

5 Identify the upper and lower bounds of these figures.
   a Attendance at a football game was 56 000 (nearest 1000).
   b Speed of sound is 1200 km per hour (nearest 100 km).
   c Beryl's height is 1.6 m (2 sf).
   d Max won about £2 million (1 sf).
   e Width of an ant is 0.093 cm (3 dp).

PLAN OF ROOM

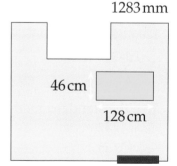

6 Jack buys a cupboard. The cupboard is 128 cm wide
   and 46 cm deep, both to the nearest cm. The space where
   Jack wants to put the cupboard is 1283 mm (nearest mm)
   wide. Explain why the cupboard might not fit.

challenge

A mini laptop screen is 22.6 cm wide and 16.9 cm high. All
measurements are to one decimal place.
a Calculate the upper and lower bounds for each measurement.
b Use your answers to calculate the maximum and minimum
   area of the screen.
c The width of the screen contains a line of 2560 pixels
   (nearest 10 pixels). What is the maximum and minimum width of a pixel?

- Add and subtract decimals
- Multiply and divide decimals using equivalent calculations

Keywords
Equivalent integer calculation
Estimate
Standard method

- You can use a standard column procedure for adding and subtracting numbers with differing numbers of decimal places.

example

Calculate $7239 + 470.004 + 0.0032$

```
7239.0000
 470.0040     Set out the calculation in columns.
   0.0032     Align the decimal points.
7709.0072
       1
```

Add zeros so that all the numbers have the same number of decimal places.

- Use a **standard method** for multiplying and dividing decimals.

example

Calculate
a 0.0632×0.047
b $0.0735 \div 0.68$ to 3 sf

Estimate the answer.

a $0.0632 \times 0.047 \approx 0.06 \times 0.05 \approx 0.003$
b $0.0735 \div 0.68 \approx 0.07 \div 0.7 \approx 0.1$

Change the decimal calculation into an **equivalent integer calculation**.

$$0.0632 \times 0.047 = \frac{632}{10\,000} \times \frac{47}{1000}$$

$$= \frac{632 \times 47}{10\,000\,000}$$

$$0.0735 \div 0.68 = \frac{0.0735}{0.68} = \frac{735}{6800}$$

$$= \frac{735}{68} \times \frac{1}{100} = \frac{735}{68} \div 100$$

Use the standard method.

```
    632
  × 47
  -----
  25280    40 × 632
   4424     7 × 632
  -----
  29704
      1
```

Remember to divide the answer by 10 000 000.

```
         10.80 ᵥ 0.6
       _____
   68 ) 735.00
      - 680.00          10 × 68 = 680
      --------
         55.00
       - 00.00          0 × 68 = 0
      --------
         55.00
       - 54.40          0.8 × 68 = 54.4
      --------
          0.60
        - 0.00          0.00 × 68 = 0
      --------
          0.60
```

$0.0632 \times 0.047 = 0.002970\,4$

$\qquad\qquad\quad = 2.9704 \times 10^{-3}$

$0.0029704 \approx 0.003$ ✓

$0.0735 \div 0.68 = 10.8 \div 100$

$\qquad = 0.108$ (3 sf) $= 1.08 \times 10^{-1}$ (3 sf)

$0.108\ldots \approx 0.1$ ✓

Exercise 7e

1 Calculate these using an appropriate method.
   a $5.63 + 435.2 + 6$ **b** $64.3 + 216.8 + 50.32$ **c** $7.12 + 0.4 + 7 + 0.46$
   d $425.1 + 38.16 + 0.027$ **e** $243.5 - 6 - 37.8$ **f** $57.6 + 284.8 - 61.92$
   g $47.3 - 2.9 - 14$ **h** $354.68 - 88 - 4.7$

2 Calculate these using a written method.
   a 32×4.37 **b** 27×1.64 **c** 63×35.7 **d** 47×0.24
   e 75×0.96 **f** 32×0.75 **g** 7.1×36.1 **h** 4.9×52.7
   i 9.3×4.48 **j** 0.83×4.45 **k** 0.63×4.71 **l** 0.18×88.4
   m 0.32×0.0311 **n** 0.28×0.678 **o** 0.63×0.504 **p** 0.045×0.63
   q 0.063×0.095 **r** 0.084×0.00572 **s** 0.00725×0.078 **t** 0.0238×0.00056

3 **a** Hanif buys 0.064 tonnes of coal. The iron costs £103.45 per tonne.
      How much does the coal cost?
  b Jason measures a microchip. It is 0.0375 m long and 0.0013 m wide.
      What is the area of the microchip in square metres?

4 Calculate these using an appropriate method. Give your answers
   to three significant figures.
   a $384 \div 5.9$ **b** $275 \div 1.9$ **c** $835 \div 6.4$ **d** $513.4 \div 0.4$
   e $713.2 \div 0.7$ **f** $419.3 \div 0.6$ **g** $326.7 \div 0.03$ **h** $586.2 \div 0.08$
   i $395.4 \div 0.09$ **j** $0.036 \div 0.0077$ **k** $0.017 \div 0.0023$ **l** $0.083 \div 0.00091$
   m $0.084 \div 0.64$ **n** $0.783 \div 6.5$ **o** $0.0624 \div 0.56$ **p** $0.375 \div 0.49$
   q $0.073 \div 0.00392$ **r** $0.0529 \div 0.36$

5 Give your answers to these calculations as decimals to 3 sf.
   a Barry the plankton is 0.037 cm long. His friend Gary is 0.027 cm
      long. How many times longer is Barry?
   b A DNA molecule measures 34 angstroms long by
      21 angstroms wide.
      What is the ratio of length to width for a DNA molecule?
      (1 angstrom = 1.0×10^{-10} metres)

21 Angstroms

34 Angstroms

You can find the square root of 5
using the sequence generated by
this term-to-term rule.
$$x_{n+1} = \frac{\left(x_n + \frac{5}{x_n}\right)}{2}$$

a Start with the estimate $x_1 = 2$ and work out x_2.
b Generate furtherer terms in the sequence $x_1, x_2, x_3, x_4, \ldots$
   until you can give $\sqrt{5}$ to 3 sf.
c Find the square root of other numbers using this method.

- Convert recurring decimals to fractions
- Recognise and use reciprocals

Keywords
Reciprocal
Recurring decimal
Terminating decimal

- You can convert a **terminating decimal** into a fraction using place value.

example

Convert these decimals into fractions in their simplest form.
a 0.4 　　　　**b** 0.325

a $0.4 = \frac{4}{10}$
$= \frac{2}{5}$

b $0.325 = \frac{325}{1000}$
$= \frac{13}{40}$

- You can convert a **recurring decimal** to a fraction using an algebraic method.

example

Convert these decimals into fractions in their simplest form
a $0.\dot{3} = 0.33333...$ 　　　　**b** $0.\dot{2}\dot{7} = 0.272727...$

If a group of n digits recur then you multiply by 10^n.

a Let $x = 0.33333...$ 　(1)
$10x = 3.33333...$ 　(2)
Subtract
$(2) - (1)$ 　$9x = 3$
$x = \frac{3}{9} = \frac{1}{3}$

b Let $x = 0.272727...$ 　(1)
$100x = 27.272727...$ 　(2)
$(2) - (1)$ 　$99x = 27$
$x = \frac{27}{99} = \frac{3}{11}$

The **reciprocal** of a number is the result of dividing it into 1.

example

Find the reciprocal of these numbers.
a 6 　　**b** 0.4 　　**c** $\frac{1}{6}$ 　　**d** $\frac{2}{5}$

Divide the number into 1.
a $= \frac{1}{6}$ 　**b** $= \frac{1}{0.4}$ 　**c** $= \frac{1}{\frac{1}{6}}$ 　**d** $= \frac{1}{\frac{2}{5}}$

To find the reciprocal of a fraction turn it upside down.

Rewrite as a division where appropriate.
$= 1 \div 0.4$ 　$= 1 \div \frac{1}{6}$ 　$= 1 \div \frac{2}{5}$
$= 2.5$ 　$= 1 \times \frac{6}{1}$ 　$= 1 \times \frac{5}{2}$
$= 6$ 　$= \frac{5}{2}$

- You can use the $\boxed{x^{-1}}$ key on your calculator to calculate the reciprocal.

Exercise 7f

1 Write each decimal as a fraction in its simplest form.

    a 0.3   **b** 1.24   **c** 0.56   **d** 0.78   **e** 0.355

    f 0.045   **g** 1.625   **h** 0.435   **i** 2.045   **j** 1.555

2 Write these fractions as decimals without using a calculator.

    a $\frac{7}{10}$ **b** $\frac{13}{20}$ **c** $\frac{16}{25}$ **d** $\frac{43}{50}$ **e** $\frac{35}{25}$

    f $\frac{9}{5}$ **g** $\frac{27}{20}$ **h** $\frac{53}{40}$ **i** $\frac{19}{16}$ **j** $\frac{165}{80}$

3 Change these fractions into decimals using division. Use an appropriate method. Give your answers to 5 sf.

    a $\frac{1}{3}$ **b** $\frac{3}{7}$ **c** $\frac{7}{11}$ **d** $\frac{6}{13}$ **e** $\frac{4}{17}$

4 Write these recurring decimals as fractions in their simplest form.

    a 0.666...   **b** 0.111...   **c** 0.2323...   **d** 0.4545...

    e 0.354354...   **f** 0.801801...   **g** 0.729729...   **h** 0.162162...

5 Find the reciprocals of these numbers without using a calculator. Leave your answers in the most appropriate form.

    a 7   **b** $\frac{1}{4}$ **c** 0.2   **d** $\frac{2}{3}$

    e 2.6   **f** $\frac{1}{13}$ **g** $\frac{72}{83}$ **h** 26.2

6 Jose thinks of a number between 0 and 100. He finds the reciprocal of the number and rounds his answer to 4 significant figures. He writes down his answer as 0.013*1.

Find Jose's number and the missing digit.

7 Write these recurring decimals as fractions in their simplest form.

    a 0.1666...   **b** 0.53333...   **c** 0.58333...   **d** 0.291666...

Did you know?

The graph of $y = \frac{1}{x}$ is an example of a conic section called a hyperbola. You make a hyperbola by slicing through a cone at a shallow angle to its axis.

---

investigation

Kelvin wants to draw the graph of $y = \frac{1}{x}$. This is called the reciprocal function. He completes a table of values.

x	0.5	1	1.5	2	2.5	3
y						

a Copy and complete the table.

b Draw the graph of $y = \frac{1}{x}$.

c Use some more values for x which are smaller than 1.
Plot these points on your graph. Describe what is happening to your graph as x gets smaller.

d Use some larger values for x which are greater than 3. Plot these points on your graph. Describe what is happening to your graph as x gets larger.

e Try some negative values for x. Describe what happens.

- Write a number as the product of its prime factors
- Find the HCF and LCM
- Multiply and divide numbers written in standard form

Keywords
Prime factors
HCF
LCM

- You can write a number as the product of its **prime factors** by using a method based upon repeated division.

example

Write 700 as the product of its prime factors.

$2)\overline{700}$
$2)\overline{350}$
$5)\overline{175}$
$5)\overline{35}$
7 STOP

$700 = 2 \times 2 \times 5 \times 5 \times 7$
$ = 2^2 \times 5^2 \times 7$

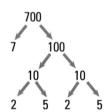

You must only divide by prime factors. Be systematic and start by testing the smallest prime: 2, 3, 5, 7, 11 . . .

The fundamental theorem of arithmetic states that all natural numbers, greater than one, can be written as a unique product of prime numbers.

- You can find the highest common factor (**HCF**) and the lowest common multiple (**LCM**) of two or more numbers by using prime factors.

example

Find the HCF and LCM of 56 and 80.

$56 = 2^3 \times 7 \qquad 80 = 2^4 \times 5$

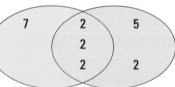

HCF $= 2 \times 2 \times 2 = 8$
LCM $= 2 \times 2 \times 2 \times 2 \times 5 \times 7 = 560$

- You can multiply and divide numbers written in standard form.

example

Calculate
a $(3 \times 10^3) \times (2 \times 10^2)$ \qquad **b** $(6 \times 10^2) \div (3 \times 10^4)$

a $(3 \times 10^3) \times (2 \times 10^2)$
$= (3 \times 2) \times (10^3 \times 10^2)$
$= 6 \times 10^5$

b $(6 \times 10^2) \div (3 \times 10^4)$
$= \dfrac{6 \times 10^2}{3 \times 10^4} = \dfrac{6}{3} \times \dfrac{10^2}{10^4}$
$= 2 \times 10^{-2}$

Separate the division into the product of two fractions.

Exercise 7g

1 Write each of these numbers as the product of its prime factors.

a 24	**b** 40	**c** 66	**d** 84
e 108	**f** 140	**g** 160	**h** 225
i 256	**j** 375	**k** 440	**l** 1440

2 Find the HCF and LCM of these numbers.

a 28 and 42   **b** 35 and 90   **c** 208 and 273

d 350 and 675   **e** 216 and 576   **f** 1189 and 1827

g 25, 45 and 65   **h** 35, 49 and 63

3 Cancel down these fractions to their simplest form.

a $\frac{84}{228}$ **b** $\frac{91}{169}$ **c** $\frac{350}{434}$ **d** $\frac{315}{525}$ **e** $\frac{124}{192}$

4 Work out the following leaving your answers as fractions in their simplest form.

a $\frac{17}{40} - \frac{12}{30}$ **b** $\frac{45}{56} + \frac{7}{80}$ **c** $\frac{37}{50} + \frac{17}{60}$

5 Calculate the following, giving your answers in standard form.

a $(2 \times 10^4) \times (4 \times 10^5)$ **b** $(3 \times 10^3) \times (3 \times 10^2)$

c $(8 \times 10^2) \div (4 \times 10^3)$ **d** $(9 \times 10^{-2}) \div (2 \times 10^3)$

6 Calculate the following. Rewrite your answers in standard form.

a $(3 \times 10^2) \times (5 \times 10^4)$ **b** $(6 \times 10^3) \times (2.5 \times 10^{-2})$

c $(9 \times 10^2) \div (6 \times 10^5)$ **d** $(2 \times 10^2) \div (5 \times 10^{-3})$

7 Write down the values of x, y and z.

$54 = 2 \times 3^x$ $45 = 5 \times 3^y$ $54 \times 45 = 2 \times 5 \times 3^z$

---

challenge

Use a calculator to answer these problems. Give your answers as numbers written in standard form to 3 sf.

a A planet takes 2.5×10^2 years to orbit its sun at a speed of 1.25×10^4 miles per hour. Assuming the orbit of the planet is a circle how far away from the sun is the planet?

b Calculate the missing side in this right-angled triangle.

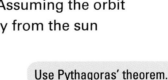
Use Pythagoras' theorem.

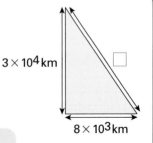
3×10^4 km

8×10^3 km

- Know and use simple laws for surds
- Use index notation for square roots and cube roots

- You can multiply numbers written in surd form
  $\sqrt{a} \times \sqrt{b} = \sqrt{a \times b} = \sqrt{ab}$.

---

example

Calculate
a $\sqrt{5} \times \sqrt{5}$ b $\sqrt{5} \times \sqrt{2}$

. . . .

a $\sqrt{5} \times \sqrt{5} = \sqrt{5 \times 5}$ b $\sqrt{5} \times \sqrt{2} = \sqrt{5 \times 2}$
$\qquad\qquad = \sqrt{25}$ $\qquad\qquad = \sqrt{10}$
$\qquad\qquad = 5$

Most square roots
cannot be written as
exact decimals
$\qquad \sqrt{9} = 3$
but $\sqrt{10} = 3.1622776\ldots$
It is more accurate to leave
these numbers in **surd**
form; $\sqrt{10}$ is a surd.

- You can use the multiplication rule to simplify surds.

---

example

Write these surds in their simplest form
a $\sqrt{27}$ b $\sqrt{32}$

. . . .

a $\sqrt{27} = \sqrt{9 \times 3}$ b $\sqrt{32} = \sqrt{16 \times 2}$
$\qquad\quad = \sqrt{9} \times \sqrt{3}$ $\qquad\quad = \sqrt{16} \times \sqrt{2}$
$\qquad\quad = 3 \times \sqrt{3} = 3\sqrt{3}$ $\qquad\quad = 4 \times \sqrt{2} = 4\sqrt{2}$

$\sqrt{ab} = \sqrt{(a \times b)}$
$\qquad = \sqrt{a} \times \sqrt{b}$

- You can multiply numbers written in simplified surd form.

---

example

Calculate
a $2\sqrt{5} \times 3\sqrt{5}$ b $2\sqrt{5} \times 3\sqrt{2}$

. . . .

a $2\sqrt{5} \times 3\sqrt{5} = (2 \times 3) \times (\sqrt{5} \times \sqrt{5})$ b $2\sqrt{5} \times 3\sqrt{2} = (2 \times 3) \times \sqrt{5 \times 2}$
$\qquad\qquad\qquad = 6 \times 5 = 30$ $\qquad\qquad\qquad = 6 \times \sqrt{10} = 6\sqrt{10}$

- You can use **fractional indices** to represent square roots and cube roots in **index form**.

---

example

Write these square roots and cube roots in index notation
a $\sqrt{4}$ b $\sqrt{10}$ c $\sqrt[3]{8}$ d $\sqrt[3]{10}$

. . . .

a $\sqrt{4} = 4^{\frac{1}{2}}$ b $\sqrt{10} = 10^{\frac{1}{2}}$
c $\sqrt[3]{8} = 8^{\frac{1}{3}}$ d $\sqrt[3]{10} = 10^{\frac{1}{3}}$

$\sqrt{4} \times \sqrt{4} = 4$
$4^{\frac{1}{2}} \times 4^{\frac{1}{2}} = 4^{\frac{1}{2} + \frac{1}{2}} = 4^1$

$\sqrt[3]{8} \times \sqrt[3]{8} \times \sqrt[3]{8} = 8$
$8^{\frac{1}{3}} \times 8^{\frac{1}{3}} \times 8^{\frac{1}{3}} = 8^{\frac{1}{3} + \frac{1}{3} + \frac{1}{3}} = 8^1$

Exercise 7h

1 Calculate the following leaving your answers in surd form.
   a $\sqrt{3} \times \sqrt{3}$ b $\sqrt{4} \times \sqrt{4}$ c $\sqrt{5} \times \sqrt{3}$
   d $\sqrt{6} \times \sqrt{2}$ e $\sqrt{7} \times \sqrt{3}$ f $\sqrt{2} \times \sqrt{18}$
   g $\sqrt{2} \times \sqrt{32}$ h $\sqrt{5} \times \sqrt{20}$ i $\sqrt{27} \times \sqrt{3}$
   j $\sqrt{8} \times \sqrt{18}$

2 Write these numbers in their simplest form.
   a $\sqrt{12}$ b $\sqrt{8}$ c $\sqrt{18}$ d $\sqrt{24}$ e $\sqrt{40}$
   f $\sqrt{48}$ g $\sqrt{32}$ h $\sqrt{50}$ i $\sqrt{72}$ j $\sqrt{98}$

3 Calculate the following leaving your answers in surd form.
   a $2\sqrt{3} \times 3\sqrt{3}$ b $3\sqrt{2} \times \sqrt{2}$
   c $4\sqrt{5} \times 2\sqrt{3}$ d $3\sqrt{6} \times 2\sqrt{2}$
   e $4\sqrt{7} \times 2\sqrt{3}$ f $3\sqrt{2} \times 4\sqrt{5}$
   g $\sqrt{2} \times 2\sqrt{3}$ h $\sqrt{5} \times 3\sqrt{20}$

4 a Calculate the area of this triangle.
   b Calculate the length
      of the missing side,
      leaving your answer
      as a surd in its simplest
      form.

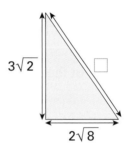

$3\sqrt{2}$

$2\sqrt{8}$

$\sqrt{2}$

Did you know?

Around 500 BC
Hippasus of
Metapontum proved
that $\sqrt{2}$ could not be
written as a fraction.
According to legend,
this so upset his
fellow Pythagoreans
that they drowned
him!

5 Write these numbers using index notation.
   a $\sqrt{8}$ b $\sqrt[3]{8}$ c $\sqrt{18}$ d $\sqrt[3]{24}$ e $\sqrt[3]{40}$

6 Work out the value of each of these expressions.
   a 3^2 b $9^{\frac{1}{2}}$ c $8^{\frac{1}{3}}$
   d $16^{\frac{1}{2}}$ e $64^{\frac{1}{3}}$ f $27^{\frac{1}{3}}$

Index laws
$$x^n \times x^m = x^{n+m}$$
$$x^n \div x^m = x^{n-m}.$$

7 Calculate the following leaving your answers in index form.
   a $8^{\frac{1}{3}} \times 8^{\frac{1}{2}}$ b $9^{\frac{1}{2}} \times 9^2$ c $16^4 \div 16^{\frac{1}{2}}$
   d $4^2 \div 4^{\frac{1}{3}}$ e $4^{-3} \div 4^{\frac{1}{2}}$

8 Give four different values for a and b which satisfy this equation.
   $$a^b = 4$$

challenge

a For each of the following write the answer in index form
   and then state the numerical value of the answer.
   i $(4^{\frac{1}{2}})^2$ ii $(8^{\frac{1}{3}})^2$ iii $(4^{\frac{1}{2}})^3$ iv $(64^{\frac{1}{3}})^2$
b Write down what you have noticed.
c Use your answer to part **b** to work out the value of $25^{\frac{3}{2}}$.

7a

1 Write these numbers in standard index form.
  a 460   **b** 813 000   **c** 98 000 000   **d** 201.4

2 Write these numbers in standard index form.
  a The population of the USA is 261 million.
  b The speed of light is 297 600 kilometres per second.

7b

3 Write these numbers in standard index form.
  a 0.27   **b** 0.000 031   **c** 0.000 003 67   **d** 0.000 001 056

4 Use a calculator to find the following, giving your answers
  in standard form where appropriate.
  a A man walks 8.76×10^4 km in an 80-year lifetime.
  How many km does he walk on average each day?
  b The population of the UK is 6.1×10^7. The UK has a land
  area of 2.45×10^5 km². On average how many people live
  in each square kilometre in the UK?

7c

5 Work out the value of each of the following.
  a $\dfrac{6^4 \times 6^3}{6^5}$ **b** $\dfrac{3^2 \times 3^4}{3^3}$ **c** $10^4 \div 10^6$

6 Simplify the following leaving your answers as a single
  power of the number.
  a $\dfrac{5^4 \times 5^3}{5^2 \times 5^3}$ **b** $\dfrac{6^2 \times 6 \times 6^7}{6^3 \times 6^4}$ **c** $\dfrac{8^3 \div 8^{-5}}{8^2}$

7 Calculate the following leaving your answers in index form.
  a $(2^{-2})^2$ **b** $(3^2)^3$ **c** $(4^{-1})^{-2}$
  d $(5^2)^{-3}$ **e** $(10^{-2})^{-5}$

7d

8 Round each of these numbers to
  i 1 sf   **ii** 2 sf   **iii** 3 sf.
  a 3.478×10^4 **b** 36 204   **c** 5.893×10^{-3}

9 Estimate the answers to these calculations by first rounding
  all the numbers to one significant figure.
  a $\dfrac{261 \times 2.3}{28.1}$ **b** $\dfrac{4.92 \times 22.5}{0.24}$ **c** $\dfrac{485 \times 3.25}{32.05}$

10 A football pitch is 70 m (nearest 10 m) wide and 103 m (nearest m) long. Calculate the maximum and minimum possible areas of the football pitch.

11 **a** Erik buys 0.43 tonnes of steel. The steel costs £186.23 per tonne. How much does the steel cost?
b Lilian designs microcircuits. A particular chip is 0.0405 m long and 0.0024 m wide. What is the area of the microchip in square metres?

12 Write these recurring decimals as fractions in their simplest form.
a 0.222... **b** 0.1313... **c** 0.732732... **d** 0.45124512...
e 0.01666... **f** 0.47777.. **g** 0.712929... **h** 0.32323...

13 Find the reciprocals of each of these numbers without using a calculator. Leave your answer in the most appropriate form.
a $\frac{1}{8}$ **b** $\frac{2}{7}$ **c** 1.4 **d** 16.4

14 Find the HCF and LCM of these numbers.
a 408 and 282 **b** 250 and 475 **c** 85, 119 and 136

15 Calculate the following, giving your answers in standard form.
a $(5 \times 10^3) \times (2.5 \times 10^5)$ **b** $(5 \times 10^3) \times (4 \times 10^5)$
c $(1.2 \times 10^2) \div (4 \times 10^2)$ **d** $(4.4 \times 10^{-2}) \div (2 \times 10^3)$

16 Write these numbers in their simplest form.
a $\sqrt{75}$ **b** $\sqrt{180}$ **c** $\sqrt{150}$ **d** $\sqrt{45}$ **e** $\sqrt{245}$

17 Calculate each of the following leaving your answer in surd form.
a $3\sqrt{2} \times 5\sqrt{2}$ **b** $4\sqrt{3} \times 2\sqrt{3}$
c $2\sqrt{5} \times 4\sqrt{2}$ **d** $4\sqrt{7} \times 3\sqrt{3}$

18 Work out the value of each of the following.
a $4^{\frac{1}{2}}$ **b** $9^{-\frac{1}{2}}$ **c** $16^{\frac{3}{2}}$ **d** $64^{\frac{2}{3}}$ **e** $27^{\frac{2}{3}}$

19 Calculate the following leaving your answer in index form.
a $2^{\frac{2}{3}} \times 2^{\frac{1}{3}}$ **b** $3^{\frac{3}{4}} \times 3^{\frac{1}{2}}$ **c** $6^{\frac{1}{2}} \div 6^{\frac{1}{4}}$ **d** $4^{\frac{3}{3}} \div 4^{\frac{1}{2}}$ **e** $4^{-\frac{2}{3}} \div 4^{\frac{1}{3}}$

Maths life

Television viewing figures

The most commonly quoted television viewing figures are gathered from 5100 homes across the UK. The households are chosen to give a representative audience. The figures are important within the television industry, both for planning the type of programmes to make and also when commercial channels are negotiating costs with advertisers.

Television viewing figures for the first week of March 2009

Channel	average daily viewers 000s	weekly viewers 000s
BBC 1	28 760	47 208
BBC 2	14 836	35 532
Total BBC 1 and 2	31 616	48 625
ITV 1	23 520	43 650
Channel 4	16 592	38 391
FIVE	10 323	28 623
Total terrestrial commercial TV	31 303	49 092
Total of non terrestrial TV	31 730	46 076
All TV	44 146	53 547

average weekly viewing time per person hrs:min	percentage of viewing time
5:38	
1:52	
7:30	
5:00	18.6%
2:02	
8:34	
10:52	
26:56	100%

- Why do the daily figures for BBC1 and BBC2 not add up to the combined total given for BBC 1 and 2?
- What extra information can you work out from this?

- What is meant by terrestrial TV and non-terrestrial TV?

- The average daily figures for ITV1 are over half the weekly figures but the daily figures for Five are well below half the weekly figures
- What does this tell you about viewing patterns for the two channels?

- Of the people who watched BBC sometime during the week, how many only watched BBC1 and how many only watched BBC2?

- Complete the missing values in the final two columns to find out what share of the viewers each channel had during the week.

- Explain why dividing the weekly viewing figure for any channel by 7 does not give you the average daily figure for that channel.

BATTLE OF THE TV RATINGS

These are the viewing figures (in millions) for the top 30 programmes on the two main channels for the first week of March 2009:

BBC1

9.64	8.97	8.78	8.44	7.05	6.90	6.78	6.73	6.48	5.99
5.93	5.84	5.75	5.57	5.41	5.32	5.24	5.15	5.12	5.01
4.95	4.94	4.90	4.88	4.86	4.86	4.84	4.81	4.73	4.72

ITV1

10.58	10.58	10.02	9.74	9.64	9.40	8.92	8.52	7.68	7.41
7.38	7.36	7.02	7.00	6.24	5.97	5.74	5.16	5.01	4.99
4.80	4.51	4.35	4.28	4.09	4.05	3.89	3.77	3.71	3.71

Which channel do you think wins the battle of the ratings for this week? Give your reasons.

- Find the mean, median and mode of the viewing figures for each channel.
- Which average do you think gives the best representation of the figures? Which gives the worst? Give your reasons.
- What can you say about the consistency of the viewing figures for each channel?
- What statistics can you give to support your statement?

- Carry out a survey to find out if the share of channels watched by viewers of your age is similar to the share given in the table.
- It would be useful if you could gather the information without everyone having to time their TV viewing. How could you do this?
- Once you have completed your survey, produce charts that make it easy to compare the results.

How do you think the channel share might change if you only surveyed people aged 30 or more?

7 Summary

Assessment criteria

- Solve problems involving calculating with powers and roots **Level 8**
- Change recurring decimals to fractions **Level 8**

Level 8 **1** Write the recurring decimal 0.83333333 ... as a fraction in its simplest form.

Millie's answer ✔

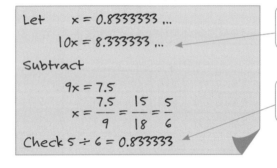

Let $x = 0.8333333$ ...
        $10x = 8.3333333$ ...

Subtract
        $9x = 7.5$
        $x = \dfrac{7.5}{9} = \dfrac{15}{18} = \dfrac{5}{6}$
Check $5 \div 6 = 0.833333$

Millie decides to multiply by 10.

Millie checks that $\frac{5}{6}$ is the correct answer.

Level 8 **2 a** Is 3^{100} even or odd?

Explain your answer.

b Tick (✔) the number below that is the same as $3^{100} \times 3^{100}$.

☐ 3^{200} ☐ 6^{100} ☐ 9^{200} ☐ $3^{10\,000}$ ☐ $9^{10\,000}$

KS3 2007 6–8 Paper 1

8 Algebra

Graphs

The Gateshead Millennium bridge spans the River Tyne between Gateshead and Newcastle. It cost £22 million and has become a major tourist attraction. It was lifted into place on November 20th 2000 using one of the world's largest floating cranes.

The reverse of a 2007 pound coin shows an image of the bridge.

What's the point? This bridge is a parabola in shape and its design required knowledge of the graph of $y = x^2$.

✓ Check in

Level 6

1 Plot the following line graphs.

  a $y = 2x + 1$ **b** $y = 5 - 3x$
  c $x + y = 12$ **d** $x + 3y = 10$

2 Put these expressions in ascending order if
  a $x = 3$ **b** $x = -2$.
  $3x^2$ x^3 $(3x)^2$ $x^3 - 2x$ $x^2 + x - 3$

Level 7

3 Give the gradient and y-axis intercept of each of the following line graphs.

  a $y = 2x + 1$ **b** $y = 5 - 3x$
  c $y - 3x = 4$ **d** $x + 3y = 15$

> Rewrite each equation in the form $y = mx + c$.

4 Solve the following pairs of simultaneous equations.

  a $x + 2y = 7$ **b** $2x + 3y = 10$
   $x - y = 1$ $3x + 2y = 5$

131

- Solve a pair of simultaneous linear equations graphically
- Link graphical representations of equations to the algebraic solutions
- Consider cases that have no solutions or an infinite number of solutions

p. 62

p. 8

Keywords
Graphically Solve
Implicit Simultaneous
Intersection equations

example

Draw the graphs $2x - y = 5$ and $x + 2y = 5$ and find their point of **intersection**. What does this point represent?

. . . .

$2x - y = 5 \Rightarrow y = 2x - 5$

x	0	1	2	3
y	-5	-3	-1	1

$x + 2y = 5$

x	0	5
y	2.5	0

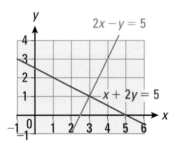

To plot a line graph write it in the form $y = mx + c$ and let $x = 0, 1, 2, 3$ (say) or leave the equation in **implicit** form and let $x = 0$ and $y = 0$.

The graphs intersect at the point (3, 1); $x = 3$ and $y = 1$ is the solution to the pair of **simultaneous equations**.

- You can **solve** a pair of simultaneous equations by representing them **graphically** and finding their point of intersection.

example

Use this graph to solve $x + 3y = 8$ and $2x + y = 1$.

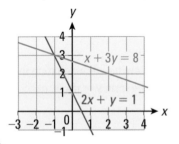

The graphs $x + 3y = 8$ and $2x + y = 1$ intersect at (-1, 3) so the solution is $x = -1$ and $y = 3$.

Give the value of each of x and y not just the coordinates of the point of intersection.

Exercise 8a

1 Use the graph to solve these pairs of simultaneous equations.

a $y = x - 1$
  $x + y = 3$

b $x + y = 3$
  $y = x + 3$

c $y = x + 3$
  $x + 2y = 3$

d $x + y = 3$
  $x + 2y = 3$

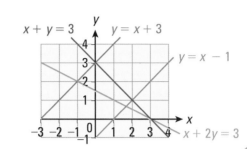

2 Plot your own graphs in order to solve these pairs of simultaneous equations.

a $y = x - 1$
  $y = 2x - 5$

b $x + y = 8$
  $y = x + 4$

c $y = 4x - 1$
  $2x + y = 2$

d $2x + 3y = 12$
  $y = x - 1$

3 Sebastian uses his mobile phone to make two calls and send five text messages. He spends 74 pence. Nicholas spends 68 pence on four calls and two text messages. They are both on the same phone tariff.

a Write two equations to represent the given information.

b Using a graphical method, find the cost of a call and of a text message.

c Check your solution using an algebraic method.

4 The graphs in the diagram intersect at the point (3, 5). What are the simultaneous equations to which $x = 3$ and $y = 5$ are the solution?

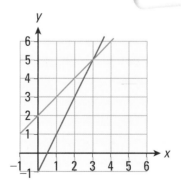

Did you know?

Architects and engineers can use straight lines to create curved surfaces for use in roofs and towers. The Kobe Port Tower uses a doubly ruled surface called a hyperboloid.

challenge

Using a graph to help you, explain why the simultaneous equations $y = 3x + 1$ and $y = 3x + 5$ have no solution. Can you give an example of a pair of simultaneous equations with two solutions? Is it ever be possible to have more than two solutions?

Think of the shapes of graphs.

- Recognise that graphs of the form $y = mx + c$ correspond to straight line graphs and find the equation of various lines
- Find the gradient of a line segment joining two points

Keywords
Gradient $y = mx + c$
Line segment   y-axis
Steepness   intercept

 p. 8

The equation of a straight line takes the form $y = mx + c$ where m represents the **gradient** and c represents the **y-axis intercept**.

- The gradient, m, is a measure of **steepness**.

You find the gradient by forming a fraction

$$m = \frac{\text{amount you go up}}{\text{amount you go across.}}$$

A gradient of $\frac{1}{2}$ represents 1 up and 2 across.

Remember TUBA
Top of the fraction is the amount you go **U**p and **B**ottom of the fraction is the amount you go **A**cross.

---

example

Find the gradient of the line joining the point (1, 3) to the point (4, 5).

Draw a diagram and count squares. The **line segment** travels 3 squares across and 2 up so the gradient is $\frac{2}{3}$.

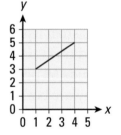

Lines which slope upwards ╱ have a positive gradient.
Lines which slope downwards ╲ have a negative gradient.

- The gradient can be found using a formula.
  For example, (1, 3) to (4, 5)   In general, (x_1, y_1) to (x_2, y_2)

$$m = \frac{5 - 3}{4 - 1} = \frac{2}{3}.$$

$$m = \frac{y_2 - y_1}{x_2 - x_1}.$$

This method is generally quicker than counting squares on a graph.

---

example

Find the equation of the line joining the points (0, 6) to (4, -2).

The gradient, $m = \dfrac{y_2 - y_1}{x_2 - x_1} = \dfrac{(-2) - 6}{4 - 0} = \dfrac{-8}{4} = -2$

The graph intercepts the y-axis at the point (0, 6).

Hence, $y = -2x + 6$ (or $y + 2x = 6$)

Check the sign of the gradient.
Imagining a line sloping from (0, 6) to (4, -2), ╲.
The line slopes downwards so the gradient is negative.

Exercise 8b

1 Match the gradients with the correct line segments.

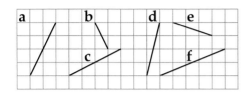

A -2	**B** 4	**C** 2
D $\frac{2}{5}$	**E** $\frac{-1}{3}$	**F** $\frac{1}{2}$

2 Four pupils found the gradient of the line joining (-2, 8) to (10, 2). Only one student did so correctly. Find the correct answer and explain why the others were incorrect.

Anil $m = \dfrac{10 - (-2)}{2 - 8}$ **Beth** $m = \dfrac{2 - 8}{(-2) - 10}$

Cheryl $m = \dfrac{2 - 8}{10 - (-2)}$ **Dev** $m = \dfrac{2 - 8}{10 - 2}$

3 a Find the gradient of the line segment joining each of the following pairs of points.
  i (4, 7) to (5, 13) **ii** (0, 9) to (2, 10) **iii** (-2, 8) to (2, 12)
  iv (-3, 6) to (-6, 9) **v** (-4, -7) to (-1, 10)
 b Put your answers in ascending order of steepness.

4 Write an expression for the gradient of the line joining
 (a, b) to (c, d).

5 Find the equations of the following lines in the form $y = mx + c$.
 a A line with gradient 5 passing through (0, 7).
 b A line with gradient $\frac{-1}{2}$ passing through the origin.
 c A line passing through the points (0, 5) and (2, 9).
 d A line passing through (0, -3) and (1, -4).
 e A line passing through (2, 7) and (3, 10).

6 Find the value of h if the gradient joining the points (h, 4h) to (3h, 30) is 1.

7 A quadrilateral ABCD is formed by joining A (2, 12), B (5, 27), C (3, 28) and D (-1, 8). Find the gradient of each of its edges. What type of quadrilateral is it?

> Draw a sketch of the quadrilateral.

> **Did you know?**
>
>
>
> The gradient of a flight of stairs is given by the rise divided by the tread. Building regulations place limits on their values. By law the gradient of new stairs must be less than 0.9.

task

The graph of x = 3 is a vertical line. Show how you would represent these inequalities on a graph.
  x ≥ 3   x > 3   x + y < 2

- Find the gradient of lines with equations of the form
  $y = mx + c$
- Investigate the gradients of parallel and perpendicular lines

Keywords
Parallel
Perpendicular
Product
Reciprocal

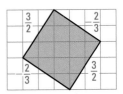

The opposite sides of a square are **parallel**. Their gradients are equal.
The adjacent sides of a square are **perpendicular**. Their gradients are 'flipped' and of opposite signs – one is positive and the other is negative.

Perpendicular lines meet at right angles.

- Parallel lines have the same gradient.

- Perpendicular lines have gradients which are the negative **reciprocal** of one another: their **product** is -1.
  $$\frac{3}{2} \times \left(-\frac{2}{3}\right) = -\frac{6}{6} = -1$$

Think of a reciprocal as "flipping" a fraction. For example, $\frac{1}{2}$ and $\frac{2}{1}(= 2)$ or $\frac{3}{4}$ and $\frac{4}{3}$ are reciprocals.

In general, lines with gradient m and $-\frac{1}{m}$ are perpendicular.

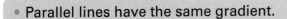

example

The equations of three lines are
$$2y = 8x + 5 \qquad y = 1 - \frac{1}{4}x \qquad x + 4y = 3.$$
Find the two lines that are parallel and the line that is perpendicular to them.

. . . .

Rewrite the equations in the form $y = mx + $ c.

$2y = 8x + 5$	$\Rightarrow y = 4x + 2.5$	This line has gradient 4.
$y = 1 - \frac{1}{4}x$	$\Rightarrow y = -\frac{1}{4}x + 1$	This line has gradient $-\frac{1}{4}$.
$x + 4y = 3$	$\Rightarrow 4y = -x + 3$	
	$\Rightarrow y = -\frac{1}{4}x + \frac{3}{4}$	This line has gradient $-\frac{1}{4}$.

The lines $y = 1 - \frac{1}{4}x$ and $x + 4y = 3$ have the same gradient, $-\frac{1}{4}$, they are parallel.
The line $2y = 8x + 5$ has gradient 4 and $4 \times \frac{-1}{4} = -1$ (4 and $-\frac{1}{4}$ are negative reciprocals of one another), so it is perpendicular to the other two lines.

Exercise 8c

1 Copy and complete this table of gradients.

Gradient of line	Gradient of parallel line	Gradient of perpendicular line
5		
$-\dfrac{1}{3}$		
$\dfrac{3}{4}$		
1.5		
$y = 4x + 3$		
$3y = 8x + 1$		

Equation of line

2 Are these statements true or false?

a The line $y = 5x + 4$ has gradient of 4.

b The lines $y = 5x + 4$ and $2y = 5x + 7$ are parallel.

c The lines $y = \dfrac{1}{4}x$ and $y = 4x$ are perpendicular.

d Lines with gradient 0.125 and $\dfrac{1}{8}$ are parallel.

e Lines with gradient $-1\dfrac{1}{3}$ and $\dfrac{3}{4}$ are perpendicular.

3 Given the equation of one line, find the equation of the other line.

a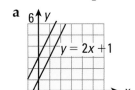

b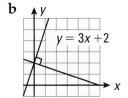

c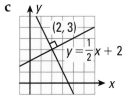

4 A triangle is formed by joining the points A (1, 1), B (3, 11) and C (6, 0). By finding the gradient of each side of the triangle, decide if ABC is a right-angled triangle.

> A diagram is useful in such problems.

5 A rectangle is drawn on coordinate axes. One edge has equation $y = 2x + 4$. Give possible equations for the other three sides.

---

challenge

Explain why perpendicular lines must have gradients that are the negative reciprocals of one another.

First, explain why one gradient must be positive and one must be negative.

Second, explain why the gradients cannot have the same numerical value.

You may find diagrams on squared paper useful to support your explanations.

8d Quadratic graphs

- Know properties of quadratic functions
- Generate points and plot graphs of quadratic functions

Keywords
Maximum   Parabola
Minimum   Quadratic

- A **quadratic** expression contains x^2 as the highest power.
  – Such functions produce **parabola** shaped graphs.

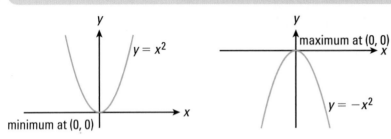

In both graphs the y-axis, $x = 0$, is the line of symmetry.

- If the coefficient of x^2 is positive the parabola has a **minimum** point.

- If the coefficient of x^2 is negative the parabola has a **maximum** point.

All parabolas have a vertical line of symmetry.

The parabola is a common shape in everyday life.

example

A goalkeeper kicks a football from his area. The height of the football at any point is given by the equation

$$y = 6x - x^2$$

where

  y is the height of the ball above the ground (m)
  x is the time from when it was kicked (s).

Plot a graph to show the path of the football and use this to work out the highest point above the ground that the ball reached.

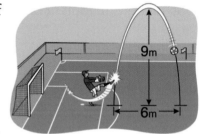

. . . .

x	0	1	2	3	4	5	6
$6x$	0	6	12	18	24	30	36
$-x^2$	0	-1	-4	-9	-16	-25	-36
y	0	5	8	9	8	5	0

y can be found by adding $6x$ and $-x^2$ since $(6x) + (-x^2)$ is the same as $6x - x^2$.

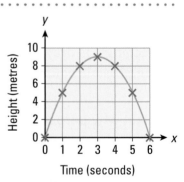

Use about **7 points** when plotting a curve.

Since only positive times are meaningful we only need to consider x values greater than zero.

The symmetry of the graph shows that the football reached a maximum height of 9 m when $x = 3$ m.

Plot the points (0, 0), (1, 5), (2, 8) etc. and join them with a smooth curve.

Exercise 8d

1 For each equation given below

    i use a completed table of values to plot a smooth parabola

    ii decide if your parabola has a maximum or minimum point and give its coordinates

    iii state the equation of the line of symmetry.

a $y = 2x^2 - 8x + 3$

x	-1	0	1	2	3	4	5
$2x^2$					18		
$-8x$					-24		
$+3$	3	3	3	3	3	3	3
y					-3		

b $y = 6x - x^2$

x	-1	0	1	2	3	4	5	6
$6x$								
$-x^2$								
y								

> **Did you know?**
>
>
>
> When a uniform load is hung from the cables of a suspension bridge they take up the shape of a parabola.

2 John throws a ball in the air. Its height, y metres, after x seconds is given by the equation $y = 16x - 4x^2$.

    a Plot a graph to show the path of the ball over 5 seconds.

    b Find the coordinate of the highest point of your graph. What does this mean in real life?

    c When does the ball hit the ground?

    d Find y when $x = 5$. Explain why your result is impossible in real life.

3 A rectangular conservatory is built on a house using 50 metres of framework.

    Let x be the width of the conservatory.

    a In terms of x, write expressions for the conservatory's

        i length   **ii** area, y.

    b Plot a graph of area y against width x.

    c Use your graph to find the largest possible area of this conservatory and explain why, in real life, a homeowner may wish to maximise area.

House

x — *Framework*

challenge

Find out the equations of the parabolas used in one or more suspensions bridges from around the world.

Can you use your findings to form an accurate scale drawing of your bridge?

Can you find out some other real-life uses of quadratic graphs?

- Know simple properties of cubic functions
- Generate points and plot graphs of cubic functions

Keywords
Cubic
S-shaped

- **Cubic** expressions contain x^3 as the highest power. They have a characteristic **S-shape** when plotted.

p. 11 The simplest cubic function is $y = x^3$.

x	-3	-2	-1	0	1	2	3
y	-27	-8	-1	0	1	8	27

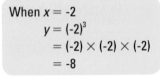

When $x = -2$
$$y = (-2)^3$$
$$= (-2) \times (-2) \times (-2)$$
$$= -8$$

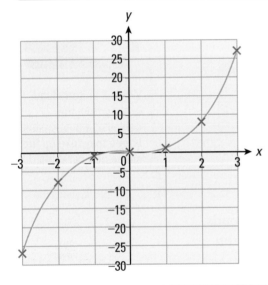

Plot the points (-3, -27), (-2, -8), (-1, -1) etc. and join them with a smooth curve.

example

Plot the graph $y = x^3 - 4x$ for values of x in the range $-3 \leq x \leq 3$.
Use your graph to estimate $2.5^3 - 4 \times 2.5$.

. . . .

Construct a table of values.

x	-3	-2	-1	0	1	2	3
x^3	-27	-8	-1	0	1	8	27
$-4x$	12	8	4	0	-4	-8	-12
y	-15	0	-3	0	-3	0	15

To find $2.5^3 - 4 \times 2.5$ find 2.5 on the x-axis.
Draw a straight line up to the graph and go across to the y-axis. Reading from the graph $y \approx 5.5$.

Exercise 8e

1 Match each equation with its graph.

a $y = x^2 + 1$ **b** $y = 1$ **c** $y = x + 1$

d $y = 1 - x^2$ **e** $y = x^3 + 1$ **f** $x = 1$

A   B   C   D   E   F

2 Copy and complete the table of values for each cubic function and use your values to plot the graph of the function.

> Think carefully about the choice of scale for each graph.

a $y = x^3 + x + 2$

x	-3	-2	-1	0	1	2	3
x^3			-1				
x			-1				
2	2	2	2	2	2	2	2
y				2			

b $y = -x^3$

x	-3	-2	-1	0	1	2	3
y						-8	

> $-x^3$ means first cube the number and then multiply by -1.

c $y = x^3 - 3x^2 + 9$

x	-3	-2	-1	0	1	2	3
x^3						8	
$-3x^2$						-12	
9						9	
y						5	

3 a Plot the graph of $y = x^3 - x + 4$ for $-3 \le x \le 3$.

   b On the same pair of axes, plot the graph of $y = x + 5$.

   c At which points do your graphs intersect?

   d Find the equation of a straight line that intersects the curve $y = x^3 - x + 4$

     i only once   **ii** three times.

Did you know?

Cubic equations are often used by engineers to describe the curves that occur in the design of many objects including roller coasters.

ICT

The graph of $y = x^2$ is a parabola and the graph of $y = x^3$ is an S-shaped curve. Using graphical software or otherwise, investigate the shape of $y = x^4$, $y = x^5$, etc. What do you notice? Can you explain why this happens?

- Plot graphs arising from real-life problems
- Interpret distance-time graphs

Keywords
Accelerate   Speed
Distance   Stationary
Gradient

- **Distance**-time graphs are used to represent journeys.

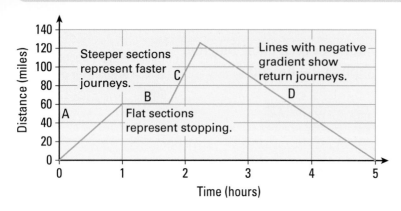

$$\text{Speed} = \frac{\text{Distance covered}}{\text{Time taken}}$$

Travelling 60 miles in one hour gives an average speed of 60 miles per hour.

This distance-time graph represents the journey of a police car.

A The police car left the station and travelled at a **speed** of 60 miles per hour for one hour.   To go to the scene of a crime.

B The car was **stationary** for 45 minutes.   Whilst they observed the suspects.

C The car then travelled 65 miles in half an hour, its speed was 130 miles per hour.   As they chased the suspects.

D The police car then returned to the station.

example

At what speed did the police car return to the police station?

. . . .

The **gradient** of a distance-time graph tells you the speed.

Use the gradient formula on the line joining $(2\frac{1}{4}, 125)$ to $(5, 0)$.

$$\text{Speed} = \frac{y_2 - y_1}{x_2 - x_1} = \frac{0 - 125}{5 - 2\frac{1}{4}} = \frac{-125}{\frac{11}{4}} = -125 \times \frac{4}{11} = -45\frac{5}{11}$$

Take care with time since it is not decimal.
$2\frac{1}{4}$ hours is not the same as 2 hours 25 minutes.

The car returned at $45\frac{5}{11}$ miles per hour.

example

Describe the speed of a car in this distance-time graph.

. . . .

The gradient of the curve gradually gets steeper so the speed is gradually increasing. The graph represents **acceleration**.

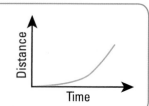

Exercise 8f

1 Match each distance-time graph sketch with a description.

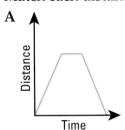
A

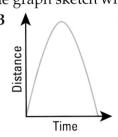
B

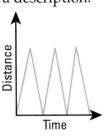
C

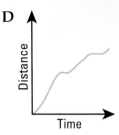
D

a A ball thrown up into the air.

b A man walking to and from the local shop.

c A car stuck in traffic.

d A swimmer doing lengths of a pool.

2 The distance-time graph shows the movements of a rabbit.

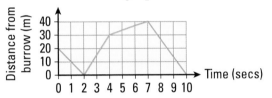

a How do you know that the rabbit did not begin its
journey at its burrow?

b Did the rabbit rest at any point during its journey?

c How often did the rabbit visit its burrow?

d What was the rabbit's speed during
  i the first second?   **ii** the final part of its journey?

e What was the rabbit's average speed during the entire journey?

3 a Make a copy of the graph from question **2**.

   b Add to this graph a second rabbit undertaking the following journey.

> The rabbit leaves the burrow and travels at a speed of 5 m/s for three seconds,
> then rests for one second. After a further two seconds, the rabbit is 40 m from
> the burrow. The rabbit then returns to the burrow at a speed of 17 m/s.

4 Make up your own journey story about an object of your choice
  and show the information on a distance-time graph.

task

For each description given in question **1**, draw
a speed-time graph.

- Sketch and interpret graphs arising from real-life problems

Keywords
Interpret
Plot
Sketch

Many real-life situations can be represented by a graph.

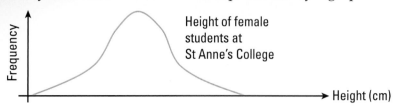

This **sketch** shows that most students' heights fall around the middle value but there are a few very short and a few very tall students.

> A **sketch** graph is not accurate but shows key features clearly.
> A **plot** is an accurate graph.

example

Sketch a graph to show your heart rate before, during and after a session of exercise

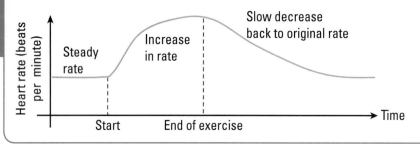

> Label the axes with relevant information.

- Straight-line graphs can be **interpreted** with more detail if you know the equation of the straight line.

example

The graph shows the mobile phone charges used by one company. Explain their charging policy.

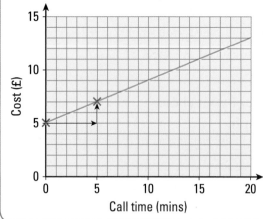

y-axis intercept is 5, gradient is $\frac{7-5}{5-0} = 0.4$

The gradient of the line joining (0, 5) to (5, 7).
Equation is $y = 0.4x + 5$.
Even if you don't make a call ($x = 0$) you are charged £5.   The intercept
This could be line rental.
Every extra minute you spend on the phone increases your bill by £0.4.   The gradient
The company charges 40 pence per minute on calls.

Exercise 8g

1 Sketch a graph to illustrate each of these situations.
In each case use the *x*-axis to represent time
 a The cost of petrol which is rising steadily.
 b The temperature of a cup of tea over half an hour.
 c The weekly amount of pocket money given throughout childhood.
 d The speed of a parachutist as she jumps from a plane.
 e The level of water in a bath as it is filled, used and emptied.

2 Sketch a graph to show the depth of water against time if water is flowing into each container at a constant rate.

a **b**  **c** **d**

3 Explain why the graph of volume against time would be the same for all the containers in question **2** and sketch this graph.

4 Explain what is happening in each of the following sketch graphs.

a 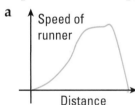 **b**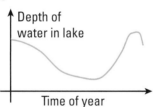

5 Nicholas hires a hall to hold his birthday party. The cost of the hall is found using the formula
$$y = 2x + 50 \qquad x = \text{number of people} \qquad y = \text{cost in pounds.}$$
 a Nicholas invites 50 friends but is not sure if they will all come. Using the formula given, plot a graph of number of people attending the party against the cost of hiring the hall.
 b Use your graph to find the number of people if the cost is £78.
 c Interpret the values of the gradient and the *y*-axis intercept on your graph.

6 The sketch graph shows the height of a baby during the first 12 weeks of its life.
Find the equation of this line graph and interpret its meaning.

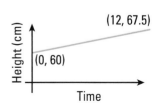

8a

1 The graph shows the lines
$y = 2x + 3$ and $x + 2y = 1$.
Use the graph to solve
$y = 2x + 3$ and $x + 2y = 1$ simultaneously.

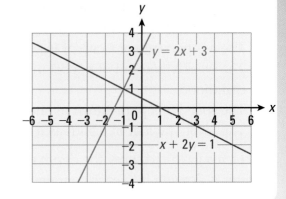

2 Solve graphically the simultaneous
equations $y = 5x - 2$ and $y - 2x = 4$.

8b

3 Find the gradient of the line segment joining the following
pairs of points.
a (2, 6) and (4, 10) **b** (7, 0) and (5, 8)
c (-4, 5) and (-2, -1) **d** (-1, -6) and (0, -5)

4 Find the equation of the line satisfying the following conditions.
a A line with gradient 8 passing through the point (0, 6).
b A line passing through the points (0, 6) and (5, 11).
c A line passing through the points (0, -3) and (-5, -9).

8c

5 Copy and complete the following table of parallel and
perpendicular gradients.

Gradient of line	Gradient of parallel line	Gradient of perpendicular line
4		
$\frac{1}{3}$		
-6		
		0.5

6 Give the equation of a line which is
a parallel to $y = 2x + 5$
b parallel to $3y = x - 1$
c perpendicular to $y = 5 - 4x$
d perpendicular to $2x + 5y = 10$.

7 Copy and complete the table of values and use it to plot the graph of $y = 2x^2 - x + 3$.

x	-4	-3	-2	-1	0	1	2	3	4
$2x^2$								18	
$-x$								-3	
$+3$	3	3	3	3	3	3	3	3	3
y								18	

Use the graph to find
a the coordinates of the maximum or minimum point
b the equation of the line of symmetry.

8 Repeat question 7 for the graph of $y = 10 - x^2$.

9 Make a table of values and use it to plot the graph of $y = x^3 + x$.
Use your graph to estimate the value of y when $x = 2.4$.

10 The graph shows the journey of a cyclist.
a What was the speed of the cyclist in the first part of the journey?
b For how long did the cyclist rest during the whole journey?
c At what speed was the cyclist travelling at after $3\frac{1}{2}$ hours?
d How far did the cyclist travel altogether?
e Ignoring rest periods, what was the average speed of the cyclist for the entire journey?
f True or false: After $1\frac{1}{2}$ hours the cyclist started to repeat part of the journey that he had just covered.

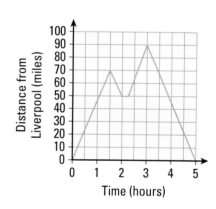

11 Make a sketch graph to show
a the average daily number of calories consumed for the first 25 years of a person's life.
b temperature against time for 24 hours on a spring day in London.
c your own choice.

8 Summary

Assessment criteria
- Use graphical methods to solve simultaneous equations in two variables **Level 7**
- Understand and use measures of speed to solve problems **Level 7**
- Sketch and interpret graphs that model real situations **Level 8**

1 Draw the graphs of $\quad x + y = 8$
$$y = x + 3.$$

Use your graphs to solve the simultaneous equations.

Niall answer ✔

Niall realises both graphs are straight lines.

Niall chooses suitable values of *x*.

He finds the point of intersection of the straight lines.

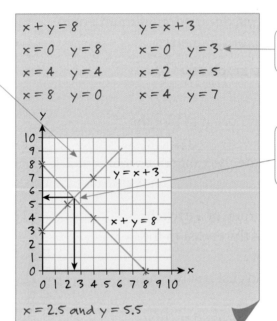

$x + y = 8 \qquad\qquad y = x + 3$

$x = 0$	$y = 8$	$x = 0$	$y = 3$
$x = 4$	$y = 4$	$x = 2$	$y = 5$
$x = 8$	$y = 0$	$x = 4$	$y = 7$

$x = 2.5 \text{ and } y = 5.5$

2 Look at this graph.
  a The gradient of the line through R and Q is 0.5.
  Show how you can work this out from the graph.
  b What is the equation of the straight line through R and Q?
  c Write the equation of a line that is parallel to the straight line through R and Q.

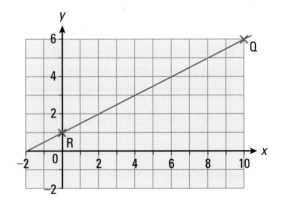

KS3 2003 6–8 Paper 1

9 Statistics

Probability

Traffic engineers use simulations to decide how to design the layout of roads.

For example at a junction, you may not know when cars will arrive or in which direction they will want to go but can assign probabilities to them. This allows possible road layouts to be modelled – a crossroads or roundabout, with or without traffic lights – and the best option chosen.

What's the point? Knowing how to combine simple probabilities allows you to describe and study much more complex situations.

✓ Check in

1 An ordinary die is rolled.
  What is the probability of the score being
  a a square number?
  b not a square number?

2 A traffic warden checks 78 parking meters and finds that the time has expired on 6 of them. Estimate the probability that the next meter he checks will have the time expired on it.

• **Understand that uncertainty is all around us in life**

Keywords
Uncertainty

How we deal with **uncertainty** depends on a combination of how likely something is to happen and the consequences of it happening.

---

example

a For each of the following, describe how big a problem it would be if you were delayed getting there when you planned to.

  i Meeting up with friends.

  ii A job interview.

  iii A flight to Spain for a holiday.

b How much time would you allow for possible delays in these situations.

. . . .

a i Not a big deal.

  ii It is important to be there on time.

  iii Missing a flight is likely to mean missing the whole holiday or paying a lot of money to rebook onto another flight.

b You would want to leave more margin in cases **ii** and **iii** because of the consequences of being late.

---

example

Yulia wants to buy a car. She sees a car she likes in a garage for £3500. She sees the same car in a local newspaper as a private sale for £2950. If she buys privately, a friend recommends getting a vehicle inspection report, costing £135.

Discuss any advantages and disadvantages you can see for buying each car and for the vehicle inspection report.

. . . .

The garage is more expensive but Yulia has some rights if there are problems with the car after she has bought it. Buying a car privately, she has no comeback after she has paid for it, but it is cheaper. The vehicle inspection report would pick up anything reasonably obvious that is wrong mechanically or with the bodywork and so is probably a good thing to get.

Exercise 9a

1 For each of the following, describe how big a problem it would be if you were delayed getting there when you planned to.
   a Getting to school on a normal school day.
   b Getting to school on a day when you have a GCSE.
   c Going to the cinema.

2 You are going out with friends to the park on a reasonably warm day but it looks as though it might rain.
   What are the reasons for and against taking a coat with you?
   Are there any other pieces of information which might make a difference to your decision?

3 You buy a new mobile phone costing £110. The cost of insuring the phone for 12 months is £34.99.
   a What are the advantages and disadvantages of taking the insurance?
   b If a group of 10 friends each took the insurance, how many would have to claim for a replacement phone for the group to save money overall. How likely do you think that is to happen?

Did you know?

Insurance is a way of paying someone else to accept a risk that you can not afford to take. Could you pay for medical treatment when abroad on holidays?

discussion

Two friends have each been offered the chance to invest £100 000 in an oil field. A survey estimates a 75% chance that there is a substantial oil deposit, in which case they would get back double their money in a year's time. However, if there is no oil then they will lose their money.
Mr Goldfinger is a millionaire businessman with enough ready cash to make the investment.
Mr Median has worked hard all his life in an office and has built up savings of £50 000 and owns his own home. He could take out a mortgage against his house to raise the other £50 000.

Discuss what difference their financial position might make to whether or not they decide to invest and what you would advise each of them to do.

9b Independent events

- Be able to identify independent outcomes and calculate probabilities

- If the outcome of one event does not affect what happens in another then the events are **independent**.

State, with reasons, whether these pairs of events are independent or not.

a Toss two coins and obtain
   i heads on the first coin
   ii tails on the second coin.
b Roll a die and obtain
   i a prime number
   ii an even number.
c At a rugby game
   i it rains
   ii the home side wins.
d You interview a final year student at university
   i they live at home
   ii they have health problems.

- -

a Yes.   What happens on one toss does not affect on the second.
b No.   The primes are 2, 3 and 5. If you know there is a prime then only one out of three is even; without this information the chance is three out of six.

> $P(\text{even given a prime}) = \frac{1}{3}$
> whilst $P(\text{even}) = \frac{1}{2}$

c Difficult to say.   The weather may change the likelihoods of the possible results but you would need to know more about the two teams to know how.
d Unlikely to be independent.   Students living at home are more likely to have a regular routine and be less likely to have health problems.

- If A and B are independent events then
   P(A and B both happen) = P(A) × P(B).

A road safety officer estimates that $\frac{1}{4}$ of bicycles used by teenagers do not have properly inflated tyres and $\frac{1}{6}$ of them don't have adequate lights.

a If these are independent, what is the probability that a bicycle belonging to a teenager, chosen at random, has both faults?
b Do you think independence is reasonable?

- -

a P(both faults) $= \frac{1}{4} \times \frac{1}{6} = \frac{1}{24}$.
b While the tyres and lights are not directly connected, they may both be dependent on how careful the owner is, so independence is not likely to be completely correct.

> Independence may be assumed, even when not strictly true, to allow you to calculate an approximate answer.

Exercise 9b

1 State, with reasons, whether these pairs of events are independent or not.

    a A person visiting their doctor
       i suffers from breathlessness
       ii is a smoker.

    b Roll a die and obtain
       i a square number
      ii an even number.

2 For the second example opposite, what is the probability that that a bicycle belonging to a teenager, chosen at random, has neither fault?

3 The probability of throwing more than a 4 on a fair dice is $\frac{1}{3}$.

    What is the probability you will get over 4 both times if you throw it twice?

4 The probability that a person chosen at random in a company is married is 0.6. One third of the company employees are female.

    a Assuming that these are independent, what is the probability that a person chosen at random in a company is a married female?

    b Give reasons why the proportions of women and men in the company who are married might be different.

Did you know?

In an airplane, the designers try to have systems work independently of one another. So, for example, if a problem affects one engine, it can continue to fly on the other engines.

---

discussion

Discuss whether you think these pairs of events are independent or not.

a Roll a die and obtain
    i an odd number
    ii an even number.

b Roll a red and a blue die and obtain
    i an even number on the red die
    ii an even number for the sum.

c You toss a coin four times and obtain
    i a head on the first toss
    ii you get the first tail on the third toss.

> These are all cases you could test experimentally. Does the proportion of times you see both events roughly equal the proportions of times you see each one multiplied together?

- Draw a tree diagram to show the possible outcomes for combined events

Keywords
Tree diagram

- A **tree diagram** is used to show the possible outcomes for combined events.
  – They are particularly useful when outcomes are not equally likely.

example

A road safety officer offered free checks on tyres and headlights for bicycles brought into school. Draw a tree diagram to show what faults a bicycle might have.

Label each tier of branches.

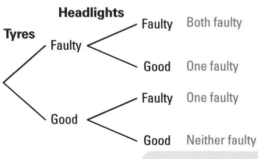

Write the outcomes at the end of the branches.

There is no limit, in theory, to the number of possible outcomes at each stage, or how many stages there are in a tree diagram. In practice, you will rarely deal with more than three of either.

example

Employees in a company are classified as manual, administrative or managerial staff and can be full-time or part-time.
Draw a tree diagram to show how employees can be classified.

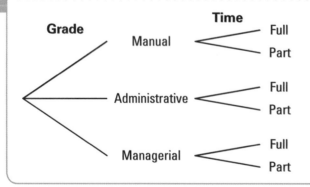

Here the two sets of branches could equally well have been drawn in the opposite order. Sometimes the situation suggests a natural order.

Exercise 9c

1 A firm wants to classify their employees by whether they are
   married or not and as male/female. Show a tree diagram they
   could use for this.

2 When James leaves the house in the morning he has a choice
   or taking an umbrella with him or not. When he comes home
   it may or may not rain. Show a tree diagram to represent this
   information.
   Which paths would result in James getting wet on his
   way home?

3 On a stretch of road, a car may or may not be breaking the
   speed limit and there may or may not be a police mobile speed
   camera.
   a Show a tree diagram to represent this information.
   b Which paths would result in the car being given a ticket for
      breaking the speed limit?
   c The police mobile camera is present one quarter of the time and
      8% of motorists break the speed limit. If 200 cars have travelled
      along this stretch of road, show how many cars are on each path
      in your diagram.
   d Using the number of cars on your diagram calculate the
      probability that on this stretch of road
      i a speeding motorist is caught on camera
      ii a speeding motorist is not caught on camera.

4 A team scores 3 points for a win, 1 for a draw and 0 for losing
   a league match. Show a possibility tree for the first two matches
   of the league.
   On which paths do the team score more than 2 points altogether
   in the two matches?

discussion

In which of the above cases do you think there is a natural
order to the stages in the tree diagrams you drew, and in
which do you think it could have been reversed without causing
a problem?

- Draw tree diagrams to represent independent events
- Use tree diagrams to calculate the probability of combined events

Keywords
Independent
Mutually exclusive
Tree diagram

- **Tree diagrams** can be used to organise the calculation of probabilities for combinations of events.

example

For the first example in spread **9c**, $\frac{1}{4}$ of bicycles used by teenagers do not have properly inflated tyres and $\frac{1}{6}$ of them don't have adequate lights. Show the probabilities for the various possibilities on a tree diagram.

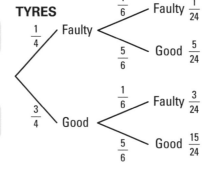

Write the probabilities on each branch.

P(good tyres) = 1 − P(bad tyres)

Assuming the two events are **independent** the individual probabilities are multiplied.

A particular bicycle must end up at one of the four endpoints.

- Two events are **mutually exclusive** if they cannot happen at the same time.
- If A and B are mutually exclusive events, then
   P(A or B) = P(A) + P(B).

Since in a tree diagram the pathways are distinct they are mutually exclusive. Therefore, for example, the probability that a bicycle fails only one of the tests is

$$\text{P(fail one test)} = \frac{5}{24} + \frac{3}{24} = \frac{8}{24} = \frac{1}{3}$$

Exercise 9d

1 Anne-Marie supports her local rugby team and goes to watch them every week. The probability that they win a match is 0.5, that they draw is 0.2 and the probability that it rains during the match is 0.2.

Assuming the team's performance is independent of whether it rains or not, what is the probability that Anne-Marie watches her team lose in the rain?

2 Colour blindness affects 8% of males. 11% of both males and females are left-handed and this is independent of colour-blindness. Copy and complete the tree diagram below and calculate the probability that a male chosen at random is left-handed and not colour-blind.

Handedness

Colour-blindness

```
         0.08        0.11    Left
              Yes  <
         <
```

3 Eve commutes to work first taking a bus to the station and then a train. The probability of getting a seat on the bus is $\frac{2}{3}$ and of getting a seat on the train $\frac{3}{5}$.

a Draw a tree diagram to represent these probabilities.

b Calculate the probability that Eve has to stand on one leg of her journey.

4 For question **4** of exercise **9c**, if the probability of a win is 0.5, and the probability of a draw is 0.3, find the probability of the team scoring more than two points from the first two matches.

PREMIERSHIP RESULTS

14th **March 2008**

Home		Away
Arsenal	4 – 0	Blackburn
Bolton	1 – 3	Fulham
Everton	3 – 1	Stoke City
Hull City	1 – 1	Newcastle Utd
Manchester Utd	1 – 4	Liverpool
Middlesbrough	1 – 1	Portsmouth
Sunderland	1 – 2	Wigan Athletic

Investigation

In question **2**, you were told that the performance of the team that Anne-Marie supports is independent of whether it rains.

Do you think it will normally be the case that the outcomes of sporting events are independent of the weather during the match?

Can you find data to help you decide?

You might take the Football league results for some Saturdays when the weather was reasonable and some where the weather was bad and compare the total number of goals for example.

- Estimate and use probabilities based on an experiment or on observations

Keywords
Experimental probability

The print out shows Sean's reaction times (in seconds) for a series of tests.

0.21	0.19	0.22	0.23	0.24	0.21
0.22	0.19	0.18	0.20	0.22	0.24
0.23	0.22	0.20	0.23	0.27	0.24
0.23	0.19	0.24	0.21	0.23	0.18
0.22	0.25	0.23	0.21	0.22	0.23
0.20	0.24	0.19	0.22	0.23	0.20
0.23	0.22	0.23	0.19	0.20	0.24
0.26	0.22	0.20	0.23	0.19	0.21
0.23	0.24	0.26	0.21	0.22	0.23
0.19	0.24	0.21	0.22	0.20	0.25

a Estimate the probability that on a randomly chosen test Sean's reaction time is less than 0.20 s.

b A prize is awarded if you can react in under 0.20 s in a maximum of two attempts. Estimate the probability Sean would win a prize.

a The **experimental probability** is estimated using

$$P(t < 0.20\,\text{s}) = \frac{\text{number of successes}}{\text{number of trials}} = \frac{9}{60} = 0.15$$

b A tree diagram shows the possibilities

First attempt **Second attempt**

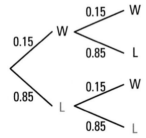

Sean will win a prize if he does not lose twice.

$$P(\text{lose twice}) = 0.85 \times 0.85$$
$$= 0.7225$$
$$P(\text{win at least once}) = 1 - 0.7225$$
$$= 0.2775$$

A road safety officer is investigating whether a busy road junction needs a cycle lane. He counted the number of cyclists arriving at the junction in each minute between 8 am and 9 am.

Estimate the probabilities for the numbers of cyclists that might arrive in a randomly chosen minute.

3, 0, 2, 2, 1, 0, 4,
2, 2, 2, 1, 3 2, 1,
0, 1, 2, 1, 4, 0, 3,
5, 2, 3, 4, 2, 1, 0,
5, 3, 2, 4, 5, 2, 4,
3, 2, 4, 5, 3, 2, 1,
0, 4, 2, 1, 3, 0, 1,
2, 4, 2, 0, 1, 3, 0,
1, 3, 4, 2

Number of cyclists	0	1	2	3	4	5
Frequency	9	11	17	10	9	4
Estimated probability	$\frac{9}{60} = \frac{3}{20}$	$\frac{11}{60}$	$\frac{17}{60}$	$\frac{10}{60} = \frac{1}{6}$	$\frac{9}{60} = \frac{3}{20}$	$\frac{4}{60} = \frac{1}{15}$

Exercise 9e

1 Shamsa repeatedly tosses a fair coin until it shows heads, each time counting how many tosses it takes. The table shows her results after 40 goes.

  a What is the relative frequency of 1s in her experiment?

  b What is probability that she will get a head on the first toss of a sequence?

  c If Shamsa was to toss the coin again, which of the answers to parts **a** and **b** would you use for the likelihood of her seeing a head on the first toss?

1	1	2	2	3
1	5	2	2	2
1	1	1	1	6
1	1	2	3	1
3	3	1	2	1
3	1	6	1	1
2	1	3	1	5
2	2	2	1	2

2 The supervisor in a factory tests samples of 25 components and records the number of faulty components in each of 30 samples. The table shows her results.

  a Find the total number of faulty components in the 750 components in these samples.

  b Estimate the probability that a component chosen at random is faulty.

0	2	1	1	0	0
2	1	2	3	1	2
1	0	1	2	0	0
3	0	0	0	1	2
1	1	0	0	0	1

3 The number of customers arriving at the checkout in a store per minute is recorded over a period of twenty minutes. The table shows the results listed in order.

2	1	0	3	5	4	2	3	4	2
0	3	1	2	2	0	2	1	2	1

  a Estimate the probability that three customers arrive in period of a minute.

  b Show that the mean number of customers arriving per minute is 2.

  c If the checkout can serve two customers per minute, make a table showing the length of the queue of customers waiting at the start of each minute.

> In the first minute the two customers who arrived can be served. In the fourth minute three customers arrive so there will be one left in the queue at the start of the fifth minute.

discussion

In question **3**, you investigated the behaviour of the queue on the basis that two customers would be served if there were two in the queue. What other information would let you give a better description of the behaviour of a queue?

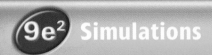
- Explore the use of random numbers to simulate a simple situation

Keywords
Simulation
Random number

How a queue behaves in the long run depends on the rate of arrival at the queue and the rate of departures.

You can model the length of a queue using a **simulation**.

new length = old length + arrivals − departures

with the condition that the length can never be negative.

Consider a simple model, where the number of arrivals and departures behave according to these probability distributions.

> If the queue starts with 1 person in it and in the next time interval 2 arrive and 4 leave then there are 0 people in the queue at the start of the next time interval not -1.

	0	1	2	3	4
Arrivals	0.2	0.25	0.3	0.15	0.1
Departures	0.05	0.4	0.25	0.2	0.1

> There is a probability of 0.2 that three people could be served (provided there are three people in the queue).

To simulate 20 time periods for the queue, generate two lists of 20 **random numbers** for the arrivals and departures. Use these pairs of random numbers, $R_\#$ and $R'_\#$, with the rules given below (which uses cumulative probabilities from the table above).

> If $R_\# = 0.783$ and $R'_\# = 0.065$ there would be 3 arrivals and 1 departure in the time period.

	0	1	2	3	4
Arrivals	$0 \leqslant R_\# < 0.20$	$0.20 \leqslant R_\# < 0.45$	$0.45 \leqslant R_\# < 0.75$	$0.75 \leqslant R_\# < 0.9$	$0.9 \leqslant R_\# < 1$
Departures	$0 \leqslant R'_\# < 0.05$	$0.05 \leqslant R'_\# < 0.45$	$0.45 \leqslant R'_\# < 0.70$	$0.70 \leqslant R'_\# < 0.9$	$0.9 \leqslant R'_\# < 1$

Running the simulation three times gave the queue histories below. You can see how very different they look even though they are all based on the same quite simple set of rules for a very simple situation.

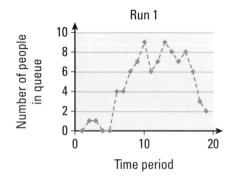

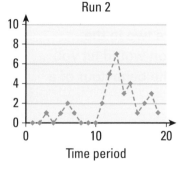

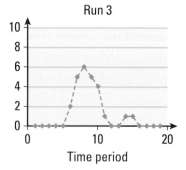

Exercise 9e^{2}

1 a Use the random number generator on your calculator 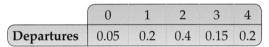,
or on a spreadsheet, to simulate the arrivals and departures
for 10 time periods, using the probabilities opposite.

b Calculate the number of people in the queue for your results
for the 10 time periods.

c Draw a graph to show your queue history.

2 Repeat the simulation in question **1** and compare the queue
histories; how similar are they?

3 The store owner feels it is important that the queues do not grow
to over five or customers will be put off using the store. A new
type of till is available for which the probabilities for departures
would be

	0	1	2	3	4
Departures	0.05	0.2	0.4	0.15	0.2

a Assuming the arrivals continue with the same probabilities
as before, use these probabilities for departures in another
simulation of 10 periods.

b Would you advise the owner to get the new type of till?

investigation

a Collect your own data in a local shop to estimate
probability distributions for customer arrivals and
departures at the checkout and then run your own
simulation.

b Use an electronic simulation to explore the behaviour
of queues for a variety of probability distributions for
arrivals and departures.

9a

1 You leave a computer memory stick on a train. In the two scenarios described below
  i how serious a problem is this?
  ii does it make a difference if the data is encrypted?
    a You work for a premier league football club and the stick contains records of the club's attendances over the past 5 years.
    b You work for the Inland Revenue and the stick contains the tax returns of 5837 individuals.

9b

2 State, with reasons, whether these pairs of events are independent or not.
  a i A person gets a grade C or higher in GCSE maths.
    ii The person becomes a doctor.
  b Roll a die and obtain
    i a factor of 6   **ii** an even number.

3 The probability that a car passing a checkpoint on a motorway is a sports car is 0.2. One quarter of the cars on the road are black.
  a Assuming that these are independent, what is the probability that a car chosen at random passing the checkpoint is a black sports car?
  b Can you think of any reasons why the proportions of sports cars which are black might be different to the proportion of family cars which are black?

9c

4 In tennis, a player can win or lose each set.
  a Draw a probability tree for the outcomes of the first two sets of a match.
  b On which paths are the two players level after two sets?

9d

5 The probability of Andy winning each set in a tennis match is 0.6. The match is 'best of three sets' so if a player wins the first two sets, the match is over.
  a Add probabilities to your diagram from question **4**.
  b Calculate the probability that Andy wins the match in two sets.
  c Calculate the probability that the match goes into a third set.

6 Arinda throws 25 darts at a dartboard, trying to score a 20. She succeeds on 10 of the throws.

  a Estimate the probability of Arinda scoring a 20.

  b Arinda throws two darts, trying to score a 20 each time, draw a tree diagram to represent this.

  c What is the probability that Arinda scores at least one 20.

7 Use the probabilities below in a queuing simulation, using the random number generator on your calculator, or in a spreadsheet.

	0	1	2	3	4
Arrivals	0.2	0.2	0.4	0.15	0.05
Departures	0.1	0.1	0.5	0.2	0.1

  a Calculate the number of people in the queue for your results for the 10 time periods.

  b Draw a graph to show your queue history.

  c What was the longest queue you had over the 10 time periods?

9 Summary

Assessment criteria

- Understand relative frequency as an estimate of probability and use this to compare outcomes of an experiment **Level 7**
- Know when to add or multiply two probabilities **Level 8**

Level 7

1 Jodi wants to find out if a dice is biased in favour of even numbers.

She decides to throw the dice 500 times, in 5 sets of 100.

Here are her results.

Number of throws out of 100 that showed an even number				
63	51	59	55	62

Jodi decides a dice is biased if the probability of throwing an even number is greater then 60%.

Is the dice biased?

Sami's answer ✔

63 + 51 + 59 + 55 + 62 = 290

There are 290 even throws out of 500 throws.

Relative frequency = $\frac{290}{500}$

$= 0.58$

$= 58\%$

The dice is not biased as the relative frequency is not greater than 60%.

> Sami finds the total of throws that showed an even number.

> Sami remembers to answer the question.

Level 8

2 I have three fair dice, each numbered 1 to 6.

I am going to throw all three dice.

What is the probability that all three dice will show the same number?

KS3 2006 6–8 Paper 2

10 Geometry

Transformations and scale

You can generate shapes with very strange mathematical properties by repeatedly applying a simple rule over and over again. This process is called *recursion*. Often this recursion results in the same structures appearing on smaller and smaller scales. A self-similar shape like this is called a fractal.

What's the point? Fractals have been found throughout nature, for example, in ice crystals, blood vessels and plants like romanesco broccoli. They are also used to generate scenery in computer games.

 Check in

Level 5

1 a Copy the diagram on square grid paper and draw the flag after a reflection in the mirror line.
  b Translate this image 3 units to the right and 1 unit up. Draw this new image on your diagram.

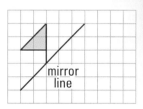

Level 6

2 A scale drawing of a door has a scale of 1 cm to represent 50 cm. The door measures 3.9 cm by 1.6 cm on the scale drawing.
Calculate the actual height and width of the door.

Scale 1 cm represents 50 cm

Level 7

3 Copy the diagram on square grid paper and draw the enlargement of the isosceles trapezium with a scale factor of $2\frac{1}{2}$.

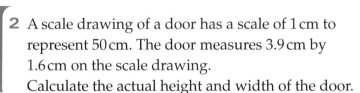

4 Use Pythagoras' theorem to calculate the length of AB.

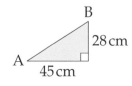

- Reflect, rotate and translate 2-D shapes
- Transform 2-D shapes using combinations of transformations

Keywords
Congruent   Reflection
Image   Rotation
Map   Transformation
Object   Translation

You can transform 2-D shapes using a

reflection (flip)	**rotation** (turn)	**translation** (slide).

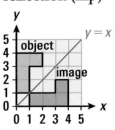

A reflection in the line $y = x$

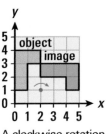

A clockwise rotation of 90° about (2, 1)

A translation of $\binom{2}{-1}$

$\binom{2}{-1}$ means 2 to the right and 1 down.

The **transformation maps** the **object** to the **image**.
The object and the image are **congruent** in reflections, rotations and translations.

Congruent figures are the same shape and the same size.

You can transform 2-D shapes using a combination of transformations.

A and B are two transformations
  A is a reflection in the line $y = x$
  B is a rotation of 180° about (0, 0).
One of the transformations is applied to the pink triangle and then the other transformation is applied to its image.
Does the order in which these transformations are applied matter?

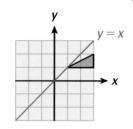

A then B

Pink $\xrightarrow{\text{Reflection}}$ Blue $\xrightarrow{\text{Rotation}}$ Green

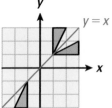

B then A

Pink $\xrightarrow{\text{Rotation}}$ Blue $\xrightarrow{\text{Reflection}}$ Green

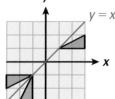

If the order in which two transformations are applied does not alter the final image, they are said to be commutative.

In this example, the order of the transformations does not matter.

Exercise 10a

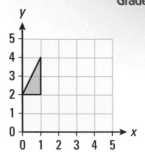

1 a Copy the diagram on square grid paper.
Reflect the green triangle in the line $x = 2$ to give
the image I_1.

b State the coordinates of the vertices of triangle I_1.

c Reflect triangle I_1 in the line $y = 2$ to give the image I_2.

d State the coordinates of the vertices of triangle I_2.

e Describe fully the single transformation that maps the
green triangle to triangle I_2.

2 A and B are two transformations.

A is a translation of $\begin{pmatrix} -1 \\ 3 \end{pmatrix}$.   B is a translation of $\begin{pmatrix} 3 \\ -2 \end{pmatrix}$.

$\begin{pmatrix} -1 \\ 3 \end{pmatrix}$ means 1 to the left and 3 up.

Find the single transformation that is equivalent to
translation A followed by translation B.

3 A and B are two transformations.

A is a reflection in the x-axis.
B is an anticlockwise rotation of $90°$ about $(0, 0)$.

The pink triangle has coordinates $(1, 1)$, $(3, 1)$ and $(3, 2)$.

a On two separate diagrams draw the following two
sequences of transformations labelling the images
I_1, I_2 and I_3, I_4.

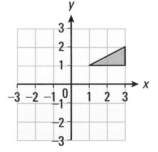

$$\text{Pink} \xrightarrow{\ A\ } I_1 \xrightarrow{\ B\ } I_2 \qquad \text{Pink} \xrightarrow{\ B\ } I_3 \xrightarrow{\ A\ } I_4$$

b Give the coordinates of the images I_1, I_2, I_3 and I_4.

c Does the order in which these transformations are
applied matter?

challenge

What single transformation is equivalent to the following
pairs of transformations?

Look at the effect of the
transformations on a 'flag'
shape.

a Reflection in $x = 2$ followed by reflection in $x = 4$.

b Reflection in $y = 1$ followed by reflection in $y = -1$.

c Reflection in $x = 1$ followed by reflection in $y = x$.

d Reflection in $y = 2$ followed by rotation through $180°$ about $(0, 2)$.

- Enlarge a 2-D shape using a centre of enlargement and a positive fractional scale factor

Keywords
Centre of enlargement
Enlargement
Image
Object
Scale factor
Similar

p. 34

- An **enlargement** is a transformation that alters the size of the shape.
  The angles of the shape do not change.

You enlarge a shape by multiplying the lengths of the shape by the **scale factor**.

The **object** and the **image** are **similar**, as they are the same shape, but different sizes.

The position of the image is fixed if you use a **centre of enlargement**.

If the scale factor > 1, the image is larger than the object.
If the scale factor < 1, the image is smaller than the object.

Always measure from the centre of enlargement.

distance to image vertex
= scale factor × distance to object vertex.

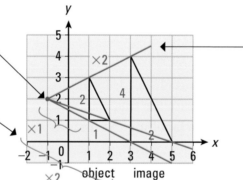

Draw lines from the centre of enlargement through the vertices of the object.

Measure the ratio of image and object sides to check the scale factor, for example,
$4 \div 2 = 2$, $2 \div 1 = 2$.

The enlargement is scale factor 2, using
$(-1, 2)$ as the centre of enlargement.

example

a Using the given centre, enlarge the pink rectangle by scale factor $\frac{1}{3}$.

b Calculate the perimeter and area of the pink rectangle and the enlargement.

Centre of enlargement

. . . .

a

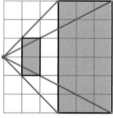

b Perimeter of the pink rectangle = 18 units
   Perimeter of the enlargement   = 6 units
   Area of the pink rectangle   = 18 square units
   Area of the enlargement   = 2 square units

All the lengths have been multiplied by $\frac{1}{3}$.

Ratio of the perimeters = 3 : 1
Ratio of the areas   = 9 : 1

Exercise 10b

1 a Calculate the perimeters and areas of the twelve pentominoes.

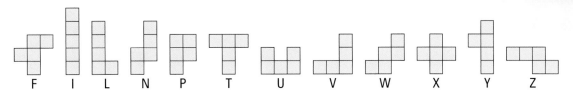

F I L N P T U V W X Y Z

Each pentomino is enlarged by scale factor 2.

b Calculate the perimeter and area of each enlarged shape.

2 In each diagram, the pink shape is an enlargement of the green shape.
Copy each of these shapes on to coordinate axes to calculate the scale
factor and to find the coordinates of the centre of enlargement.

a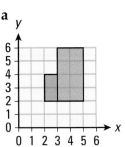

b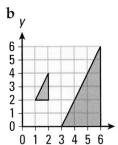

c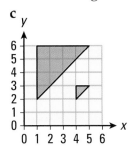

Did you know?

Look carefully at the
nurse's tray. The box
shows a fractional
enlargement of the
main image. Nesting
the same image like
this is called the
Droste effect.

3 Draw the enlargement of each shape using the dot as
the centre of enlargement and the given scale factor.

a

Scale factor 3

b

Scale factor $\frac{1}{3}$

c

Scale factor $\frac{1}{2}$

4 This triangle is enlarged by scale factor p.
The image is then enlarged by scale factor q.
What is the scale factor of the single enlargement that is
equivalent to these successive transformations?

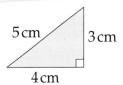

5 cm   3 cm

4 cm

activity

Fold a sheet of A4 paper in half. The size of the paper is now A5.
Folding a sheet of A5 paper gives A6 size and so on.
A sheet of A4 paper measures 297 mm by 210 mm.
The different sizes of paper can be arranged with opposite
corners along a diagonal, so that A4 is an enlargement of A5 *etc.*
Find the scale factor of the enlargement.

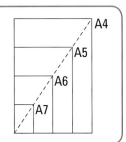

• Enlarge a 2-D shape using a centre of enlargement
  and a negative scale factor

Keywords
Centre of enlargement
Negative
Scale factor
Similar

You can enlarge a shape with a **negative scale factor**.

• If the scale factor is negative, the image and the object
  are on opposite sides of the **centre of enlargement**.

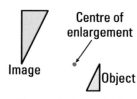

The scale factor is -2.

The object and the image are **similar**
  – the lengths increase in proportion
  – the angles stay the same.

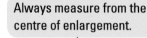

Always measure from the
centre of enlargement.

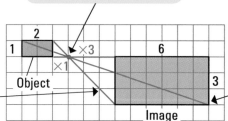

Draw lines from the centre
of enlargement through the
vertices of the object.

The enlargement is scale factor -3,
The lengths have been multiplied by 3.

distance to image vertex
= scale factor
× distance to object vertex.

Measure the ratio of image
and object sides to check
the scale factor, for example,
6 ÷ 2 = 3, 3 ÷ 1 = 4.

<blockquote>
example

The green triangle is an enlargement
of the orange triangle.
Find
a the centre of enlargement
b the scale factor.

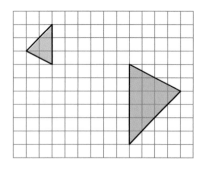

a Join the corresponding vertices to find the
centre of enlargement.
b Compare corresponding lengths of the
triangles to find the scale factor and insert
the negative sign.

Scale factor = $\frac{-6}{3}$ = -2

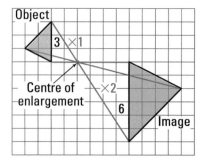
</blockquote>

Exercise 10c

1 Each pink shape is an enlargement of the blue shape.
Copy these shapes on to coordinate axes to calculate the scale
factors and find the coordinates of the centres of enlargement.

a 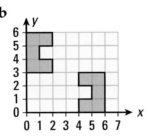   **b**   **c**

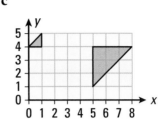

2 Draw the enlargement of each shape using the dot as
the centre of enlargement and the given scale factor.

a 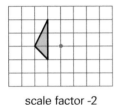   **b**    **c**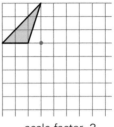

scale factor -1

scale factor -2

scale factor -3

3 Draw triangle ABC on a coordinate grid.

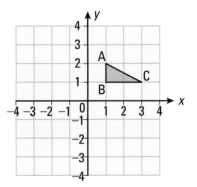

  a Write down the coordinates of the points
    A, B and C.
  b Enlarge the triangle by scale factor -2 using (0, 0) as the
    centre of enlargement.
    Label the image A′, B′ and C′.
  c Write down the coordinates of the points A′, B′ and C′.
  d What do you notice about the coordinates of the
    vertices of the object and the image?

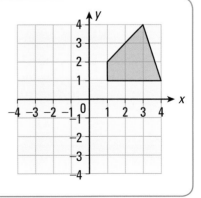

a Enlarge the green quadrilateral by scale factor
   -1 using (0, 0) as the centre of enlargement.
b Describe a single different transformation that is
   equivalent to this enlargement.
c Are this enlargement and your transformation still
   equivalent if the object is in a different quadrant
   of the coordinate grid?

investigation

- Use and interpret maps and scale drawings

Keywords
Map   Scale
Ratio   Scale drawing

You use **maps** and **scale drawings** to represent real-life distances.

- Real-life distances are reduced in proportion using a **scale**.
- All the angles remain the same.
- The scale enables you to interpret the map or scale drawing.

30 metres

The length of the blue whale is 30 metres.

- A scale can be written as a **ratio**.

In a map or scale drawing, corresponding lengths are in the same ratio.

The real-life lengths are an enlargement, scale factor 500, of the scale drawing.

The lengths in the scale drawing are 500 times smaller than in real life.

$30\,m \div 500 = 3000\,cm \div 500 = 6\,cm$

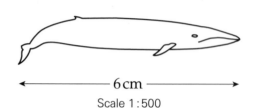

6 cm

Scale 1 : 500

---

example

The distance from Leeds to York is 40 km.
The distance from Leeds and York on the map is 2.5 cm.
Express the scale of the map as
a 1 cm represents _____
b as a ratio in the form 1 : n.

York

2.5 cm

Leeds

. . . .

a 2.5 cm represents 40 km
    1 cm represents 40 ÷ 2.5 km
    1 cm represents 16 km
b Scale is 2.5 cm : 40 km
        2.5 cm : 40 000 m
        2.5 cm : 4 000 000 cm
           1 : 1 600 000

> You need to change 40 km to cm so that the units are the same in the ratio.

The real-life distances are 1 600 000 times longer.

Exercise 10d

1 A London Routemaster bus has these dimensions
  length 9.14 m   height 4.37 m   width 2.44 m.
  A scale model is made using a scale of 1:50.
  Calculate the length, height and width of the model in
  centimetres, giving each answer to the nearest millimetre.

2 A map has a scale of 1:25 000.
  Calculate the real-life distance in kilometres that these
  lengths represent
  a 4 cm **b** 0.5 cm **c** 8.5 cm **d** 25 cm **e** 35 cm.
  Calculate the distance in centimetres on the map for a
  real-life distance of
  f 5 km **g** 7.5 km **h** 4.4 km **i** 10.5 km **j** 0.5 km.

3 Write each of these scales in the form 1:n.
  a 1 cm represents 1 m   **b** 1 cm represents 5 m
  c 1 cm represents 0.25 m   **d** 4 cm represents 1 km
  e 10 cm represents 5 km   **f** 1 cm represents 0.25 km

4 The centre of the dartboard must be 1.73 m from the floor.
  A darts player must stand behind the oche, which
  is 2.37 m from the wall.
  Use this information to
  a draw a scale drawing using a scale of 1:25
  b measure and calculate the distance
    from the oche to the centre of the dartboard
  c calculate the distance from the oche to the centre
    of the dartboard using Pythagoras' theorem.

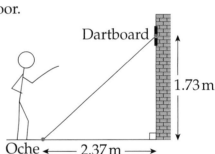

The Highway Code gives the distances in
metres a driver needs to stop a vehicle at
various speeds.
Each stopping distance is calculated by adding
the thinking distance and the braking distance.
a Draw a poster to illustrate the thinking
  distance, the braking distance and the
  stopping distance for each speed.
  Use a scale of 1:500 for the distances.
  A car's length can be 5 metres.
b Superimpose cars on the distances on your scale drawing.

Speed (mph)	Thinking distance (metres)	Breaking distance (metres)
20	6	6
30	9	14
40	12	24
50	15	38
60	18	55
70	21	75

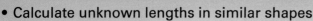
- Calculate unknown lengths in similar shapes
- Find points that divide a line in a given ratio

Keywords
Enlargement Scale factor
Ratio   Similar

p. 34

- In an **enlargement**, the object and the image are **similar**.
  - The lengths increase in proportion.
  - The angles stay the same.

You use corresponding lengths to find the **scale factor** of the enlargement.

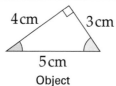

Object

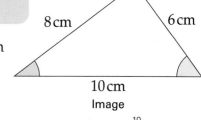

Image

- Scale factor = $\dfrac{\text{length on the image}}{\text{corresponding length on the object}}$

scale factor $= \dfrac{10}{5} = 2$

scale factor $= \dfrac{6}{3} = 2$

scale factor $= \dfrac{8}{4} = 2$

example

Calculate the length a in these similar triangles.

Scale factor $= \dfrac{35}{10} = 3.5$

$a = 7 \times 3.5 = 24.5\,\text{cm}$

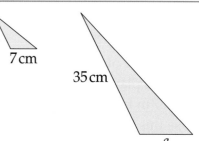

You can use similar triangles to divide a line in a given **ratio**.

example

A and B have coordinates (5, 10) and (25, 20) respectively.
Find the coordinates of the point P that divides the line
AB in the ratio 2:3.

Extract two similar triangles from the grid.

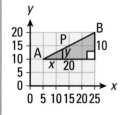

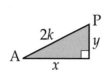

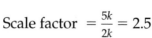

Scale factor $= \dfrac{5k}{2k} = 2.5$

$x = 20 \div 2.5 = 8$ $y = 10 \div 2.5 = 4$

The coordinates of P are (5 + 8, 10 + 4) or (13, 14).

$AP = \dfrac{2}{5} \times AB$

Exercise 10e

1 Each rectangle is an enlargement of the blue rectangle.
Calculate the scale factor of each enlargement.

a
15 cm
24 cm

b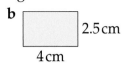
2.5 cm
4 cm

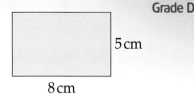
5 cm
8 cm

c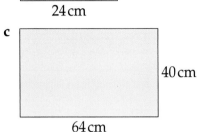
40 cm
64 cm

d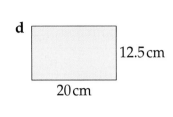
12.5 cm
20 cm

2 Calculate the scale factor and the missing length in each pair of
similar triangles.

a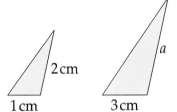
2 cm
a
1 cm   3 cm

b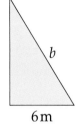
10 m
b
4 m   6 m

c
8 cm
c
6 cm   1.5 cm

3 A and B have coordinates (2, 3) and (18, 15) respectively.
  a Find the coordinates of the point P that divides the line AB in the ratio 1 : 3.
  b Find the coordinates of the midpoint of AB.
  c Use Pythagoras' theorem to calculate the length of AB.

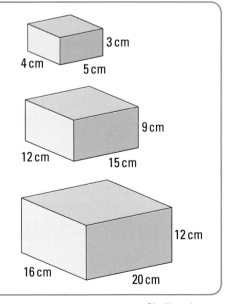

investigation

A pink cuboid has dimensions 3 cm by 4 cm by 5 cm.
The lengths of the pink cuboid are enlarged by scale
factor 3 to give the blue cuboid, scale factor 4 to
give the green cuboid and scale factor k to give an
orange cuboid.
Calculate the ratio of
   i lengths   ii surface areas   iii volumes
  a for the pink and blue cuboids
  b for the pink and green cuboids
  c for the pink and orange cuboids.

3 cm
4 cm   5 cm

9 cm
12 cm   15 cm

12 cm
16 cm   20 cm

10a

1 A and B are two transformations.

A is a reflection in the line $y = x$.
B is a reflection in the line $y = -x$.

The green triangle has vertices $(1, 1)$, $(3, 1)$ and $(3, 2)$.

a On two diagrams draw the following two sequences of transformations labelling the images I_1, I_2 and I_3, I_4.

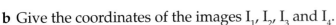

Green $\xrightarrow{\text{A}}$ I_1 $\xrightarrow{\text{B}}$ I_2 Green $\xrightarrow{\text{B}}$ I_3 $\xrightarrow{\text{A}}$ I_4

b Give the coordinates of the images I_1, I_2, I_3 and I_4.

c Does the order in which these transformations are applied matter?

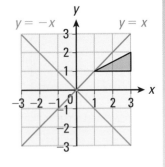

2 The right-angled triangle is reflected in the line AB.
The triangle ABC and its image are now reflected in the line CB produced.
State, with reasons, the mathematical name of the shape formed by the object and the images.

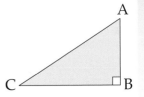

10b

3 Calculate the dimensions of the photograph after these enlargements.

a 20" by 30" enlarged by scale factor $\frac{1}{5}$

b 16" by 24" enlarged by scale factor $\frac{1}{2}$

c 16" by 24" enlarged by scale factor $\frac{1}{4}$

4 Draw the enlargement of each shape using the dot as the centre of enlargement and the given scale factor.

a

Scale factor 3

b

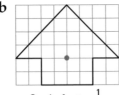

Scale factor $\frac{1}{2}$

c

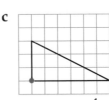

Scale factor $\frac{1}{3}$

5 Draw the enlargement of each shape using the dot as the centre of enlargement and the given scale factor.

a

Scale factor -2

b

Scale factor -1

c

Scale factor -2

d

Scale factor -1

6 Write each of these scales in the form $1:n$.
a 1cm represents 0.2m   **b** 1cm represents 25m
c 1cm represents 2.5km   **d** 1cm represents 50m
e 5cm represents 10km   **f** 2cm represents 250m

7 The velociraptor was a dinosaur measuring about 2 metres long and about 0.5 metres high. Calculate the length and height of the dinosaur in a scale drawing, if the scale is
a 1:20   **b** 1:5   **c** 1:50   **d** 1:25   **e** 1:4.

8 Calculate the scale factor and the missing length in each pair of similar triangles.

a

8cm   4cm   a   12cm

b

20cm   15cm   b   3cm

c
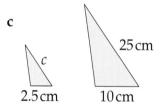
c   25cm   2.5cm   10cm

9 A and B have coordinates (1, 10) and (10, 4) respectively.
Find the coordinates of the point P that divides the line AB in the ratio 1:2.

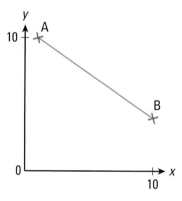

10 Summary

Assessment criteria

- Enlarge 2-D shapes given a centre of enlargement and a fractional scale factor **Level 7**
- Understand and use mathematical similarity **Level 8**

Level 7

1 Enlarge the shape by scale factor $3\frac{1}{2}$ using point P as the centre of enlargement.

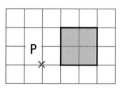

Tim's answer ✔

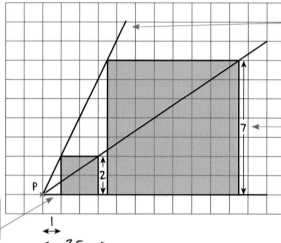

Tim draws the lines from P through the vertices.

Tim checks the image is a square with side length $2 \times 3\frac{1}{2} = 7$.

He multiplies each length along the lines by $3\frac{1}{2}$.

3.5

Level 8

2 The diagram shows two shapes that are mathematically similar.

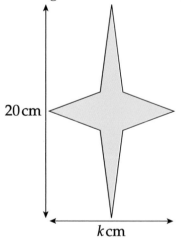

20 cm

k cm

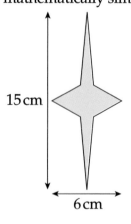

15 cm

6 cm

Not drawn accurately

a What is the value of k?

b I want to draw another shape that is mathematically similar to the ones in the diagram, but of a different size.
Give the length and width of a shape I could draw.

Geometry Transformations and scale

KS3 2005 6–8 Paper 1

11 Algebra

Expressions and formulae

In December of 2001, a high school student from Pomona, California derived a formula to calculate the minimum required length, *L*, of a piece of paper in order to fold the paper *n* times. Challenged by her maths teacher to show that the formula worked Britney Gallivan, set a new world record by achieving 12 folds in gold foil and then paper in January of 2002.

What's the point? New formulae that change the way the world works and thinks are being derived all the time.

✅ Check in

Level 5

1 Simplify these algebraic expressions, where possible.

a $x + x + x$ **b** $6y + 3y$

c $12a - 5a$ **d** $5b - 2$

e $p + 5p - 2p$ **f** $4a + 5b - 3a$

g $x^2 - 3x + 5x$ **h** $10y - y^2 + 2y^2 - 4y$

2 The formula to find the perimeter, *P*, of a rectangle with length, *l*, and width, *w*, is

$$P = 2(l + w).$$

Find *P* when

a $l = 12\,\text{cm}$ and $w = 9\,\text{cm}$ **b** $l = 16\,\text{cm}$ and $w = 7\,\text{cm}$.

Level 6

3 Expand these brackets.

a $2(x + 5)$ **b** $7(p - 3)$ **c** $5(2k + 1)$ **d** $3(4 - y)$

e $x(x + 2)$ **f** $a(b - 6)$ **g** $4p(p + q)$ **h** $3t(5 - 2t)$

Index laws 1

- Use index notation for integer powers
- Know and use the general forms of the index laws for multiplication and division of integer powers

Keywords

Base   Indices
Index   Power

p. 114

- Repeated multiplications of the same number can be written in **index** form.
  $5 \times 5 \times 5 = 5^3$ has **base** number 5 and index number or **power** 3.
  $n \times n \times n \times n \times n \times n \times n = n^7$ has base n and index 7.

---

example

Evaluate
a $3^2 \times 3^4$ **b** $5^6 \div 5^4$ **c** $(4^2)^3$

....

a $3^2 \times 3^4$

$= (3 \times 3) \times (3 \times 3 \times 3 \times 3)$

$= 3^6$

Add the indices $2 + 4 = 6$.

b $5^6 \div 5^4$

$= \dfrac{\cancel{5} \times \cancel{5} \times \cancel{5} \times \cancel{5} \times 5 \times 5}{\cancel{5} \times \cancel{5} \times \cancel{5} \times \cancel{5}}$

$= 5^2$

Subtract the indices $6 - 4 = 2$.

c $(4^2)^3$

$= (4^2) \times (4^2) \times (4^2)$

$= (4 \times 4) \times (4 \times 4) \times (4 \times 4)$

$= 4^6$

Multiply the indices $2 \times 3 = 6$.

- The index laws state
  $$p^a \times p^b = p^{a+b} \qquad p^a \div p^b = p^{a-b} \qquad (p^a)^b = p^{ab}.$$

You can only use the index laws when the base numbers are the same.

---

example

Simplify
a $2^6 \times 2^3$ **b** $7^8 \div 7^3$ **c** $(6^3)^4$

When you are confident you can miss out the working, for example, $2^6 \times 2^3 = 2^9$.

....

a $2^6 \times 2^3 = 2^{6+3} = 2^9$ **b** $= 7^8 \div 7^3 = 7^{8-3} = 7^5$ **c** $(6^3)^4 = 6^{3 \times 4} = 6^{12}$

- **Indices** in algebra follow the same rules as they do in arithmetic.

---

example

Simplify
a $2x^3 \times 5x^2$ **b** $12y^7 \div 4y^3$ **c** $4a^3 \times 2b^2$

....

a $2x^3 \times 5x^2 = 2 \times 5 \times x^{3+2}$

$\qquad\qquad = 10x^5$

b $12y^7 \div 4y^3 = (12 \div 4) \times y^{7-3}$

$\qquad\qquad = 3y^4$

c $4a^3 \times 2b^2 = 8a^3b^2$

The index laws do not apply here as a and b are different base numbers. Simplify using the rules of algebra.

Exercise 11a

1 Evaluate these expressions without using a calculator.

a 5^2	**b** 2^3	**c** 10^4	**d** 3^4
e 2^7	**f** 1^{12}	**g** $(-1)^5$	**h** $(-4)^3$

> Write each question as a repeated multiplication and then evaluate this product.

2 Simplify these expressions, leaving your answer in index form.

a $3^2 \times 3^5$ **b** $4^6 \times 4^3$ **c** $8^{12} \div 8^5$

d $(2^3)^4$ **e** $x^{10} \div x^4$ **f** $a^3 \times a^6$

g $(y^2)^9$ **h** $\dfrac{n^9}{n^7}$

3 Simplify these expressions, leaving your answer in index form.

a $3a^2 \times 2a^5$ **b** $10b^6 \div 5b^4$ **c** $(2x^4)^2$

d $\dfrac{12y^5}{3y^4}$ **e** $5p^4 \times 3p^{10}$ **f** $(3q^7)^4$

g $2m^3 \times 3m^2 \times 4m$ **h** $\dfrac{4n^{10} \times 3n^5}{6n^3}$

4 Write simplified expressions for the areas of each of these shapes.

a
$8k^5$, $3k^2$

b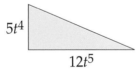
$5t^4$, $12t^5$

c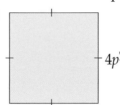
$4p^7$

d
$10w^3$

5 Copy and complete each of these equations.

a $3^3 \times \square = 3^{10}$ **b** $\square \div 5^9 = 5^4$ **c** $(x^\square)^3 = x^{12}$

d $\square t^{10} \div 3t^\square = 2t^3$ **e** $5k^\square \times \square k^6 = 20k^8$ **f** $(3a^5)^\square = 81a^\square$

6 Are these statements true or false? Give reasons for each answer.

a $a^5 + a^2$ simplifies to a^7

b $2x^3 \times 5y^7$ simplifies to $10x^3y^7$

c $2^a \times 2^b$ simplifies to 4^{a+b}

---

challenge

Solve these equations.

a $x^2 = 36$	**b** $x^{10} = 1$	**c** $2^x = 64$	**d** $3^x = 27$
e $x^3 = -125$	**f** $x^5 = -32$	**g** $4^{x-1} = 16$	**h** $2^{x-2} = 128$
i $3^{5-x} = 81$	**j** $5^{4-x} = 25$	**k** $x^2 = 3^4$	**l** $2^6 = x^3$

- Apply index notation to negative and fractional powers and recognise that the index laws can be applied to these as well

Consider $x^4 \div x^4$ (with $x \neq 0$)

$x^4 \div x^4 = x^{4-4} = x^0$ By the laws of **indices**.

$x^4 \div x^4 = 1$ By the laws of arithmetic.

Comparing $x^0 = 1$

When you divide, subtract the indices.

A (non-zero) number divided by itself is always equal to 1.

- For **zero** powers, $x^0 = 1$ for all non-zero values of **x**.
  - For example, $5^0 = 1$, $1234^0 = 1$ and $(-10)^0 = 1$.

Consider $2^3 \div 2^6$

$2^3 \div 2^6 = 2^{3-6} = 2^{-3}$ By the laws of indices.

$\dfrac{2^3}{2^6} = \dfrac{2 \times 2 \times 2}{2 \times 2 \times 2 \times 2 \times 2 \times 2} = \dfrac{1}{2^3}$ By the laws of arithmetic.

Comparing $2^{-3} = \dfrac{1}{2^3}$

- For **negative** powers, $x^{-n} = \dfrac{1}{x^n}$.

For a negative index, write the **reciprocal** with a positive index.

Consider $3^{\frac{1}{2}} \times 3^{\frac{1}{2}}$ and $5^{\frac{1}{3}} \times 5^{\frac{1}{3}} \times 5^{\frac{1}{3}}$

$3^{2 \times \frac{1}{2}} = 3$ $= 5^{3 \times \frac{1}{3}} = 5$ By the laws of indices.

But $\sqrt{3} \times \sqrt{3} = 3$ $\sqrt[3]{5} \times \sqrt[3]{5} \times \sqrt[3]{5} = 5$ By definition.

Comparing $3^{\frac{1}{2}} = \sqrt{3}$ and $5^{\frac{1}{3}} = \sqrt[3]{5}$

- For **fractional** powers, $x^{\frac{1}{n}} = \sqrt[n]{x}$.

The *n*th root, is that number which multiplied by itself *n* times, gives the original value.

example

Evaluate

a 10^0 **b** 3^{-2} **c** $32^{\frac{1}{5}}$ **d** $(x^3)^{-5}$

When a power is in brackets, multiply the indices.

a $10^0 = 1$ **b** $3^{-2} = \dfrac{1}{3^2}$ **c** $32^{\frac{1}{5}} = \sqrt[5]{32}$ **d** $(x^3)^{-5} = x^{-15}$

$= \dfrac{1}{9}$ $= 2$ $= \dfrac{1}{x^{15}}$

Exercise 11b

1 Evaluate these expressions without using a calculator.

a 4^0 **b** $9^{\frac{1}{2}}$ **c** 7^1 **d** $8^{\frac{1}{3}}$

e 5^{-2} **f** 100^0 **g** $49^{\frac{1}{2}}$ **h** 4^{-3}

2 Simplify these expressions.

a $2^8 \times 2^{-3}$ **b** $5^2 \times 5^{-4}$ **c** $3^2 \div 3^5$ **d** $\dfrac{8^3}{8^7}$

> Write your answer in the form $\dfrac{1}{p^n}$ where appropriate.

e $\left(2^4\right)^{-3}$ **f** $a^3 \times a^{-3}$ **g** $\left(x^{-5}\right)^2$ **h** $\dfrac{n^3}{n^{-4}}$

3 Simplify these expressions, leaving your answer in index form.

a $3^{\frac{1}{2}} \times 3^{\frac{1}{2}}$ **b** $\left(8^{\frac{1}{3}}\right)^2$ **c** $10 \div 10^{\frac{1}{4}}$ **d** $4^{\frac{1}{3}} \times 4^{-1\frac{1}{3}}$

e $\left(x^2\right)^{\frac{1}{5}}$ **f** $y^{\frac{5}{4}} \div y$ **g** $\left(a^3\right)^{\frac{1}{2}} \times a^{\frac{1}{2}}$ **h** $\dfrac{b^{-\frac{1}{4}} \times b^2}{b^{\frac{3}{4}}}$

4 A group of friends write these cards.

$x^3 \times x^{-2}$
Isla

$\left(x^{\frac{1}{4}}\right)^2$
Grace

$\dfrac{x^9}{x^{10}}$
Flora

$x^7 \times x^{-7}$
Isobel

$x^{-3} \div x^{-5}$
Jason

a Simplify each expression and write it on a new cards.

b Arrange the friends so that their expressions are in ascending order if

   i $x = 4$ **ii** $x = \dfrac{1}{4}$.

5 Given that $a = 4$ and $b = 8$ find the value of these expressions.

a $a^{\frac{1}{2}}$ **b** b^{-2} **c** $2a^{-3}$ **d** $a^2b^{\frac{1}{3}}$ **e** $ab^{-1} + 1$

6 Write simplified expressions for the areas of these shapes.

a

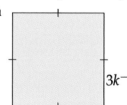
$3k^{-3}$

b

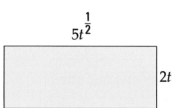
$5t^{\frac{1}{2}}$
$2t$

Solve these equations for x.

a $x^{\frac{1}{2}} = 4$ **b** $x^{\frac{1}{3}} = 2$ **c** $2x^{\frac{1}{2}} = 10$ **d** $5x^{\frac{1}{3}} = 20$

e $x^{-2} = \dfrac{1}{4}$ **f** $x^{-3} = 8$ **g** $18x^{-2} = 2$ **h** $81x^{-3} = 3$

- Multiply a single term over a bracket
- Square a linear expression
- Expand and simplify the product of two linear expressions

Keywords
Bracket   Expand
Double   Quadratic
brackets

- To **expand** a **bracket** multiply each term inside the bracket by the term outside the bracket.

example

Write an algebraic expression for the total area of this shape.
Simplify your answer.

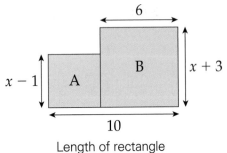

....

Area of rectangle A = $4(x - 1)$
Area of rectangle B = $6(x + 3)$
Total area of shape = $4(x - 1) + 6(x + 3)$
               = $4x - 4 + 6x + 18$
               = $10x + 14$

Length of rectangle
A = $10 - 6 = 4$

Consider the large rectangle.
Area of rectangle = length × width
                  = $(x + 3)(x + 2)$

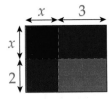

Consider the four small rectangles.
Areas of rectangles = $x \times x + 3 \times x + x \times 2 + 3 \times 2$
                   = $x^2 + 3x + 2x + 6$
                   = $x^2 + 5x + 6$

The result is a **quadratic** expression as the highest power of x involved is x^2.

Comparing $(x + 3)(x + 2) = x^2 + 5x + 6$

- To expand **double brackets**, multiply each term in the first bracket by each term in the second bracket.

To help you remember: draw a 'smiley face'

or use the mnemonic FOIL multiply the First terms
                      Outer terms
                      Inner terms
                      Last terms.

example

Expand these double brackets and implify your answer.
a $(x + 3)(x + 5)$ **b** $(x + 2)(x - 3)$ **c** $(x - 4)^2$

....

a $(x + 3)(x + 5)$ **b** $(x + 2)(x - 3)$ **c** $(x - 4)^2$
   = $x^2 + 3x + 5x + 15$ = $x^2 + 2x - 3x - 6$ = $(x - 4)(x - 4)$
   = $x^2 + 8x + 15$ = $x^2 - x - 6$ = $x^2 - 4x - 4x + 16$
                                            = $x^2 - 8x + 16$

Exercise 11 C

1 Copy and complete the diagrams to expand these double brackets.

a $(x + 5)(x + 1)$

b $(a + 2)(a + 7)$

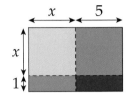 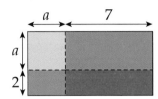

2 Expand these double brackets and simplify your answers.

a $(x + 1)(x + 3)$ **b** $(a + 3)(a + 4)$ **c** $(k + 2)(k + 9)$

d $(t + 6)(t + 3)$ **e** $(p + 5)^2$ **f** $(n + 10)^2$

3 Expand these double brackets and simplify your answers.

a $(y + 4)(y - 3)$ **b** $(b - 2)(b + 5)$ **c** $(d + 3)(d - 5)$

d $(g + 2)(g - 4)$ **e** $(q + 3)(q - 3)$ **f** $(m + 5)(m - 5)$

4 Expand these double brackets and simplify your answers.

a $(a - 1)(a - 2)$ **b** $(t - 5)(t - 2)$ **c** $(x - 3)(x - 8)$

d $(m - 4)(m - 7)$ **e** $(n - 5)^2$ **f** $(p - 7)^2$

5 Write an algebraic expression for the area of each shape. Expand the brackets and simplify your answer.

a 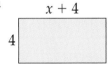   **b** 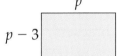   **c** 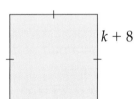   **d**

6 Expand the brackets and simplify these expressions.

a $(x + 2)(x + 1) + (x + 5)(x + 3)$ **b** $(y + 2)^2 + (y + 2)(y - 1)$

c $(a - 3)(a + 8) + (a - 4)(a + 2)$ **d** $(b - 7)(b + 2) + (b - 3)^2$

e $(p - 5)(p + 6) - (p + 2)(p + 5)$ **f** $(q - 7)^2 - (q + 6)(q - 6)$

g $(2x + 1)(x + 3) + (x + 1)(2x + 5)$ **h** $(3x - 2)(x + 4) + (2x - 1)(2x + 3)$

a Show that $(n + 1)^2 = n^2 + 2n + 1$.

b Use this result to calculate

   i 11^2 **ii** 51^2 **iii** 101^2.

c Write and expand a similar linear expression in order to calculate

   i 19^2 **ii** 49^2 **iii** 99^2.

challenge

- Simplify or transform algebraic expressions by taking out single-term common factors
- Factorise into two brackets using the difference of two squares

Keywords

Brackets · Factorise
Difference · Highest
of two · common
squares · factor, HCF
Expand

> • To **expand** an expression you remove **brackets**.

For example, $5(x + 3) = 5x + 15$ Multiply each term inside the bracket by 5.

> • To **factorise** an expression you insert brackets.

Factorising is the reverse of expanding.

For example, $8x - 20 = 4(2x - 5)$.   Each term is divided by 4.

To fully factorise an expression, the term outside the brackets should be the **highest common factor (HCF)** of all terms inside the brackets.

---

example

Factorise

a $6p + 15$ **b** $5x^2 + 2x$ **c** $4mn - 12m^2$.

· ·

a $6p + 15$
  $= 3(2p + 5)$

b $5x^2 + 2x$
  $= x(5x + 2)$

c $4mn - 12m^2$
  $= 4m(n - 3m)$

Check your factorisation by expanding the brackets.

The common factors of 6p and 15 are 1 and 3. The HCF is 3.

In some cases, when you expand a pair of double brackets some terms cancel out. For example,

$(x + 5)(x - 5) = x^2 + 5x - 5x - 25 = x^2 - 25$.

> • $(a + b)(a - b) \equiv a^2 - b^2$ is called the **difference of two squares**.

---

example

Factorise

a $x^2 - 16$ **b** $4y^2 - 36$ **c** $2p^2 - 18$.

· ·

a $x^2 - 16$
  $= (x + 4)(x - 4)$

b $4y^2 - 36$
  $=(2y + 6)(2y - 6)$

c $2p^2 - 18$
  $= 2(p^2 - 9)$
  $= 2(p + 3)(p - 3)$

To work out what goes in the brackets, calculate

$\sqrt{x^2} = x$ and $\sqrt{16} = 4$ $\sqrt{4y^2} = 2y$ and $\sqrt{36} = 6$.

Take out the HCF of 2 and factorise into one bracket. Then use the difference of two squares.

Algebra Expressions and formulae

Exercise 11c^2

1 Copy and complete these factorisations.

a $2x + 8 = 2(x + \square)$

b $6a - 10 = 2(3a - \square)$

c $12 - 3p = 3(\square - p)$

d $8b + 12 = \square(2b + \square)$

e $5mn + 3m = m(\square + \square)$

f $4a - 7ab = \square(4 - \square)$

g $6x + 18xy = 6x(\square + \square)$

h $15pq - 12p = \square(\square - 4)$

2 Fully factorise these expressions.

a $3x + 12$

b $5y - 20$

c $24a - 16$

d $21b - 7$

e $14 - 8p$

f $10 - 10q$

g $3x + 4xy$

h $12mn + 9n$

i $4a + 12b + 20c$

j $25a + 10ab - 15ac$

3 Alexander and William have each written a formula for the number of red squares, r, in a rectangle of height, n.

> View each rectangle as a set of horizontal 'strips'. How many squares are coloured red in each 'strip'?

Alexander wrote the formula $r = 2(n - 1)$.

William wrote the formula $r = 2n - 2$.

a Use factorisation to explain why they are both right.

b Justify each formula by referring to the diagrams.

4 Fully factorise these expressions.

a $x^2 + 2x$

b $3y^2 - 4y$

c $5p^2 + p$

d $a^2 - ab$

e $2n^2 + 4n$

f $12m^2 + 9m$

g $5pq - 15p^2$

h $20x^2y - 12x$

i $10a^2 + 20ab + 12a$

j $6x^2 - 12x^2y + 3xy$

5 Use the difference of two squares to factorise these expressions.

a $x^2 - 9$

b $x^2 - 25$

c $y^2 - 49$

d $y^2 - 100$

e $4x^2 - 25$

f $9a^2 - 16$

g $4p^2 - 49$

h $16a^2 - 81$

i $x^2 - 4y^2$

j $9m^2 - 64$

challenge

Use factorisation to simplify these algebraic fractions.

a $\dfrac{x^2 - y^2}{x + y}$

b $\dfrac{a^2 - b^2}{2a - 2b}$

c $\dfrac{5m + 5n}{m^2 - n^2}$

- Distinguish between a formula, an equation and an identity
- Transform and simplify an algebraic expression
- Derive and use identities for the product of two linear expressions

Keywords
Difference of two squares
Equation
Formula
Identity
Variable

- A **formula** shows the connection between two or more **variables**.

Temperatures in Fahrenheit and Celsius are connected by the formula.

$$F = \frac{9}{5}(C + 40) - 40$$

The variables are
F = temperature in °F
and C = temperature in °C.

- An **equation** is true for particular values of the unknown.

$9(x - 5) = 27$ is true only when $x = 8$
$4(5t - 9) = 3(t + 5)$ is true only when $t = 3$

When $t = 3$,
LHS = $4(15 - 9) = 24$
RHS = $3(3 + 5) = 24$.

- An **identity** is true for all values of the unknown.

$9(x - 5) \equiv 9x - 45$ is true for all values of x
$4(5t - 9) \equiv 20t - 36$ is true for all values of t

Write $\equiv$ to mean 'is identically equal to'.

---

example

Prove that these are identities.
a $7(a - 9) - 3(a - 4) = 4a - 51$ **b** $(b - 4)(b + 5) = b^2 + b - 20$

. . . .

a $7(a - 9) - 3(a - 4)$
  $= 7a - 63 - 3a + 12$
  $= 4a - 51$
  $7(a - 9) - 3(a - 4) \equiv 4a - 51$

b $(b - 4)(b + 5)$
  $= b^2 - 4b + 5b - 20$
  $= b^2 + b - 20$
  $(b - 4)(b + 5) \equiv b^2 + b - 20$

Expand any brackets and check that the left-hand side (LHS) is identical to the right-hand side (RHS).

---

example

Prove that these are identities.
a $(x + 5)(x - 5) = x^2 - 25$ **b** $(p - q)(p + q) = p^2 - q^2$

. . . .

a $(x + 5)(x - 5)$
  $= x^2 + 5x - 5x - 25$
  $= x^2 - 25$
  $(x + 5)(x - 5) \equiv x^2 - 25$

b $(p - q)(p + q)$
  $= p^2 - pq + pq - q^2$
  $= p^2 - q^2$
  $(p - q)(p + q) \equiv p^2 - q^2$

- The identity $(a + b)(a - b) \equiv a^2 - b^2$ is called the **difference of two squares**.

Expand
$(x + 10)(x - 10) \rightarrow x^2 - 100$
Factorise
$x^2 - 9 \rightarrow (x + 3)(x - 3)$

Exercise 11d

1 Find the value of the required variable in each of these formulae.

  a $A = l^2$ Find A when $l = 2.5$

  b $P = 2l + 2w$ Find P when $l = 4\frac{1}{2}$ and $w = 2\frac{1}{4}$

  c $V = \pi r^2 h$ Find V when $r = 3$ and $h = 8$

  d $s = ut + \frac{1}{2}at^2$ Find s when $u = 0$, $a = 5.8$ and $t = 2$

2 Solve these equations to find the value of the unknown.

  a $3x + 5 = 23$ **b** $5(y + 4) = 35$ **c** $25 = 7a - 3$

  d $20 - 4b = 8$ **e** $6(5 - p) = 18$ **f** $9q - 5 = 7q + 5$

  g $3(m + 7) = 5m - 3$ **h** $22 - n = 5(n - 4)$

3 Prove that these are identities.

  a $6(a + 5) \equiv 6a + 30$ **b** $9(b - 6) \equiv 9b - 54$

  c $10k + 5(k - 7) \equiv 15k - 35$ **d** $3(t + 6) + 7(t + 1) \equiv 5(2t + 5)$

  e $3(p - 4) + 6(p + 3) \equiv 3(3p + 2)$ **f** $8(q + 3) - 6(q - 3) \equiv 2(q + 21)$

  g $4(2x + 3) - 3(x - 6) \equiv 5(x + 6)$ **h** $7(2 - y) + 8(5 + 2y) \equiv 9(y + 6)$

4 Write an algebraic expression for each area. Expand and simplify your answers using the difference of two squares.

  a

$x + 3$

$x - 3$

  b

$2y + 5$

$2y - 5$

5 Pair the factorised form of the difference of two squares with their expanded equivalents.

  A $(x + 5)(x - 5)$ **B** $x^2 - 16$ **C** $(3x + 4)(3x - 4)$

  D $9x^2 - 16$ **E** $(2x + 5)(2x - 5)$ **F** $4x^2 - 25$

  G $x^2 - 25$ **H** $(x + 4)(x - 4)$

6 Write an identity for each of these products.

  a $(a + b)^2$ **b** $(a + b)(c + d)$ **c** $(a + b)(c - d)$

---

challenge

Use the difference of two squares to do these calculations.

  a $101^2 - 99^2$ **b** $1002^2 - 998^2$ **c** $10\,003^2 - 9997^2$

  d $0.8^2 - 0.2^2$ **e** $8.7^2 - 1.3^2$

11e Formulae

- Use formulae from mathematics and other subjects
- Explain the meaning of and substitute numbers into formulae
- Derive algebraic expressions and formulae

Keywords

Derive | Substitute
Formula | Variable

- A **formula** is a relationship or rule expressed in symbols.

To find the surface area, S, of a cuboid with width w, depth d and height h you use the formula
$S = 2dw + 2dh + 2hw$.

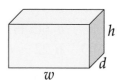

S, w, d and h are the **variables** in this formula.

You can **substitute** values into this formula to find an unknown variable.

A variable is a quantity that can vary.

> **example**
>
> Find the surface area of these cuboids.
>
> **a**
> 5 cm, 4 cm, 8 cm
>
> **b**
> 10 mm, 6 mm, 8 mm
>
>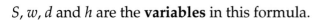
>
> **a** $S = 2dw + 2dh + 2hw$
> $= 2 \times 4 \times 8 + 2 \times 4 \times 5 + 2 \times 5 \times 8$
> $= 64 + 40 + 80$
> $S = 184\,\text{cm}^2$
>
> **b** $S = 2dw + 2dh + 2hw$
> $= 96 + 120 + 160$
> $S = 376\,\text{mm}^2$

- You may need to **derive** a formula in order to solve a problem.

Derive means work out from the information given.

> **example**
>
> A garden has a lawn, bordered on either side by flowerbeds.
> **a** Derive a formula for the area, A, of the lawn.
> **b** Use this formula to work out the area of the lawn if each flowerbed has a depth of 75 cm.
>
>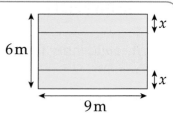
>
> **a** $A = lw$ The width of the lawn is
> $= 9(6 - 2x)$ 6 m minus two lots of x m
> $A = 54 - 18x$ (one for each flowerbed).
>
> **b** $A = 54 - 18x$
> $= 54 - 18 \times 0.75$ Change 75 cm
> $= 40.5\,\text{m}^2$ into metres.

186   **Algebra** Expressions and formulae

Exercise 11e

1 Use the formula
$S = 2dw + 2dh + 2hw$ to
find the surface areas of
these cuboids.

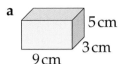

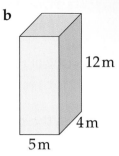

2 The area of an ellipse is given by the formula
$A = \pi ab$.

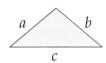

Use your formula to find the area of an ellipse when
a $a = 6$ cm and $b = 4$ cm　　**b** $a = 8.2$ cm and $b = 3.7$ cm.
Give your answers in terms of π.

3 Hero, a Greek mathematician, derived this formula
for the area of a triangle with sides a, b and c

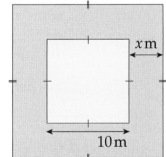

$$A = \sqrt{s(s - a)(s - b)(s - c)}$$

where $s = \frac{1}{2}(a + b + c)$.

Use Hero's formula to find the area of a triangle with sides
a 3 cm, 4 cm and 5 cm　　**b** 4 cm, 4 cm and 6 cm.

4 A garden consists of a square lawn
of length 10 m, bordered by a path
of width, x m.

> Multiply out the brackets
> $(10 + 2x)(10 + 2x)$

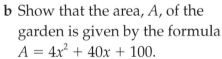

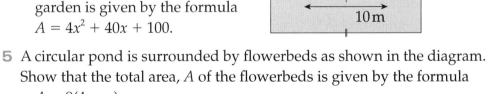

a Explain why the total length
of the garden is $(10 + 2x)$ m.
b Show that the area, A, of the
garden is given by the formula
$A = 4x^2 + 40x + 100$.

5 A circular pond is surrounded by flowerbeds as shown in the diagram.
Show that the total area, A of the flowerbeds is given by the formula
$A = 9(4 - \pi)$.

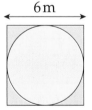

---

investigation

Find out more about the Greek mathematician Hero, whose
formula is used in question **3**.
Hero also described a Babylonian method of finding square roots. Try to
use this method to find some square roots yourself.

- Use formulae from mathematics and other subjects
- Explain the meaning of and substitute numbers into formulae
- Change the subject of a formula

Keywords
Change the subject
Inverse operations

The subject of a formula is the variable that stands alone on one side of the equals sign.

p. 60 • You can **change the subject** of a formula by rearranging it.

In the formula $\quad y = mx + c \quad\quad$ y is the subject.

An equivalent formula is $\quad x = \dfrac{y - c}{m} \quad\quad$ x is the subject.

Addition and subtraction are inverses of one another. Multiplication and division are inverses of one another.

• You can use **inverse operations** to rearrange a formula.

example

Rearrange these formulae to make x the subject.

a $a = p + qx$ $\quad\quad\quad\quad\quad$ **b** $m = \dfrac{x + y}{n}$

. . . .

a $a = p + qx$

This reads 'start with x, multiply by q and add p to get a'.

$a - p = qx \quad$ Subtract p.

$\dfrac{a - p}{q} = x \quad$ Divide by q.

$x = \dfrac{a - p}{q}$

b $m = \dfrac{x + y}{n}$

This reads 'start with x, add y and divide by n to get m'.

$mn = x + y \quad$ Multiply by n.

$mn - y = x \quad$ Subtract y.

$x = mn - y$

'Read' the formula starting with the variable you want to make the subject.

example

A formula that connects temperature in °F to temperature in °C is
$F = \dfrac{9}{5}C + 32$.
Use this formula to convert 64.4 °F to °C.

. . . .

Substitute 64.4°F into the formula and solve the resulting equation.

$\dfrac{9}{5}C + 32 = 64.4 \quad$ Rewrite the formula with the subject on the RHS.

$\dfrac{9}{5}C = 32.4 \quad$ Subtract 32 from both sides.

$9C = 162 \quad$ Multiply by 5 on both sides.

$C = 18 \quad$ Divide by 9 on both sides.

64.4°F is 18°C

An alternative method is to change the subject of the formula and *then* evaluate the variable.

Exercise 11f

1 Make x the subject of these formulae.

a $x + p = q$ **b** $5y = x + y$ **c** $x + a = b + c$

d $k = x - t$ **e** $x - g^2 = h$ **f** $p = x - mn$

g $x + \sqrt{a} = b^2$ **h** $k + x = k + t^2$

2 Make y the subject of these formulae.

a $ay = b$ **b** $\dfrac{y}{p} = x$ **c** $xy = w + z$

d $\dfrac{y}{a} = b + c$ **e** $r = py + q$ **f** $ky - t^2 = x$

g $\dfrac{y}{g + h} = k$ **h** $\dfrac{y}{m} - x = n$ **i** $xyz = k^2$

j $aby = m + n$ **k** $p + mny = q - p$ **l** $y(a - b) = c^2$

3 The formula $v = u + at$ connects the variables

v = final velocity a = acceleration

u = initial velocity t = time.

Find the acceleration, a, of a train which starts from rest and passes a station 22 seconds later with a velocity of $33\,\text{m s}^{-1}$.

> If an object starts from rest then its initial velocity is zero.

4 Make a the subject of these formulae.

a $x = y(a + b)$ **b** $q(a - r) = p$ **c** $a(m + n) = k$

d $t^2(a - v) = w$ **e** $S = 2\pi(a + b)$ **f** $y = \dfrac{1}{2}(a - x)$

g $m = \dfrac{1}{10}(mn + a)$ **h** $k^2 = \dfrac{1}{\pi}(a - h)$

5 The surface area of a closed cylinder is given by the formula

$$S = 2\pi r(h + r)$$

where r = radius and h = height.

a Show that $h = \dfrac{S - 2\pi r^2}{2\pi r}$.

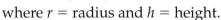

b Find the height of a cylinder with a surface area of 72π cm² and a radius of 13 cm.

> Leave π in your working.

Pair these formulae so that one is a rearrangement of the other.

A $a = b(x + y)$

B $x = \dfrac{a - y}{b}$

C $x = \dfrac{b + ay}{a}$

D $y = a - bx$

E $b = ax + y$

F $x = \dfrac{b - y}{a}$

G $x = \dfrac{a - by}{b}$

H $b = a(x - y)$

- Use formulae from mathematics and other subjects
- Change the subject of a formula

Keywords
Denominator
Squared
Subject

example

Make x the **subject** of these formulae.

a $\quad b = a - x$ $\qquad$ **b** $p = \dfrac{q}{x}$ $\qquad$ **c** $x^2 = t$

The subject of a formula is the variable that stands alone to one side of the equals sign.

. . . .

a $\quad b = a - x \quad +x$ $\quad$ **b** $\quad p = \dfrac{p}{x} \quad \times x$ $\quad$ **c** $\quad x^2 = t \qquad$ square root both sides

$\quad b + x = a \qquad -b \qquad px = q \quad \div p \qquad x = \pm\sqrt{t}$

$\qquad x = a - b \qquad\qquad\qquad x = \dfrac{p}{q}$

A positive number, n, has two square roots: $+\sqrt{n}$ and $-\sqrt{n}$.

- If the intended subject is negative add sufficient terms to make it positive.
- If it appears in a **denominator** cross-multiply to remove the fractions.
- If it appears **squared** make it the subject and then take the square root.

---

example

Make x the subject of these formulae.

a $\quad m = p - px$ $\qquad$ **b** $\dfrac{a}{x} + b = c$ $\qquad$ **c** $x^2 - k = t$

. . . .

a $\quad m = p - qx$ $\qquad$ **b** $\dfrac{a}{x} + b = c$ $\qquad$ **c** $x^2 - k = t$

$\quad m + qx = p \qquad\qquad\qquad \dfrac{a}{x} = c - b \qquad\qquad x^2 = k + t$

$\qquad qx = p - m \qquad\qquad\quad a = x(c - b) \qquad x = \pm\sqrt{k} + t$

$\qquad x = \dfrac{p - m}{q} \qquad\qquad\quad x = \dfrac{a}{c - b}$

- When the intended subject appears on both sides of the formula you can use factorisation to collect those terms together.

---

example

Make x the subject of the formula $ax + b = px + q$

. . . .

$ax - px = q - b$ $\quad$ Collect the terms in x on one side of the formula.

$x(a - p) = p - b$ $\quad$ Factorise to isolate the term in x.

$\qquad x = \dfrac{q - b}{a - p}$ $\quad$ Divide both sides by $a - p$.

Exercise 11g

1 Make x the subject of these formulae.

a $q = p - x$　　**b** $g = h - x$　　　**c** $t = mn - x$　　**d** $r^2 = c - x$

e $a = b - xy$　**f** $t = v - wx$　　　**g** $p = k(y - x)$　**h** $r = \dfrac{1}{\pi}(a - x)$

2 The equation $y = c - 2x$, where c is a constant, produces
a set of straight-line graphs.

> A constant is a number.

a Write the gradient of all straight-line graphs in this set.
b Rearrange the equation to make x the subject.
c Find the value of x when $c = 5$ and $y = 1$.

3 Make y the subject of these formulae.

a $\dfrac{a}{y} = c$　　　**b** $t = \dfrac{k}{y}$　　**c** $\dfrac{p}{y} = \dfrac{q}{r}$　　**d** $e = \dfrac{x}{yz}$

e $\dfrac{t}{y} + r = s$　**f** $a = \dfrac{b}{y} - c$　**g** $k^2 = t + \dfrac{x}{y}$　**h** $\dfrac{c}{y} - n = -m$

i $\dfrac{f}{g + y} = h$　**j** $x = \dfrac{a}{y - b}$　**k** $p = q - \dfrac{r}{y}$　**l** $n = x - \dfrac{m}{y}$

> Take care with parts **k** and **l** as the intended subject is both negative and a denominator.

4 Make p the subject of these formulae.

a $p^2 = t$　　　**b** $p^2 - q = k$　**c** $m = p^2 - n^2$　**d** $\sqrt{p} = x$

e $ap^2 = b$　　**f** $p^2x = y$　　　**g** $t - p^2 = k$　　**h** $f = g - p^2$

> Take care with parts **g** and **h** as the intended subject is both negative and a square.

5 Rearrange these formula which have x on both sides to
make x the subject.

a $ax + b = cx + d$　　**b** $px + q = r - tx$　　　**c** $hx - g = m - nx$

6 The surface area of an isosceles triangular prism is given
by the formula
$$A = bh + 2ls + lb.$$

a Find the surface area, A, of an isosceles triangular prism with
$b = 6\,cm$, $h = 4\,cm$, $l = 10\,cm$ and $s = 5\,cm$.
b Rearrange the formula $A = bh + 2ls + lb$ to make
　i s the subject　　　**ii** b the subject.

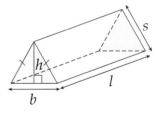

The cosine rule is used to find lengths and angles in triangles.
One form of the cosine rule is
$$c^2 = a^2 + b^2 - 2ab\cos C$$
Rearrange this formula to make $\cos C$ the subject.
Investigate this formula further.

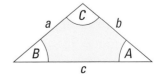

1 Simplify these expressions leaving your answers in index form.

a $2^5 \times 2^3$ **b** $4^2 \times 4^7$ **c** $3^6 \div 3^4$ **d** $\dfrac{8^{10}}{8^7}$

e $\left(5^3\right)^4$ **f** $x^5 \times x^4$ **g** $\dfrac{a^6}{a^5}$ **h** $\left(n^5\right)^2$

2 Simplify these expressions leaving your answers in index form.

a $4x^3 \times 3x^2$ **b** $\dfrac{6y^7}{2y^5}$ **c** $\left(2p^6\right)^3$ **d** $\dfrac{2n^5 \times 6n}{4n^3}$

3 Evaluate these powers without a calculator.

a 9^0 **b** 3^{-2} **c** 5^{-3} **d** 12^0

e $36^{\frac{1}{2}}$ **f** $100^{\frac{1}{2}}$ **g** $27^{\frac{1}{3}}$ **h** $64^{\frac{1}{3}}$

4 Simplify these expressions leaving your answers in index form.

a $3^4 \times 3^{-7}$ **b** $10^{-2} \div 10^3$ **c** $\left(9^5\right)^{-4}$ **d** $\dfrac{7^3}{7^{-9}}$

5 Expand these double brackets and simplify.

a $(x + 2)(x + 3)$ **b** $(y + 5)(y + 2)$ **c** $(t + 7)(t + 6)$
d $(a + 4)^2$ **e** $(b + 5)(b - 3)$ **f** $(d + 7)(d - 5)$
g $(m + 2)(m - 4)$ **h** $(n + 10)(n - 10)$ **i** $(p - 3)(p - 4)$
j $(q - 5)(q - 1)$ **k** $(f - 3)(f - 9)$ **l** $(k - 3)^2$

6 Write an algebraic expression for the area of each circle.
Expand the brackets and simplify your answer.

a

$x + 3$

b

$k - 2$

7 Fully factorise these expressions.

a $4x + 8$ **b** $12y - 9$ **c** $15p - 10$
d $12 - 12q$ **e** $7m + 11mn$ **f** $20ab - 24b$
g $12x + 15y + 9z$ **h** $18xy - 27yz + 9y$

8 Fully factorise these expressions.

a $x^2 + 10x$ **b** $y^2 - 5y$ **c** $mn + n^2$ **d** $a^2b + a$
e $2k^2 - 5k$ **f** $7t^2 + 14t$ **g** $16xy^2 - 20y$ **h** $9p^2q + 15pq - 12p$

9 Solve these equations to find the value of the unknown.

    a $5x + 7 = 22$ **b** $26 = 3y - 4$ **c** $4(a + 6) = 28$

    d $3(2b - 1) = 21$ **e** $18 - 2p = 4$ **f** $5(7 - 3q) = 20$

    g $10m - 11 = 7m - 2$ **h** $17 - 2n = 3(n - 1)$

10 Copy and complete these identities.

    a $5(x - 9) \equiv \square - 45$ **b** $8(y + 4) \equiv \square + \square$

    c $6a + 3(a - 4) \equiv \square - \square$ **d** $9(b + 2) - \square \equiv 4b + \square$

    e $4(m + 3) + 6(m - 1) \equiv 2(\square + \square)$ **f** $8(n - 1) - 5(n - 4) \equiv \square(\square + 4)$

11 The volume of a cone is given by the formula
$V = \frac{1}{3}\pi r^2 h$.

Use the formula to find the volume of a cone when

    a $r = 2$ and $h = 6$

    b $r = 5$ and $h = 12$.

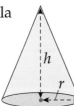

Leave your answer in terms of π.

12 Make x the subject of these formulae.

    a $x + a = b$ **b** $x + y + z = k$ **c** $q = x - p$

    d $x + t^3 = r$ **e** $nx = m$ **f** $\dfrac{x}{ab} = c$

    g $xy = a + b + c$ **h** $ax - b = k$ **i** $p(x + y) = r$

    j $k = \pi(x - t)$

13 Make k the subject of these formulae.

    a $a - k = b$ **b** $t = xy - k$ **c** $p - kt = q$

    d $m = n(t - k)$ **e** $\dfrac{a}{k} = b$ **f** $x = \dfrac{y}{kw}$

    g $y = \dfrac{a}{k} + b$ **h** $\dfrac{d}{k + f} = e$ **i** $k^2 = x$

    j $ak^2 = b$

Maths life

Golden ratio

The golden ratio has fascinated scholars for over 2000 years. It's a special mathematical ratio, which is often found in nature and used in art.

INTRODUCTION

A

B   C

This line is split so that the ratio of A to B equals the ratio of B to C. This ratio is known as the **golden ratio**.

A rectangle using the same proportions is know as the **golden rectangle**.

$$A:B = B:C$$
or
$$\frac{A}{B} = \frac{B}{C}$$

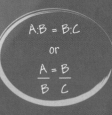

C

B

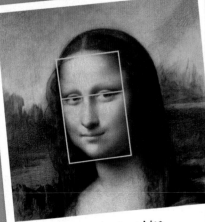

Leonardo da Vinci, Mona Lisa
The face fits within a golden rectangle. A smaller golden rectangle splits the face at the eye line.

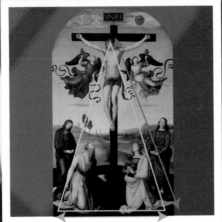

Raphael, The Crucifixion
The main focus fits within a golden triangle (an isosceles triangle with the shorter side in golden ratio to the longer sides).

The Parthenon, Athens
Contains many examples of the golden rectangle.

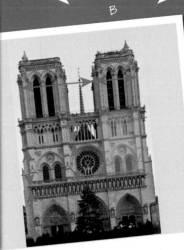

Notre Dame, Paris
There are many examples where proportions match the golden ratio, some of which are shown here.

Find further examples of the golden ratio in art and architecture.

Do you think that these works deliberately made use of the golden ratio or do you think that it is just coincidence that the ratio appears so often? Give reasons for your conclusion.

CONSTRUCT A GOLDEN RECTANGLE

Draw a square.
Mark the mid point
of the base.

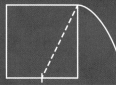

Set a pair of compasses to
the distance between the
mid point and the top
corner and draw an arc.

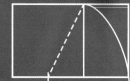

Extend the base of
the square to the arc
and complete the
rectangle.

Without measuring, find the value of the golden ratio from this construction.

Did you Know?
You can use 3 identical interlocking golden rectangles to make a regular icosahedron.

In the Fibonacci series, each term is generated by adding the previous two numbers.

0, 1, 1, 2, 3, 5, 8, 13, . . .

Find the ratio of any two adjacent numbers from the series, dividing the larger one by the smaller one.

Try this for several pairs of adjacent numbers, working towards the larger numbers.

What do you notice as you use larger and larger numbers?

The Fibonacci series can be shown as a set of squares.

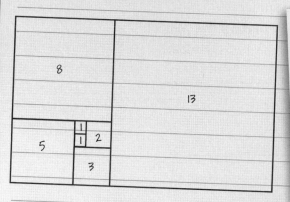

Draw your own set of squares in this way.

For each new size of rectangle that you produce, find the ratio of its length to its width.

What do you notice about the ratios?

What does this tell you about the rectangle?

You can draw arcs in each square to produce a Fibonacci spiral.

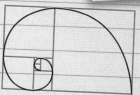

MATHSLINKS

Assessment criteria
- Simplify the product of two linear expressions **Level 7**
- Derive a formula and change its subject **Level 7**

1 Samantha says that $(x + 5)^2$ is the same as $x^2 + 25$.
Explain why she is wrong.

Mirijam's answer ✔

$(x + 5)^2 \qquad = (x + 5) \times (x + 5)$

$= (x + 5) \times (x + 5)$

$= x^2 + 5x + 5x + 25$

$\qquad$ F $\quad$ O $\quad$ I $\quad$ L

$= x^2 + 10x + 25$

This is Samantha's mistake.

Mirijam multiplies the brackets using the 'smiley face' method.

This is the same as using FOIL.

Only the $+ 5x$ and the $+ 5x$ simplify.

2 a The subject of the equation below is p.
$$p = 2(e + f)$$
Rearrange the equation to make e the subject.
b Rearrange the equation $r = \frac{1}{2}(c - d)$ to make d the subject.
Show your working.

KS3 2002 6–8 Paper 1

12 Statistics

Interpreting statistics

Three hundred years ago statistics grew out of the need of governments to have information on their populations and economies in order to more properly administer them.

Today almost all organisations collect data and we are bombarded by statistics designed to influence our decisions. However statistics do not always have a good reputation.

What's the point? You need to know how statistics should be calculated and presented in order not to be misled by other people's statistics.

Check in

Level 6

1 Draw a pie chart to shows the number of MPs at Westminster for the four countries in the United Kingdom (in the 2005 election).

England	Wales	Scotland	Northern Ireland
529	40	59	18

Level 7

2 The table shows the ages of members of the teaching staff in an outdoor activity centre.

Age x years	$20 \leq x < 25$	$25 \leq x < 30$	$30 \leq x < 35$	$35 \leq x < 40$	$40 \leq x < 45$
Frequency	6	8	5	2	1

a Draw a frequency polygon for the data.

b What is the modal class for the ages of the staff?

• Describe distributions in context

Keywords
Variability

When describing a distribution you should mention qualitative features of the graph and if possible back these up with quantitative statements.

> **Things to discuss**
> What are the typical values
>   Can you quote the mode, median or mean?
> How spread out are the values?
>   Can you quote the range?
> Is the distribution symmetric or is it skewed?
> Does the distribution have tails?
>   At the low end, high end or both?
> Are there any exceptional values?

example

The graph shows a summary of distances travelled by Arsenal to Premier League away games during the 2008–09 season. Describe the distribution of distances.

· ·

Arsenal have a number of away matches which are not far to travel but many of their matches require a long journey and there is a lot of **variability** in the length of the journeys. The estimated range of journey distances is 300 km.

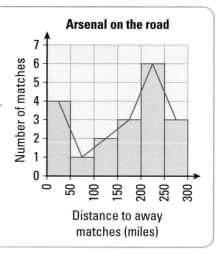

Arsenal on the road

Number of matches / Distance to away matches (miles)

example

The graph shows the weights of dunnocks (hedge sparrows) in April. Describe the distribution of weights.

· ·

Dunnocks typically weigh a little more than 20 grams in April and there is not a lot of variation in their weights. The range is approximately 7 grams. There is a small tail at the top end with a few birds weighing a little more than typical.

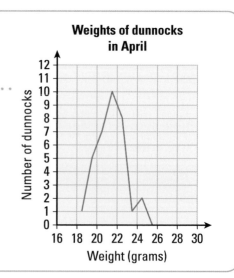

Weights of dunnocks in April

Number of dunnocks / Weight (grams)

Exercise 12a

1 The graph shows the average running speeds, over 5.2 km, for the top 200 competitors in a triathlon.
Describe the distribution of their average speeds.

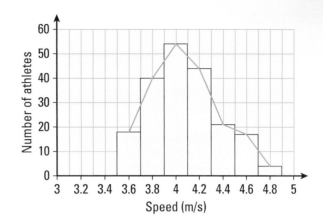

2 The graph shows the times between successive eruptions of the Old Faithful geyser in Yellowstone National Park. Describe the distribution of times between eruptions.

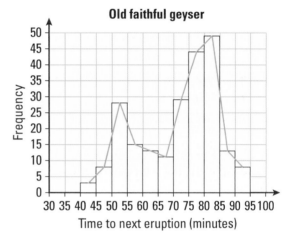

3 The table shows the total score on a pair of fair dice which were thrown 100 times.

Score	2	3	4	5	6	7	8	9	10	11	12
Frequency	2	6	9	12	14	17	12	12	8	6	2

  a Draw a frequency polygon to show this data.
  b Describe the distribution of the scores.

puzzle

  a In question **1**, if all the competitors in the triathlon had been included in the graph what do you think it would look like?
  b In question **3**, what would you expect the scores on a single die to look like? Why should the distribution of the sum of two dice look so different?

- Describe different types of correlation
- Know that correlation does not imply causation

Keywords
Causation   Linear
Correlation   correlation
Confounding   Negative
    variable   Positive
Line of   Strength
    best fit

A hypothesis that connects two variables typically claims that the data will show a particular type of **correlation**.

- Data shows a **linear correlation** if it tends to lie along a straight line in a scatter graph.
- A correlation is **positive/negative** if the **line of best fit** has a positive/negative gradient.
- The **strength** of a correlation measures how close the data is to lying exactly on the line of best fit.
- Knowing that two variables are correlated is not sufficient to tell you that changing one variable will **cause** the other to change nor does it tell you the direction of any relationship.

Exceptionally, data lying on vertical or horizontal lines are not correlated.

The strength of a correlation does **not** measure the steepness of the line of best fit.

example

A new principal is considering altering the schools' class sizes. He thinks that pupils in smaller classes obtain better exam results.

The scatter diagram shows the average GCSE score (A* = 8, A = 7,..., U = 0) and the class size for last year's Year 11.
a Describe any correlation.
   Does it support the hypothesis?
b After he sees this data, the principal says the current Year 10 should all be taught in classes of 30 to improve their chances at GCSE. Do you agree?

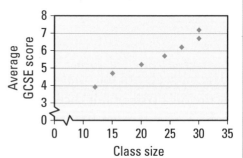

Relationship between class size and performance

....

a The correlation is strong and positive: classes with more pupils tend to have higher average GCSE scores. It does not support the hypothesis given.
b No, here the direction of the cause and effect is actually the other way round – the school has put the weaker academic pupils into smaller classes to offer them more support and putting them into a large class is likely to worsen their performance.

The ability of the pupils is a **confounding variable**. Both variables are related to this third factor which is not shown.

Exercise 12b

1 A geography student thinks that after a long eruption in a geyser there will be a longer wait for the next eruption to allow the pressure to build up. The graph shows the duration of an eruption, and the interval until the next eruption for 'Old Faithful'.

Describe the correlation. Does this data support the student's claim?

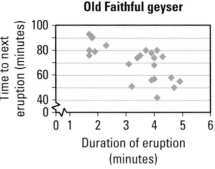

Old Faithful geyser

2 Lewis thinks that cars with smaller engines will have better fuel consumption. The graph shows the fuel consumption for a sample of new cars produced in May 2008.

a Does the data support Lewis' conjecture?

b Jensen says that heavier cars have bigger engines and it is actually the weight of the car which is important. That is, lighter cars use less fuel. Can you tell whether he is right from the graph?

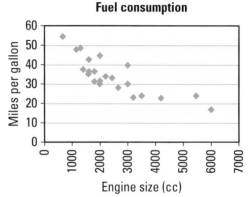

Fuel consumption

3 The table shows the distribution of two statistics for the nine regions of England.

a Draw a scatter graph and describe any correlation.

b Does this mean that the government could hope to reduce violence against persons by road safety measures which reduce the number of pedestrian casualties on roads?

	Pedestrians killed or seriously injured on roads	Violence against persons
North East	345	40 562
North West	1152	128 041
Yorkshire & Humber	764	94 290
East Midlands	477	73 290
West Midlands	758	107 364
East of England	575	81 951
London	1498	186 686
South East	816	113 395
SouthWest	472	76 252

task The population (in 1000s) in each of the regions in the last census were 2515, 6730, 4965, 4172, 5267, 5388, 7172, 8001 and 4928 (in the same order as the table). Calculate rates per thousand for the two statistics for each region and plot them on another scatter graph. What does this show?

- Construct a cumulative frequency graph
- Find the median, quartiles and interquartile range from the graph

Keywords
Cumulative   Median
frequency   Quartile
Interquartile
range (IQR)

The range is often a poor measure of a data set's spread due to its sensitivity to extreme values. A more robust measure of spread is based on using **quartiles**.

- The first, second and third quartiles are those values of the data below which lie 25%, 50% and 75% of the data.
  - The second quartile is the **median**.
- The **interquartile range (IQR)** is the difference between the third and first quartiles.
  - The IQR measures the spread of the middle 50% of the data.

The first and third quartiles are also called the upper and lower quartiles.

Quartiles can be read off a **cummulative frequency** diagram.

example

The table shows normal pulse rates for some Year 9 pupils.

a For this data draw a
  i frequency diagram
  ii cumulative frequency graph.
b Find the
  i median
  ii upper and lower quartiles
  iii interquartile range.

Normal pulse rate	Frequency	Cumulative frequency	
60–69	5	5	
70–79	13	18	= 5 + 13
80–89	30	48	= 18 + 30
90–99	20	68	= 48 + 20
100–109	12	80	= 68 + 12

a i

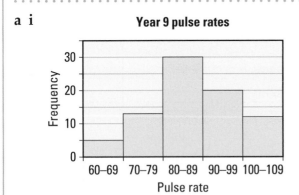

ii

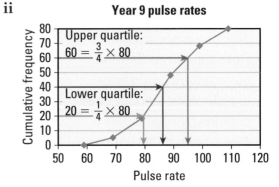

b i $\frac{1}{2} \times 80 = 40$, the 40th pupil has the median pulse rate.
  median   = 87   read off using the blue line
  ii upper quartile   = 95   read off using the red line
  lower quartile   = 80   read off using the green line
  iii interquartile range = 15

Points are plotted at the upper end of each interval. The first point is plotted at 59 – the highest value for which there is no recorded data.

Exercise 12c

Grade B

1 The table shows the numbers of people of different ages who were staying in a holiday resort during one particular week.

Age (*x* years)	<10	10–19	20–29	30–39	40–49
Number of people	15	8	35	12	7

Calculate the cumulative frequencies and use these to plot a cumulative frequency graph.

2 The cumulative frequency polygon shows the number of characters in text messages sent by Alicia.

If the points are joined by straight lines it is called a cumulative frequency polygon.

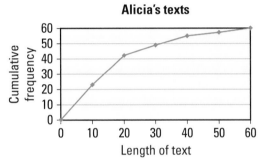

Alicia's texts

Estimate the median and the interquartile range of the text message lengths.

3 The table shows the amount of money a number of pupils raised for charity in a sponsored walk.

Be careful plotting the first point.

Sponsorship (£)	<20	20–29	30–39	40–49	50–79
Number of people	12	18	13	10	7

a Draw a cumulative frequency graph.

b Estimate the median and the interquartile range of the amount of sponsorship raised.

discussion

The diagram shows some information about the weights of a group of boys and girls.
Orla says that the boys' graph is always to the left of the girls' graph, so all the girls are lighter than the boys. Is Orla right?

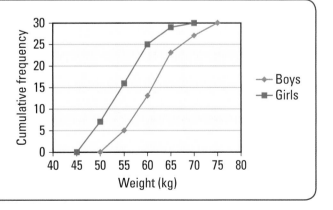

- Describe patterns or trends over time in data
- Use sources of official statistics to understand the world we live in

Keywords
Proportions
Trend

example

The table shows the **proportions** (percentages) of boys and girls aged between 11 and 15 who said they had had an alcoholic drink in the week before the survey was taken.

Data from the *Health Information Service.*

	Boys				Girls			
	1994	1998	2002	2006	1994	1998	2002	2006
11	8	5	7	5	4	4	4	3
12	10	11	12	11	9	11	9	9
13	22	18	20	17	15	22	21	19
14	34	34	34	32	26	35	34	33
15	52	51	49	44	46	50	45	46

a Draw two graphs to show this data for boys and girls.
b Is there any difference in the proportions of boys who drank alcohol for different ages?
c Is there any **trend** in the proportions of boys who drank alcohol over the period of these surveys?
d Compare the proportions of boys and girls who drank alcohol in these surveys.

· ·

a
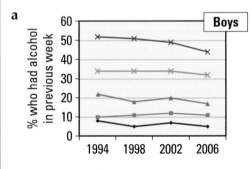
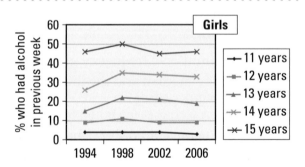

b The older the boys are, the higher the proportion who drank alcohol.
c There has been a decrease in the proportions at all ages except 12, but the changes have been of different sizes.
d As with boys, more older girls drink but there has not been the same general decrease in proportions over time, so the proportion of 13-, 14- and 15-year-old girls drinking alcohol has become higher than the proportion of boys who are the same age, whereas in 1994 there were more boys drinking than girls at all ages.

Exercise 12d

1 The table shows the percentages of adults in the UK (in 2007), who had used the internet in the previous three months and for what purposes.

Data from the *Omnibus Survey, Office for National Statistics.*

	16–24	25–44	45–54	55–64	65+
Using email	84	87	86	86	80
Obtaining information from public authority websites	30	51	49	50	36
Internet banking	34	52	46	43	31
Playing/downloading games/images/films/music	58	40	25	14	-
Telephoning over the internet	15	13	10	-	-

a Draw a graph to show this data.

b Describe any differences between the different age groups.

2 The table shows the percentages of men and women of different age groups living alone in Great Britain in 1986/87 and in 2006.

	Men		Women	
	1986/87	2006	1986/87	2006
16–24	4	3.6	3.0	2.5
25–44	7	14.1	4.0	7.5
45–64	8	16.2	13.0	14.3
65–74	17	20.6	38.0	31.4
75 and over	24	32.1	61.0	61.3

Data from the *General Household Survey (Longitudinal), Office for National Statistics (table 2.5 from Trends 38).*

a Draw a graph to compare the proportions of men and women living alone in 2006.

b Describe any differences between the proportions of men and women living alone in 2006.

c Draw another graph to show the proportions in 1986/87 and comment on any changes there have been in the 20 years.

The graph show the proportions of 15-year-old boys and girls who had an alcoholic drink the previous week, for the surveys in 1994, 1998, 2002 and 2006. Do you think this representation (with similar graphs for the other ages) makes it easier to make comparisons than the graphs used in the example?

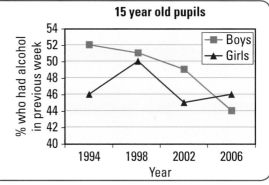

15 year old pupils

• Comparisons distributions in context

Keywords
Bimodal
Distribution

When comparing **distributions** from graphs try to be both qualitative and quantitative and to relate the comparisons to the context.

p. 84

> Things to compare
> Typical values mode, median, mean
> Spreads range, IQR
> Shapes symmetric, skewed, bimodal

example

The graph shows the time between eruptions for two geysers in Yellowstone National Park. Give two similarities and two differences in the times between their eruptions.

Times between geyser eruptions

Both distributions are **bimodal**, that is they have two distinct peaks and they have very similar spreads, the range ≈ 1 hour.
The times between eruptions for Riverside are much greater than for Old Faithful by about 5 hours. Old Faithful has intervals skewed towards lower times whilst Riverside has intervals skewed towards longer times.

example

The graph shows the distances travelled by Arsenal and Aston Villa to Premier League away games during the 2008–09 season. Compare the distances they have to travel for away games over the season.

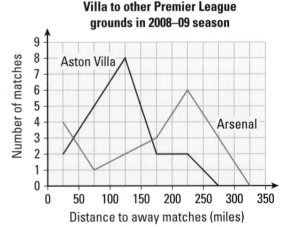

Distances from Arsenal and Aston Villa to other Premier League grounds in 2008–09 season

Aston Villa have fewer matches that are only a short distance away than Arsenal does and they also have many fewer matches that are a long distance away. On average Arsenal have to travel further to their matches, median distance 198 miles compared to 115 miles for Aston Villa and there is more variability in their journeys.

Exercise 12e

1 The graph shows average running and cycling speeds for the first 200 competitors in a triathlon race. Compare the distributions of speeds in the two disciplines.

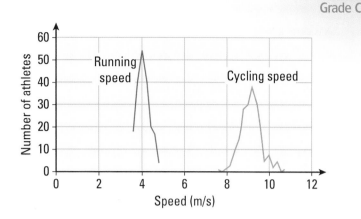

2 The graphs show a comparison between the weights of two samples of dunnocks (hedge sparrows) taken in January and in April. Compare the distributions of weights.

3 A transport company records the punctuality of its trains and buses over a week and the results of a random sample from each are summarised in the table (-5 means arrived 5 minutes early).

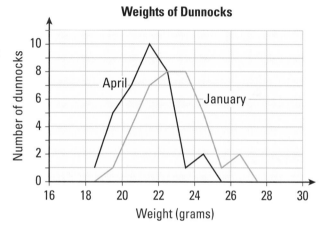

	$-10 \leq t < 0$	$0 \leq t < 10$	$10 \leq t < 20$	$20 \leq t < 30$	$30 \leq t < 40$	$40 \leq t < 50$
Number of buses	4	20	12	3	2	1
Number of trains	5	22	7	2	0	1

a On one graph, draw a frequency polygon for each type of transport.

b Compare the performances of the two types of transport.

challenge

The graph shows the fuel consumption and engine size of samples of new cars in 2002 and 2008.
Describe at least one similarity and at least one difference between the samples for 2002 and 2008.

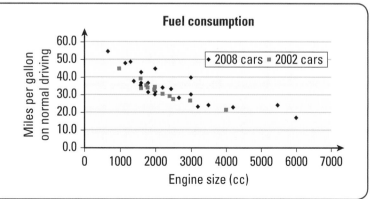

- Construct and interpret box plots
- Use box plots to compare distributions

Keywords
Box Plot   Median
Cumulative   Quartile
    frequency   Range
Interquartile
    range (IQR)

- A **box plot** is a way to summarise the location, spread and shape of the distribution of data.

example

Construct a box plot to summarise this **cumulative frequency** data on the annual salaries of scientists.

> Box plots are also known as box-and-whisker plots.

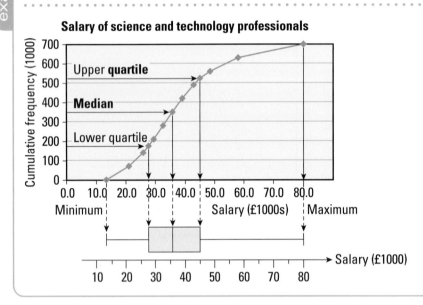

> A box plot must always have a scale.

A box plot allows the **interquartile range (IQR)** and **range** to be easily calculated.

example

This box plot summarises the data on the salaries of graphic designers

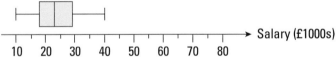

Comment on the difference in salaries between the two groups of workers.

The typical salaries of designers are much less than those of scientists:
    median, £23k versus £36k.

> Always try to support your statements with statistics.

The spread in salaries is also smaller for designers than scientists:
    IQR, 45 − 27 = £17k versus 28 − 18 = £10k.

For scientists, the long tail for high salaries indicates that some scientists earn significantly more than the average for their profession; this is not the case for designers.

Statistics Interpreting statistics

Exercise 12e²

1 For the height data summarised
In the box plot what are the
  a minimum   **b** median
  c range   **d** IQR.

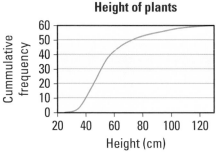

Height (m)

2 Draw a box plot given the following information.
  median = 25 cm   upper quartile = 31 cm   range = 27 cm
  minimum = 7 cm   IQR = 13 cm

3 Construct box plots given the following information.

a

Height of plants

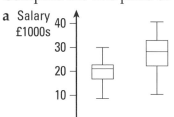

b

Value	Frequency
0–9	0
10–19	5
20–29	5
30–39	10
40–49	20
50–59	25
60–69	10
70–79	5

4 Match the box plots to the graphs of their distributions.

  a   **b**   **c**   **d**

5 Compare the two pairs of distributions given their box plots.

  a Salary £1000s   **b** Weight (kg)

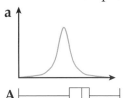 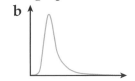 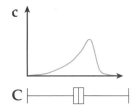 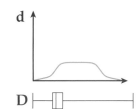

Clergy   Social workers   Wild   Domestic

Given these box plots sketch a bar chart for the possible data distributions.

  a

  b

  c

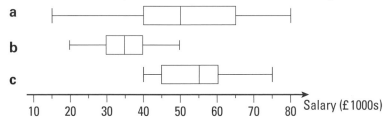

10   20   30   40   50   60   70   80   Salary (£1000s)

- Justify choice of statistical graph
- Relate interpretation of statistical information back to the original questions

Keywords
Comparative bar chart
Pie chart
Stacked bar chart

Different types of statistical graph allow you to see different features of the data more easily.

Pie charts allow proportions of groups to be seen most easily.

Comparative bar charts are best for comparing the numbers in groups.

Stacked bar charts are useful when the groups are ordered because you can also compare cumulative values.

In 2008 the number of candidates getting each grade in A level Maths and English were as follows.

	A	B	C	D	E	U
Maths	28 421	14 275	9818	6524	3746	1809
English	20 317	23 793	24 684	14 971	4545	802

The pie charts make it is easy to see that a similar proportion of candidates got E grades in both subjects.

The comparative bar chart clearly show the shapes of the two distributions. There are more grade As in Maths than in English or any other grade in Maths. Whereas C is the modal grade in English.

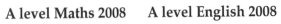

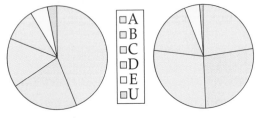

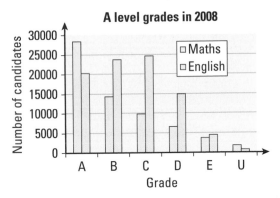

Does this mean that Maths is easier than English at A-level? That would be consistent with the data. However it could be that Maths teachers are better than English teachers or that pupils taking Maths are better on average than those taking English, so you need to be careful in giving reasons when you interpret data.

Exercise 12f

1 a What would you make of a newspaper headline which said this?

SUNDAY NEWS

Mathematics is the easiest A-level!

b The two graphs show the number of candidates and the percentage of candidates getting each grade in the five most popular A level subjects. Give two features of the graphs which are consistent with the headline.

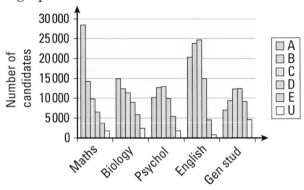

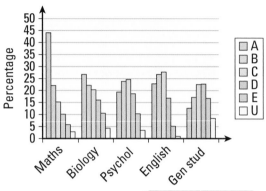

2 The table shows the responses (to the nearest thousand) to the 2001 Census question about religion in Birmingham and in Liverpool.

a To show this data draw

   i a comparative bar chart

   ii a pair of pie charts.

b Which of these would you use to compare the proportions of people who say they have no religion in the two cities?

   Explain your choice.

c What information is the other representation better at showing?

	B'ham	L'pool
Christian	578	349
Hindu	19	1
Muslim	140	6
Sikh	29	0
Other	10	5
No religion	122	43
No response	82	36

discussion

The two stacked bar charts show the data for Maths and English from question **1** as cumulative numbers of candidates and cumulative percentages.

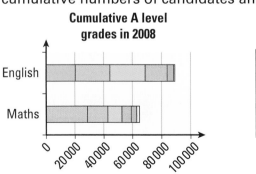

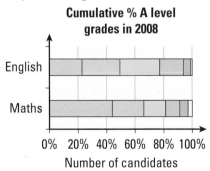

What can you see more easily in the left-hand graph and what is easier to see in the right-hand hand graph?

12a

1 The graph shows a summary of the distances that pupils in a primary school live from the school.

Describe the distribution of distances.

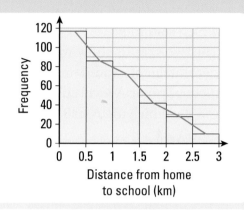

12b

2 A financial advisor wants to recommend investments which have low correlation as part of a portfolio of investments. The graph shows the monthly returns on two investments over the past year. Do you think he should recommend these investments on the basis of this data?

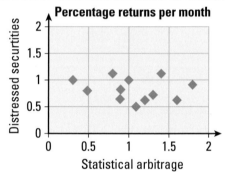

12c

3 The table shows the amount of money a number of events raised for a national charity in their centenary year.

Sponsorship(£1000s)	<10	$10 \leq x < 20$	$20 \leq x < 30$	$30 \leq x < 40$	$40 \leq x < 50$
Number of events	4	14	29	16	8

a Draw a cumulative frequency graph.
b Estimate the median and the interquartile range of the amount of money raised in the different events.

Data from Office for National Statistics (Social Trends 38, table 6.9).

12d

4 Use the graph to answer the following questions.

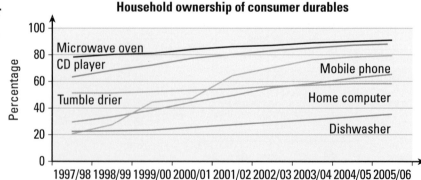

a Which item has seen the largest increase in the decade between 1997 and 2006?

b Describe the trend in ownership of tumble driers.

c Anil says that ownership of microwaves has gone up from 80% to 90% between 1999 and 2006, so everyone will have a microwave by 2013. Explain why Anil is wrong.

5 The chart below shows a comparison of
the weights of bags checked in on a
long-haul and on a short-haul flight.
Compare the distribution of weights
of the bags on the two flights.

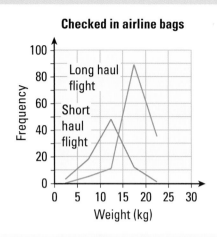

Checked in airline bags

6 The boxplots are for the same data as
in question **5**.
   a How much did the lightest bag on the
   long-haul flight weigh?
   b Amir says 'All the bags on the long-haul
   flight are about 4 kg more than the bags
   on the short-haul flight'. Explain what is
   wrong with Amir's claim.

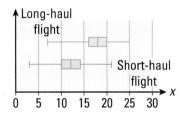

7 The table shows the number of economically active people in the
UK in 2007, in millions.

	Men	Women
Full time employees	11.6	7.1
Part time employees	1.3	5.1
Self employed	2.8	1.0
Others in employment	0.1	0.1

Data from Office for
National Statistics (Social
Trends 38, table 4.2).

   a To show this data draw
      i a comparative bar chart
      ii a pair of pie charts.
   b Which of these charts would you use to compare the proportions of
   men and women in different categories. Explain your choice.
   c What information is the other representation better at showing?

12 Summary

Assessment criteria

- Compare distributions, using the shape of the distributions **Level 7**
- Compare distributions, using measures of average and spread **Level 8**

Level 7

1 The graph shows the ages of members of a table tennis club and a badminton club.

Compare the distribution of ages at both clubs.

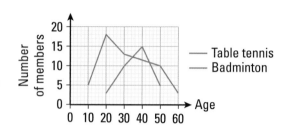

William's answer ✔

> Mode age for the table tennis club = 20
>
> Mode age for the badminton club = 40
>
> So on average, the table tennis club have
>
> younger members.
>
> Range for the table tennis club = 60 – 10 = 50
>
> Range for the badminton club = 50 – 20 = 30
>
> So ages are more spread out for the table tennis club.

William compares the mode for each distribution.

He compares the spreads of each distribution.

Level 8

2 The box plots show the marks in a test for pupils in Year 10 and Year 11.

Year 10

Year 11

0 10 20 30 40 50 60 70 80 90 100

a The lowest mark in Year 11 was greater than the lowest mark in Year 10. How much greater?

b Show that the median mark in Year 11 is 9 marks greater than the median mark in Year 10.

c The teacher says

> The marks were more consistent in Year 11 than in Year 10.

Do you agree?
Explain your answer.

KS3 2006 6–8 Paper 2

13 Geometry

3-D shapes and trigonometry

In April 1802 the great trigonometric survey of India began. Staring from a base line $7\frac{1}{2}$ miles long surveyors measured the angles to a distant point allowing them to accurately calculate its position. Using an expanding series of such triangles they mapped vast areas of India.

The survey also established the heights of many mountains. Indeed peak XV was named in honour of the survey's second superintendent, Colonel George Everest.

What's the point? Triangles are still used extensively in science and engineering making trigonometry an invaluable tool.

Check in

Level 5

1 State the mathematical names of these 3-D shapes.

a   b 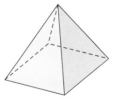   c 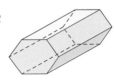   d

Level 6

2 Calculate the sizes of the unknown angles.

a 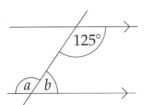   b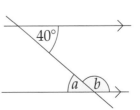

Level 7

3 Calculate the length of the unknown sides in the right-angled triangles.

a 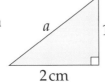   b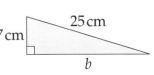

213

- Analyse 3-D shapes through 2-D projections
- Draw the net of a 3-D shape
- Identify planes of symmetry

Keywords

Front | Plane of
elevation | symmetry
Net | Side elevation
Plan | Solid

- A **solid** is a shape formed in three-dimensions (3-D).

You can describe a solid through projections of the 3-D shape onto a 2-D surface. These projections are called

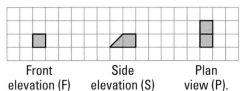

Front elevation (F) | Side elevation (S) | Plan view (P).

The plan is the 'birds-eye view'.

The solid is drawn on isometric paper.

- A **net** is a 2-D shape that folds to form a solid.

Net of a tetrahedron

Regular tetrahedron

Some solids have reflection symmetry.

- A **plane of symmetry** divides a 3-D shape into two halves, each of which is the mirror image of the other.

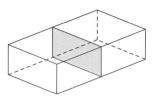

This is the net of a solid.

a State the mathematical name of the solid.

b Draw diagrams to show any planes of symmetry.

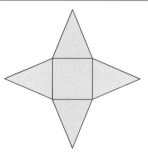

. . . .

a A square-based pyramid.

b

A square-based pyramid has four planes of symmetry.

Exercise 13a

1 A regular octahedron is made from eight equilateral triangles. The solid has five planes of symmetry.

  a Describe the 2-D shape formed when you slice the octahedron through each plane of symmetry.

  b Draw the front elevation (F), the side elevation (S) and the plan view (P).

  c Draw a net of the octahedron.

2 a State the number of faces, edges and vertices of this prism.

  b Draw a net of the prism.

3 These are the shadows of some solids. Describe possible solids for each shadow. There may be more than one answer in each case.

  a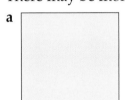
  b
  c
  d

4 On isometric paper, draw the solid that has these 2-D projections.

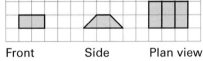

Front elevation   Side elevation   Plan view

5 The centre point of each face of a solid is marked with a dot. Straight lines are drawn from each dot to other dots on adjacent faces. State the mathematical name of the 3-D shape generated by these lines if the solid is

  a a cube   **b** a regular tetrahedron.

Did you know?

The protein shells of many viruses are in the shape of (semi-) regular polyhedra. The high degree of symmetry means that as few as five genes can code for the shell.

activity

  a Construct a cube with edges of length 5 cm.

  b Use your model to decide the number of planes of symmetry of a cube.

- Calculate the surface area and volume of a cylinder and other prisms
- Use Pythagoras' theorem in three dimensions

Keywords

Cross-section | Surface
Prism | area
Pythagoras | Volume

You calculate the **surface area** of a **prism** by finding the area of each surface.

- **Volume** of a prism = area of **cross-section** × length
  = $A × \ell$.

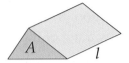

example

A cylinder has a radius of 5 cm and a height of 6 cm. (Use π = 3.14)

Calculate   **a** the surface area

               b the volume of the cylinder.

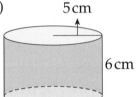

a

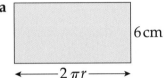

The curved surface unfurls to form a rectangle.

The circumference of a circle is 2πr.

Area of the rectangle = $2πr × 6 = 2 × π × 5 × 6 = 60π$

Area of one circular end = $πr^2 = π × 5^2 = 25π$

Surface area = $60π + 25π + 25π = 110π$

                  = 345.4 cm² (1 dp)

b Volume = area of circular cross-section × length

        = $25π × 6 = 150π$

        = 471 cm³

example

A cuboid measures 3 cm by 4 cm by 12 cm. Calculate the length of the diagonal AD.

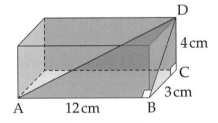

You can only use **Pythagoras'** theorem in right-angled triangles.

p. 48

In triangle BCD
$BD^2 = 3^2 + 4^2$
     = 9 + 16
$BD^2 = 25$
$(BD = \sqrt{25} = 5\,cm)$

In triangle ABD
$AD^2 = 5^2 + 12^2$
     = 25 + 144
     = 169
$AD = \sqrt{169} = 13\,cm$

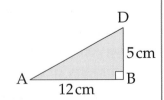

Exercise 13a²

1 A cube has sides of length 16 cm.
Calculate the surface area
and the volume of the
shaded prism.

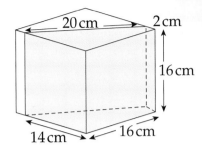

2 A prism has a right-angled
triangle as the cross-section.
Calculate
   a the length AC
   b the area of triangle ABC
   c the total surface area of the prism
   d the volume of the prism.

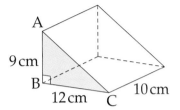

3 The diagram shows a triangular prism.
Calculate
   a the height h
   b the surface area
   c the volume.

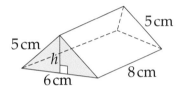

4 A cylinder has a radius of 6 cm and a height of 8 cm.
Calculate
   a the surface area
   b the volume of the cylinder.

Use π = 3.14.

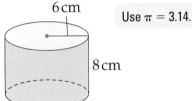

5 A cuboid measures 8 cm by 9 cm by 12 cm.
Calculate
   a the length AB
   b the length CA.

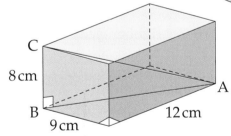

6 Calculate the length of the longest straight rod that will fit
completely inside a cubical box of side length 10 cm.

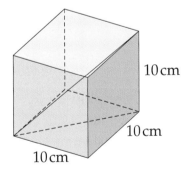

A cylinder has radius r and height h.

a In terms of r, h and π, calculate
   i the surface area and
   ii the volume of the cylinder.
b Check your formulae have the correct dimensions.

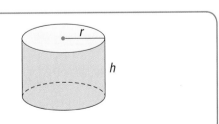

13b Trigonometry 1

- Consider sine, cosine and tangent as ratios
- Begin to use sine, cosine and tangent to solve problems

Keywords
Adjacent · Ratio
Cosine (cos) · Right-angled triangle
Hypotenuse · Sine (sin)
Opposite · Tangent (tan)

You can name the sides in a **right-angled triangle** according to their positions with respect to one of the acute angles.

- The **hypotenuse** is the longest side of the triangle.
- The **opposite** side faces the angle marked θ.
- The **adjacent** side is beside the angle marked θ.

Hypotenuse / Opposite / θ / Adjacent

The green triangle and the pink triangle are similar. The scale factor of the enlargement is s.

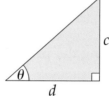

Two triangles are similar if two pairs of angles are equal.

$$a \times s = c \quad \text{and} \quad b \times s = d$$

Dividing these equations gives

$$\frac{a}{b} = \frac{c}{d} \quad \left(= \frac{\text{opposite}}{\text{adjacent}} \right)$$

For all similar right-angled triangles, the **ratio** $\dfrac{\text{opposite}}{\text{adjacent}}$ is constant.

This ratio is called the **tangent**.

- $\tan \theta = \dfrac{\text{opposite side}}{\text{adjacent side}}$

tan is the abbreviation for tangent.

You can find two more constant ratios in a right-angled triangle.

- $\sin \theta = \dfrac{\text{opposite side}}{\text{hypotenuse}}$ $\qquad \cos \theta = \dfrac{\text{adjacent side}}{\text{hypotenuse}}$

sin is the abbreviation for sine.
cos is the abbreviation for cosine.

example

Calculate the value of $\sin \theta$, $\cos \theta$ and $\tan \theta$ in the right-angled triangle.

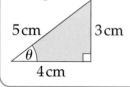

$$\sin \theta = \frac{\text{opposite}}{\text{hypotenuse}} = \frac{3}{5} = 0.6$$

$$\cos \theta = \frac{\text{adjacent}}{\text{hypotenuse}} = \frac{4}{5} = 0.8$$

$$\tan \theta = \frac{\text{opposite}}{\text{adjacent}} = \frac{3}{4} = 0.75$$

(Hypotenuse) 5 cm / 3 cm (Opposite) / θ / 4 cm (Adjacent)

Exercise 13b

1 a Explain why these triangles are similar.
  b Accurately construct each triangle.
  c Measure the lengths *a*, *b*, *c* and *d*.
  d Calculate the values of $\frac{a}{b}$ and $\frac{c}{d}$.
  e Which trigonometric ratio have you found?

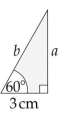

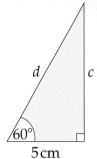

2 For each right-angled triangle, calculate as a decimal to 3 significant figures, the values of sin θ, cos θ and tan θ. All measurements are in centimetres.

a   **b**   **c**   **d**

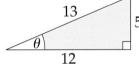

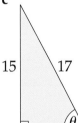

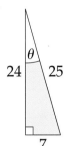

3 ABC is an equilateral triangle. Calculate
  a the length XC
  b the ratio cos C
  c the value of cos 60°.

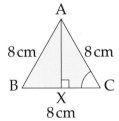

On graph paper draw a quadrant of a circle with radius 10 cm.
Use a protractor to construct a triangle OAB so that angle AOB = 50°.
Measure the length AB.
Compare your answer for $\frac{AB}{10}$ with the calculator value of sin 50°.
Repeat the process for other angles to complete the table.

Angle	AB	$\frac{AB}{10}$	Calculator value of sin of the angle to 2dp
0°			
10°			
20°			
30°			
40°			
50°	7.7	0.77	
60°			
70°			
80°			
90°			

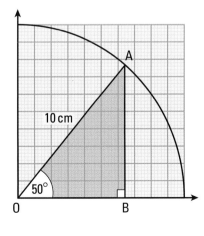

13c Trigonometry 2

- Understand and use the sine, cosine and tangent ratios in right-angled triangles

Keywords
Cosine (cos)
Sine (sin)
Tangent (tan)
Trigonometric

You use **trigonometric** ratios to calculate an angle or a side in a right-angled triangle.

- $\sin \theta = \dfrac{\text{opposite}}{\text{hypotenuse}}$ $\cos \theta = \dfrac{\text{adjacent}}{\text{hypotenuse}}$

  $\tan \theta = \dfrac{\text{opposite}}{\text{adjacent}}$

  A mnemonic is SOH CAH TOA
  $S = \dfrac{O}{H} \quad C = \dfrac{A}{H} \quad T = \dfrac{O}{A}.$

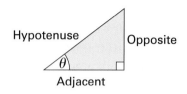

example

Calculate the angle θ in each right-angled triangle.

a

8 cm, 4 cm, θ

b

θ, 7 cm, 10 cm

a (Hypotenuse) 8 cm, 4 cm (Opposite), θ

Use the inverse button on your calculator.

b θ, 7 cm (Adjacent), 10 cm (Hypotenuse)

Sin uses opposite and hypotenuse.

$\sin \theta = \dfrac{\text{opposite}}{\text{hypotenuse}} = \dfrac{4}{8} = 0.5$

$\theta = \sin^{-1} 0.5 = 30°$

Cos uses adjacent and hypotenuse.

$\cos \theta = \dfrac{\text{adjacent}}{\text{hypotenuse}} = \dfrac{7}{10} = 0.7$

$\theta = \cos^{-1} 0.7 = 45.6°$ (1 dp)

example

Calculate the lengths a and b in these right-angled triangles.

a 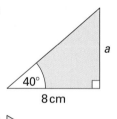 40°, 8 cm, a

b 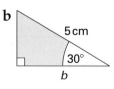 5 cm, 30°, b

a a (Opposite), 40°, 8 cm (Adjacent)

Rearrange the equation to find the unknown length.

b 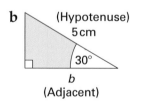 (Hypotenuse) 5 cm, 30°, b (Adjacent)

Tan uses opposite and adjacent.

$\tan 40° = \dfrac{\text{opposite}}{\text{adjacent}} = \dfrac{a}{8}$

$a = 8 \times \tan 40° = 6.7\,\text{cm}$ (1 dp)

Cos uses adjacent and hypotenuse.

$\cos 30° = \dfrac{\text{adjacent}}{\text{hypotenuse}} = \dfrac{b}{5}$

$b = 5 \times \cos 30° = 4.3$ (1 dp)

Exercise 13c

1 Use a calculator to find these values, rounding your answers to 3 significant figures.
   a sin 60°   **b** cos 45°   **c** tan 37.5°   **d** sin 36°
   e tan 48.5°   **f** cos 40.4°   **g** sin 70.6°   **h** cos 20.3°

2 Find the angle θ, correct to one decimal place, if
   a $\sin \theta = 0.5$ **b** $\cos \theta = 0.5$ **c** $\tan \theta = 1$
   d $\sin \theta = 0.75$ **e** $\cos \theta = 0.25$ **f** $\tan \theta = 1.5$

3 Calculate the angle θ in each right-angled triangle.
Give your answers to one decimal place.

a
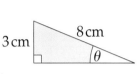

b

c
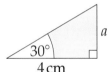

d
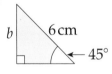

Did you know?

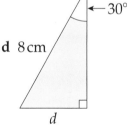

Using trigonometry, the height of the hill Mynydd Graig Goch in North Wales was calculated as 609 m (< 2000 feet). In 2008 it was re-measured using GPS to be 609.75 m. It is now officially a mountain!

4 Calculate the unknown length in each triangle.
Give your answers to one decimal place.

a

b

c

d 8 cm

5 ABC is an isosceles triangle, so that AB = AC = 5 cm.
Angle ABC is 30°.
Calculate
   a the length h
   b the length BX
   c the area of triangle ABC.

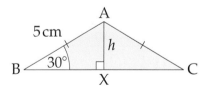

The sides of a regular pentagon are 10 cm long.
Calculate the length of a diagonal.

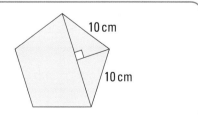

- Use bearings to specify direction
- Use trigonometry to solve problems involving bearings

Keywords
Bearing
Three-figure bearing
Trigonometry

You use a **bearing** to give the direction of one point from another point.

- A **three-figure bearing** is the angle
  - measured from north (N)
  - in a clockwise direction
  - and written with three digits, for example, 047°, 147°.

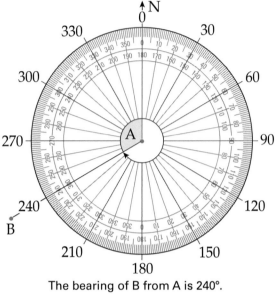

You can use angle properties to solve problems using bearings. The bearing of A from B is 060°.

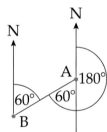

The bearing of B from A is 240°.

Notice that 240° − 180° = 60° and 60° + 180° = 240°
You either add or subtract 180° to find the reverse bearing.

You can use **trigonometry** to solve problems using bearings.

> The reverse bearing is sometimes called the back bearing.

---

example

Sayed walks north for 400 metres, then west for 450 metres.
Calculate the bearing of the starting point from the finishing point.

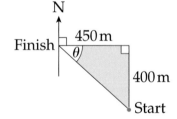

. . . .

First calculate the angle θ.
Tan uses opposite and adjacent.

$$\tan \theta = \frac{\text{opposite}}{\text{adjacent}} = \frac{400}{450} = 0.888\ldots$$

$$\theta = \tan^{-1} 0.888\ldots = 41.6° \text{ (1 dp)}$$

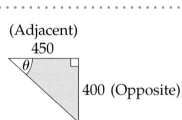

The bearing of the Start from the Finish is 90° + 41.6° = 131.6°

Exercise 13d

1 Calculate the bearing of **i** B from A **ii** A from B.

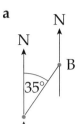

a

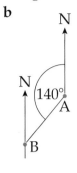

b

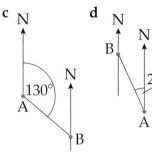

c

d

2 Calculate the bearing of
  a Belfast from Dublin
  b Sligo from Dublin
  c Sligo from Belfast
  d Dublin from Sligo
  e Belfast from Sligo.

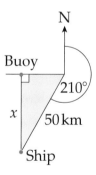

Did you know?

Magnetic north does not point in the direction of true north and even varies with place and time. Whenever you use a compass you will need to make an adjustment for this.

3 Lance runs west for 5 km and then south for 8 km.
  Calculate
  a the distance Lance is from his starting point
  b the bearing of the starting point from the finishing point.

4 A ship is due east of a buoy.
  It sails on a bearing of 210° for 50 km until it is due south of the buoy.
  How far is the ship from the buoy now?

A yacht sails from a harbour on a bearing of 060° for 8 nautical miles.
It then sails on a bearing of 150° for a further 6 nautical miles.
  a Draw a scale drawing to show the voyage.
  b Measure the distance and bearing of the boat from the harbour.
  c Use trigonometry to calculate the distance and bearing of the boat from the harbour.

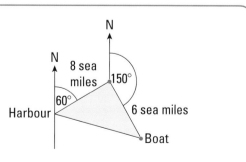

13a

1 This cuboid has three planes of symmetry.

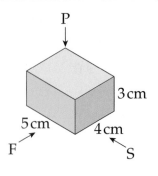

a Draw a diagram to show each plane of symmetry.

b Draw a net of the cuboid.

c Draw accurate drawings of the front elevation, the side elevation and the plan view of the solid.

2 Calculate the surface areas and volumes of these prisms.

a

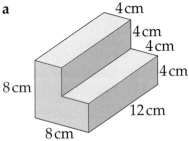

b

$r = 3.7\,\text{cm}$

c

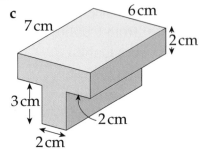

13a²

3 A cuboid measures 16 cm by 18 cm by 24 cm.

Calculate

a the length PQ

b the length RP.

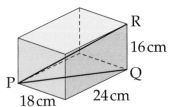

13b

4 a Construct the right-angled triangle ABC.

b Measure the length BC.

c Calculate the value of $\dfrac{BC}{AC}$.

d Use a calculator to find the value of tan 40°.

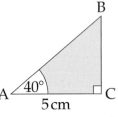

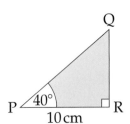

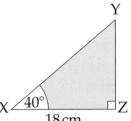

e Explain why triangles PQR and XYZ are similar to triangle ABC.

f Calculate the lengths QR and YZ.

5 **a** If $\sin 30° = \frac{1}{2}$, what values could a and b take?

b Write down an equation relating a to b.

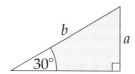

6 Calculate the angle θ in each right-angled triangle.
Give your answers to one decimal place.

a

b

c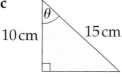

d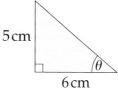

7 Calculate the unknown length in each triangle.
Give your answers to one decimal place.

a

b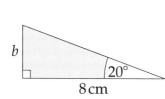

c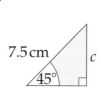

d

8 Toledo and Madrid are equidistant from Salamanca.
Calculate the bearing of

    a Madrid from Toledo

    b Salamanca from Toledo

    c Toledo from Salamanca

    d Madrid from Salamanca

    e Toledo from Madrid.

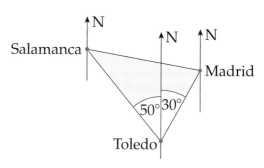

9 A ship is 40 km due north of a lighthouse.
It sails until it is 20 km due east of the lighthouse.
Use trigonometry to calculate

    a the bearing the ship sailed on

    b the distance the ship sailed.

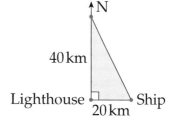

Assessment criteria
- Calculate lengths, areas and volumes in prisms **Level 7**
- Use trigonometrical ratios in right-angled triangles **Level 8**

Level 7

1 A cube of side 6 cm is sliced in two to form two congruent shapes.

Calculate the area of the shaded rectangle.

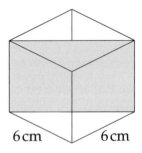

6 cm   6 cm

Hannah's answer ✔

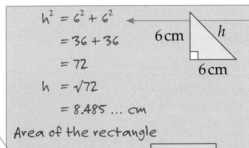

$h^2 = 6^2 + 6^2$

$= 36 + 36$

$= 72$

$h = \sqrt{72}$

$= 8.485 \ldots$ cm

6 cm

6 cm

h

Hannah finds the length of the diagonal using the right-angled triangle on the base of the cube.

Hannah uses 8.485 … in her calculation, not 8.5

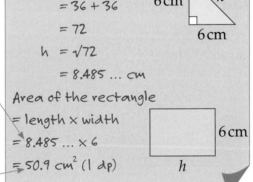

Area of the rectangle

$= $ length $\times$ width

$= 8.485 \ldots \times 6$

$= 50.9$ cm^2 (1 dp)

6 cm

h

She rounds to 1 decimal place at the end of the calculation.

Level 8

2 Engineers have worked on the leaning tower of Pisa to make it safe.

A website gave this information about the tower before the work.

> The height of the tower is 56 m.
> The angle of tilt is 5.5°
> The tower leans 5.2 m from the perpendicular.

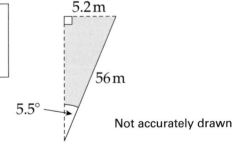

5.2 m

56 m

5.5°

Not accurately drawn

Give calculations to show that the information cannot all be true.

KS3 2006 6–8 Paper 2

14 Number

Calculation plus

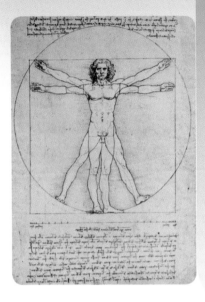

Proportion is one of the most useful ideas in mathematics and science.
- The circumference of a circle is proportional to its radius and its area is proportional to its radius squared.
- The volume of a gas filled balloon is directly proportional to its (absolute) temperature and inversely proportional to its pressure.
- The size of your head is proportional to your height.

What's the point Whenever you enlarge a shape, use trigonometry, convert between units, find gradients or rates of change etc. you are using the idea of proportion.

✓ Check in

1 Calculate the percentage change using a single multiplier.
   a Increase £220 by 7.2%.   b Decrease 45 kg by 3.75%.

2 a A newborn baby weighs 2.91 kg. After 7 days the baby weighs 2.65 kg. Calculate the percentage reduction in the baby's weight.
   b At age 3, Olivia is 68 cm tall. At age 5, she is 1 m tall. How many times taller has Olivia become?

3 Round each number to one significant figure.
   a 27.5   b 0.0772   c 2786
   d 3.78×10^2 e 4.68×10^{-2}

4 Round each number to the degree specified.
   a 5.495 m (nearest metre)   b 12.054 (1 dp)
   c 3678.25 kg (nearest kg)   d 29.4949 (3 sf)

- Calculate a percentage increase or decrease
- Calculate a repeated percentage increase or decrease
- Calculate a percentage change

Keywords
Decimal multiplier
Percentage

p. 26

- You can calculate a repeated **percentage** increase or decrease using a single **decimal multiplier**.

example

Chad invests £34 in a savings bond for three years with a guaranteed interest rate of 8%. How much money will he have after three years?

Each year the money grows by 8%

Year by year

$\times 1.08$ $\times 1.08$ $\times 1.08$

£34.00 ⟶ £36.72 ⟶ £39.6576 ⟶ £42.830208

Increase by 8%   Increase by 8%   Increase by 8% = £42.83 (2 dp)

As one calculation

$\times(1.08)^3$

£34.00 ⟶ £42.830208

Increase by 8% = £42.83 (2 dp)
for 3 years

Each year the money is multiplied by 1.08. After three years this gives

£34 × 1.08 × 1.08 × 1.08
= £34 × 1.08³.

The calculation is for three years, so the multiplier is raised to the power of 3.

- You can use the decimal multiplier to solve percentage problems in reverse.

example

John goes on a diet and changes his lifestyle. He loses 32% of his body weight and now weighs 57.8 kg. What was his original weight?

His weight has decreased by 32%

Decrease by 32%

$\times 0.68$

Original weight ⟶ New weight

= □   ÷ 0.68   = 57.8 kg

Original weight = new weight ÷ 0.68

= 57.8 ÷ 0.68

= 85 kg

The inverse of multiplying by 0.68 is dividing by 0.68

Check using percentage change

$= \dfrac{\text{Change in weight}}{\text{Original weight}}$

$= \dfrac{85 - 57.8}{85}$

$= \dfrac{27.2}{85} = 0.32 = 32\%$ ✓

Exercise 14a

1 **a** A DVD costs £16. In a sale the price is reduced by 12%.
      What is the sale price of the DVD?
   b A DVD is reduced in price from £18 to £13.68.
      What is the percentage reduction in price?
   c A DVD is reduced in price in a sale by 18%. The new price of the
      DVD is £13.12. What was the original price of the DVD?
   d A packet of biscuits is increased in weight from 240 g to 375 g.
      What is the percentage increase in weight?
   e A packet of biscuits is increased in weight by 15%. The new
      weight of the packet is 299 g. What was the original weight of
      the biscuits?
   f A packet of biscuits weighs 280 g. The packet is increased in
      weight by 21%. What is the new weight of the packet?

2 Work out the values of these items after the number of years stated.

Item	Cost	Time	Yearly change
Plasma TV	£1000	3 years	15% decrease
BMW car	£35 000	4 years	4.1% increase
Holiday in Florida	£3000	4 years	3.5% increase

3 Annual inflation is +4.1% and this year's prices are
   Bread 95p   Petrol (litre) £1.15   Electricity bill (month) £28.
   a How much will each item cost in three years' time?
   b What is the overall percentage increase in price after three years?
   c How much did each item cost three years ago?

> Inflation is the percentage
> by which prices rise or fall
> in a year.

4 A rectangle is increased in length by 15% and decreased in width by
   15%. By what percentage has the area changed?

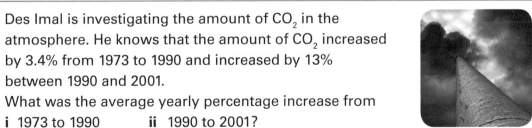

investigation

   a Des Imal is investigating the amount of CO_2 in the
      atmosphere. He knows that the amount of CO_2 increased
      by 3.4% from 1973 to 1990 and increased by 13%
      between 1990 and 2001.
      What was the average yearly percentage increase from
      i 1973 to 1990   **ii** 1990 to 2001?
   b In 1815 a soldier put his life savings of £2 into a bank. In 1994 his relatives found
      his bank book which showed that no money had ever been withdrawn.
      i How much money was in the account in 1994?
         Show your working out and explain any assumptions you make.
      ii What was the real value of the money in 1994 if you take inflation into account?

- Identify when proportional reasoning is required in a problem
- Calculate the result of any proportional change using a single multiplier

Keywords
Direct proportion
Multiplier
Ratio

p. 34

- When two quantities are in **direct proportion** the ratio between them is fixed. You can use the **ratio** to change from one quantity to another using a single **multiplier**.

example

A picture is enlarged by a scale factor of 1.5. What is the ratio of lengths in the original picture to corresponding lengths in the enlargement.

$\times 1.5$
$\times \frac{3}{2}$

3 cm

8 cm

4.5 cm

Original : Enlarged
length   length
2   :   3

$\div \frac{3}{2}$
$\div 1.5$

12 cm

$\div \frac{3}{2}$ is the same as $\times \frac{2}{3}$. $\frac{3}{2}$ and $\frac{2}{3}$ are multiplicative inverses.

Write the scale factor as a fraction.
Scale factor $= 1.5 = 1\frac{1}{2} = \frac{3}{2}$
Original : Enlargement $= 2 : 3$

- You can also use the ratios between lengths in the original shape or the enlarged shape to solve direct proportion problems.

example

A picture measures 8 cm by 3 cm. The picture is enlarged so that the new picture has a length of 12 cm. What is the width of the enlarged picture?

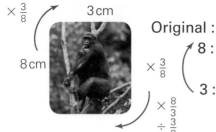

$\times \frac{3}{8}$

3 cm

8 cm

$\times \frac{3}{8}$

Original : Enlarged
8 : 12

3 : ☐

$\times \frac{8}{3}$
$\div \frac{3}{8}$

☐ cm

$\times \frac{3}{8}$

12 cm

$\times \frac{3}{8}$

$\times \frac{8}{3}$
$\div \frac{3}{8}$

width $= \frac{3}{8} \times$ length
length $= \frac{8}{3} \times$ width

Express the ratios in fractional form

$\dfrac{\text{width}}{\text{length}} = \frac{3}{8} = \frac{\square}{12}$

Enlarged width $= \frac{3}{8} \times 12 = 4.5$ cm

Exercise 14b

1 Solve these problems.

a Joe mixes seven parts of black paint with four parts of white paint to make grey paint. If he has 30 litres of black paint, how many litres of white paint does he need to mix with it to make grey paint?

b In a sale all the prices in the shop are reduced by the same percentage. A pair of trainers is reduced in price from £120 to £79.20. A pair of football boots cost £49.50 in the sale. What was the price of the football boots before the sale?

2 A triangle is enlarged by a scale factor.

a Calculate the ratio of lengths in the original triangle to those in the enlarged triangle.

b Calculate the lengths of the sides marked x and y.

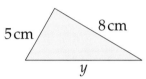
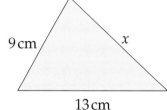

3 A ship sails across the Pacific Ocean. It has an average speed of 31 miles per hour. It uses fuel at the rate of 1 litre every 2.4 feet travelled. Calculate to the nearest litre how much fuel the ship uses to travel

1 mile = 5280 feet
= 1.609 km

a for 1 hour   **b** in a journey of 4300 km.

4 Henry fills a glass with blackcurrant cordial and water in the ratio 1 : 4. He drinks $\frac{1}{4}$ of the liquid and then fills the glass with more water. What is the ratio of blackcurrant cordial to water in the glass now?

Mandy makes a box

a Calculate the volume and surface area of the box. She makes a second box 1.5 times larger than the first.

b Calculate the volume and surface area of the new box.

c How have the surface area and volume changed after the enlargement?

d Investigate enlarging the original box by different scale factors and in each case note how the surface area and volume have changed.

e Mandy makes a third box which is an enlargement of the original box. The volume of this box is 1312.5 cm³. What are the dimensions of the new box?

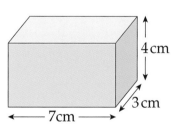

The length, width and height are all 1.5 times longer.

- Use rounding to make estimates
- Round numbers written in standard form
- Calculate the percentage error in an estimate
- Solve problems involving upper and lower bounds

Keywords
Bound   Significant
Estimate   figure
Round

- You can use **significant figures** to **estimate** the answer to a calculation with numbers written in standard form.

example

Estimate $\dfrac{(2.67 \times 10^3) \times (4.3 \times 10^2)}{5.8 \times 10^{-2}}$

· ·

$$\dfrac{(2.67 \times 10^3) \times (4.3 \times 10^2)}{5.8 \times 10^{-2}} \approx \dfrac{(3 \times 10^3) \times (4 \times 10^2)}{6 \times 10^{-2}}$$

$$\approx \dfrac{12 \times 10^5}{6 \times 10^{-2}}$$

$$\approx 2 \times 10^7$$

Round each number to one significant figure.

- You can use the upper and lower **bounds** on quantities in a calculation to place bounds on the answer.

example

Josiah can run 100 m (to the nearest metre) in 12.4 seconds (3 sf).
Find   **a** his maximum possible speed in m/s
      b his minimum possible speed in m/s.

$\text{Speed} = \dfrac{\text{Distance}}{\text{Time}}$

· ·

First calculate the upper and lower bounds for each quantity.

Distance ≈ 100 m   Time taken ≈ 12.4 s
Upper bound = 100.5 m   Upper bound = 12.45 s
Lower bound = 99.5 m   Lower bound = 12.35 s

a maximum speed $= \dfrac{\text{maximum distance}}{\text{minimum time}} = \dfrac{100.5}{12.35} = 8.14 \, \text{m/s}$

b minimum speed $= \dfrac{\text{minimum distance}}{\text{maximum time}} = \dfrac{99.5}{12.45} = 7.99 \, \text{m/s}$

Since 12.4 is rounded to 3 sf, the upper and lower bounds must lie within $\pm \frac{1}{2}$ of a tenth of a second, that is. ±0.05.

The maximum speed is when you travel the most distance in the least amount of time.

Exercise 14c

Exercise 14c

1 Estimate the answer to each problem.

a Niall's heart beats at 65 beats per minute.
How many times does his heart beat in a year?

b Jack's cat eats four pouches of cat food a day. Each pouch costs 32p.
How much does it cost to feed Jack's cat each month?

2 Estimate the answer to each calculation by first rounding each number to one significant figure.

a $\dfrac{29 \times 2.9}{27.3}$

b $\dfrac{6.98 \times 4.9}{9.57}$

c $\dfrac{4334 \times 0.58}{5.76}$

d $\dfrac{2.8 \times 10^7 \times 1.47 \times 10^{-2}}{1.97 \times 10^3}$

e $\dfrac{6.08 \times 10^3 \times 9.73 \times 10^{-4}}{3.6 \times 10^{-2}}$

3 Hercules is carrying out an experiment to see which member of his building team is the best at estimating measurements.

Measurements	Mark's estimate	Barry's estimate	Padraig's estimate	True measurement
Length of room	5 m	520 cm	500 cm	508 cm
Width of room	4 m	430 cm	420 cm	424 cm
Height of room	2.5 m	260 cm	240 cm	248 cm
Area of floor	20 m²	23 m²	21 m²	21.54 m²

a Work out the percentage error of each estimate.

b Who is the best and who is the worst person at estimating? Explain and justify your answers.

$$\% \text{ error} = \frac{\text{error}}{\text{true measurement}} \times 100$$

4 Calculate the maximum and minimum speed if

a Jack runs 1.4 km (1 dp) in 4 minutes (nearest 10 secs)

b a plane flies 3200 miles (2 sf) in 8 hours (nearest hour).

a Identify the upper and lower bounds of these quantities

i speed of light, 3×10^8 m/s (1 sf)

ii speed of sound, 1.2×10^3 km/hour (2 sf)

iii the distance of the Sun from the Earth 1.47×10^8 km (3 sf)

iv the distance to Proxima Centauri, the closest star to the earth, 4×10^{13} km (1 sf).

b Using these measurements estimate the maximum and minimum values for

i the time it would take light to travel from the Sun to the Earth

ii the time it would take sound to travel from the Sun to the Earth

iii the time it would take light and sound to travel from Proxima Centauri to the Earth.

- Use a calculator efficiently and appropriately to perform complex calculations
- Know not to round during the intermediate steps of a calculation
- Enter fractional powers onto a calculator

Keywords
Calculation
Calculator
Rounding errors

- When a **calculation** contains more than one operation, you must do the operations in the correct order.

example

Calculate $\dfrac{(7.6 \times 10^{15}) - (3.2 \times 10^{7})^{2}}{3.4 \times 10^{4} + \sqrt{1.44 \times 10^{8}}}$

Work out any powers or roots

$\dfrac{(7.6 \times 10^{15}) - (1.024 \times 10^{15})}{3.4 \times 10^{4} + 1.2 \times 10^{4}}$

$= \dfrac{6.576 \times 10^{15}}{4.6 \times 10^{4}}$

$= 1.429\,565\,217 \times 10^{11} = 1.4 \times 10^{11}$ (2 sf)

You can use a calculator to work with numbers written in standard form by using the ⌃ or EXP key.

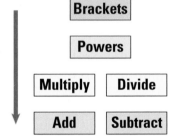

Brackets

Powers

Multiply   Divide

Add   Subtract

- Always set out a problem as a set of mathematical calculations. Then use the functions on your **calculator** to work out the answer.

example

This diagram shows a circle inside a square. The circle touches the edge of the square. What percentage of the diagram is shaded?

Area of circle $= \pi \times \text{radius}^{2} = \pi \times 6^{2} = 113.097\,335\,5\,\text{m}^{2}$
Area of square $= \text{length}^{2} = 12^{2} = 144\,\text{m}^{2}$

Fraction shaded $= \dfrac{\text{area of circle}}{\text{area of square}} = \dfrac{113.0973355}{144}$

Percentage shaded $= 0.785\,398\,163\,4 \times 100\% = 78.5\%$ (3 sf)

←12 cm→

Leave all the digits of your answer on your calculator to avoid **rounding errors**.

example

Find the value of $12^{\frac{2}{3}}$.

Enter $12^{\frac{2}{3}}$ on your calculator.

$12^{\frac{2}{3}} = 5.24$ (3 sf)

An alternative approach is to use the ANS key.

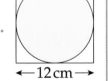

Exercise 14d

1 a Use your calculator to evaluate

   i $16^{\frac{1}{2}}$ **ii** $8^{\frac{2}{3}}$ **iii** $16^{\frac{3}{4}}$ **iv** $9^{\frac{3}{2}}$ **v** $27^{\frac{2}{3}}$.

  b What does the denominator of a fractional power do?

  c What does the numerator of a fractional power do?

2 Rachel says that when a circle fits just inside a square it will always cover about $\frac{3}{4}$ of the square.
Work out the percentage of the square covered by the circle for squares of different lengths.

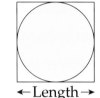

← Length →

3 Calculate the following giving your answers to 2 dp.

  a $\dfrac{(5.1 \times 10^2 + 3.2 \times 10^3)^2}{(2.1 \times 10^2)^3}$ **b** $\dfrac{(3.2 \times 10^4 - 1) \times (7.05 \times 10^{-2})^2}{9 - 3.3 \times 10^{-2}}$

  c $\dfrac{4 \times 10^7 \times (1.8^{\frac{3}{2}} + 4.2^{\frac{1}{2}})^{\frac{2}{3}}}{1.05 \times 10^{-5}}$ **d** $\dfrac{(3.03 \times 10^{26})^2 \times 3.14}{2}$

4 Hortence says that the square of a number is always bigger than the number. For example the square of 3 is 9.

  a Find some numbers for which this statement is not true.

  b Describe the type of number you found in part **b**.

5 a The speed of the fastest spacecraft is 4×10^4 km per hour. How long would it take for this spacecraft to travel to

    i the Moon (distance = 238 855 miles)

    ii Proxima Centauri (distance = 4.0×10^{13} km)?

  b How fast would the spacecraft have to travel to reach each destination in

    i 1 year   **ii** 1 week?

Did you know?

The fastest speed possible is, *c*, the speed of light. That this is the same for every observer no matter how fast they are moving lead Albert Einstein to the theory of special relativity and his equation $E = mc^2$.

---

investigation

Karen wants to investigate the graphs of these different functions.

$$y = \frac{1}{x} \qquad y = \frac{1}{(x-4)} \qquad y = \frac{1}{x^2}$$

x	0.5	1	1.5	2	2.5	3
y						

She completes a table of values for each function.

a Copy and complete a table for each function.

b Draw a graph for each function.

c Use some more values for *x* which are either less than 0.5 or greater than 3 and plot these points on your graphs.
Describe what is happening to your graph
"As *x* gets smaller ..."   "As *x* gets bigger..."

d Try some negative values for *x*. Describe what happens.

1 **a** A CD costs £11.50. In a sale the price is reduced by 35%.
What is the sale price of the CD?
b A CD is reduced in price from £13 to £8.84.
What is the percentage reduction in price?
c A CD is reduced in price in a sale by 15%.
The new price of the CD is £11.05.
What was the original price of the CD?
d Jolene has increased in weight from 51 kg to 57 kg.
What is the percentage increase in her weight?

2 Work out the value of each of these items after the number of years stated.

Item	Cost	Time	Yearly percentage change
Car	£12749	3 years	Decrease 11.5%
House	£299999	25 years	Increase 3.4%
Loan	£6500	3 years	Increase 15.49%

3 The table shows the current prices of some items together with the yearly percentage change in their prices.
Calculate the price of each item
a 2 years ago   **b** 5 years ago
c 10 years ago.

Item	Yearly percentage change	Price now
Mobile Phone	Decrease 17%	£29.99
House	Increase 7.1%	£315 000
Football Ticket	Increase 8.5%	£45

4 A piece of A4 paper measures 210 mm by 297 mm. A piece of A3 paper
is in proportion and has a length of 420 mm. What is the width of A3 paper?
Write down what you notice.

5 The larger triangle is an enlargement of the smaller triangle in each
of these diagrams. Give your answers to 1 dp.

a

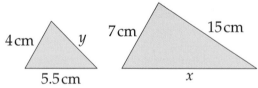

b

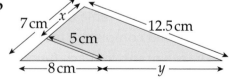

For each pair of triangles
i calculate the ratio of the lengths in the original triangle to the lengths
in the enlarged triangle
ii calculate the lengths of the sides marked x and y.

6 Estimate the answer to each of these calculations by first rounding each of the numbers to one significant figure.

a $\dfrac{3.9 \times 7.2}{1.6}$

b $\dfrac{6.2 \times 10^2 \times 4.9 \times 10^3}{0.48}$

c $\dfrac{4.3 \times 10^{-2} \times 458}{1.78}$

d $\dfrac{4.48 \times 3.37 \times 10^7}{5.54 \times 10^4}$

e $\dfrac{2.078 \times 10^2 \times 4.73 \times 10^{-3}}{1.56 \times 10^{-3}}$

7 Hiro is carrying out an experiment to see which member of his interior design team is the best at estimating the cost of a house improvement.

Upgrade	George's estimate	Kevin's estimate	Sarah's estimate	Real Cost
Living room	£5000	£8000	£7000	£7839
Kitchen	£20000	£18000	£25000	£21542
Bathroom	£5000	£10000	£8000	£8429
Bedroom	£4000	£3000	£5000	£3475

a Work out the percentage error of each estimate to 1 dp.
b Who is the best and who is the worst person at estimating? Explain and justify your answers.

$$\% \text{ error} = \frac{\text{error}}{\text{true measurement}} \times 100$$

8 For each of the following calculate the maximum and minimum possible areas.
a Football pitch 72 m wide (nearest m) by 104 m long (nearest m).

1 inch = 2.5 cm

b Piece of paper 8 inches wide (nearest inch) by 30 cm long (nearest cm).

9 Calculate the following giving your answer to 2 dp where appropriate.

a $\dfrac{(3.2 \times 10^3 + 4.1 \times 10^4)^3}{(1.2 \times 10^3)^4}$

b $\dfrac{(5.3 \times 10^5 - 1) \times (6.13 \times 10^{-1})^3}{37 - 2.3 \times 10^{-1}}$

10 The Earth's speed as it travels around the Sun is 1.08×10^5 km per hour. The Sun's speed as it travels around our galaxy is 7.2×10^5 km per hour. The speed of light is 3×10^5 km per second.
a How many times faster is the Sun compared to the Earth?
b How many times faster than the Sun is the speed of light?

Maths Life

How things fall

When something is in free fall, gravity causes it to fall downwards. It starts falling slowly and then speeds up as it falls.

THE WORLD FAMED HANLON TROUPE – IN THE MOST ASTONISHING MIDAIR ACHIEVEMENTS EVER ACCOMPLISHED.

FOREPAUGH & SELLS BROTHERS

THE AVERAGE SPEED OF A FALLING OBJECT INCREASES BY 4.9 M/S FOR EVERY SECOND THAT IT DROPS.

Complete this table giving the average speed and distance covered by a falling object that starts from rest:

REMEMBER: DISTANCE = SPEED X TIME

time (seconds)	0	1	2	3	4	5	6
mean speed (metres/second)	0	4.9	9.8		19.6		
distance (metres)	0		19.6	44.1	78.4		

★ What happens to the distance as the time doubles?
★ What happens to the distance as the time trebles?
★ What does that tell you about the relationship between distance and time?

★ How far would an object fall in 10 seconds?
★ How far in 20 seconds?

You have already found out how far it will fall in 5 seconds. That could help you here.

DRAW A GRAPH OF DISTANCE AGAINST TIME FOR A FREE FALLING OBJECT.

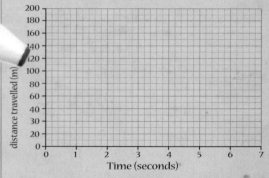

★ Is the graph the shape that you expected?
★ Why is it that shape?
★ How long does it take the object to fall 100m?
★ How long would it take to fall 200m?
★ How far does it take to fall the second 100m of a 200m drop?

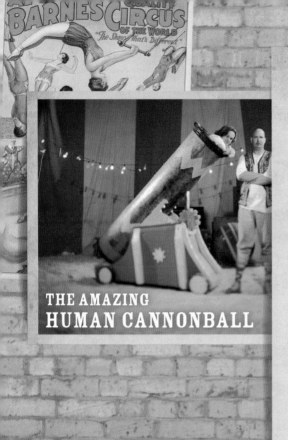

THE AMAZING
HUMAN CANNONBALL

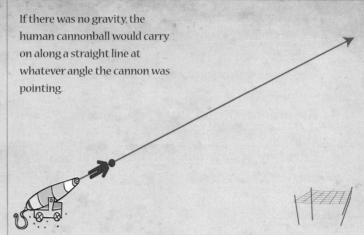

If there was no gravity, the human cannonball would carry on along a straight line at whatever angle the cannon was pointing.

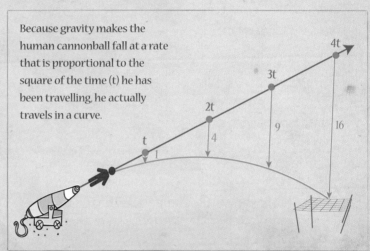

Because gravity makes the human cannonball fall at a rate that is proportional to the square of the time (t) he has been travelling, he actually travels in a curve.

MAKE YOUR OWN DRAWINGS TO SHOW WHAT HAPPENS IF:

★ The human cannonball is fired more quickly from the cannon.

Hint: Think about whether the space between the red vertical lines will increase or decrease if the cannonball travels more quickly.

★ The human cannonball is fired at the same speed as before, but at a steeper angle.

Hint: Where would a ball land if you threw it up at a very steep angle? What would happen if the human cannonball was launched at a very steep angle?

14 Summary

Assessment criteria

- Calculate fractions and percentages of quantities **Level 8**
- Use fractions and percentages to solve problems involving repeated proportional changes **Level 8**

Level 8

1 The number of ants in a nest increases by 6% each day.
There are 5000 ants in the nest.
After how many days will there be at least 6000 ants in the nest?

Izaan's answer ✔

Each day the ants increase by 6%

Day 1 5000 × 1.06 = 5300

Day 2 5300 × 1.06 = 5618

Day 3 5618 × 1.06 = 5955.08

Day 4 5955.08 × 1.06 = 6312.3848

There are at least 6000 ants in the nest after 4 days.

> Izaan finds 106% by using the multiplier 1.06

> Izaan does not round this number at this stage of the calculation.

> Izaan remembers to write the answer.

Level 8

2 The table shows the data about births in the UK.

Year	Number of births
1910	1.05×10^6
1920	1.13×10^6
1930	7.69×10^5
1940	7.02×10^5
1950	8.18×10^5
1960	9.18×10^5
1970	9.04×10^5
1980	7.54×10^5
1990	7.99×10^5

a In which year was the number of births the highest?

b How many more births were there in 1990 than in 1980?
Show your working and write your answer in standard form.

KS3 2004 6–8 Paper 1

15 Functional maths

Real life, functional maths relies on using mathematical processes and applications.

Using mathematical reasoning

Representing

Using mathematical procedures

Buy one Get one free on Pomegranates

50% off Porridge

€0.86

Interpreting and evaluating

Communicating and reflecting

Eating chocolate halves the risk of dying...

Retired men have a 1 in 50 chance of having a heart attack

239

The AfriLinks project links schools in Europe with schools in Africa.

Six British students travel to Kangera in East Africa.

Greg   Ella   Imran   Maxine   Josh   Wah Wah

The local school has been destroyed in a mudslide. The students will help build a new school.

Before they depart, the students find out about the Kangera region.

1 The population is 9953.
The table shows the population by age

Age group	0 – 20	21 – 40	41 – 60	60+
Number	3490	2988	2450	1025

a Round these numbers to the nearest 100.

b Draw a pie chart to display the rounded data values.
  Make sure you provide a key.

c To the nearest whole number, what percentage of the population is over 60?

2 The graph shows average temperature and rainfall over a 30 year period in the Kangera region.

a What is the range of temperatures?

b What is the range of rainfall measurements?

c What is the median average rainfall for a year?

d What is the mean average temperature for a year?

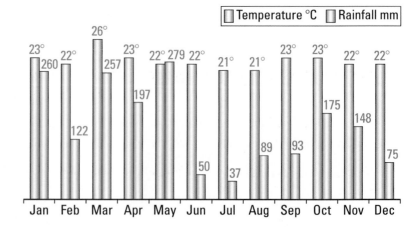

3 The table shows rainfall measurements for the first five months of this year.

Month	Jan	Feb	Mar	Apr	May
Rainfall (mm)	180	242	368	492	481

  a What do you notice when you compare these figures with the average rainfall?

  b Explain why you think the school building was destroyed.

Most pupils walk to school in Kangera.
The map shows the journey for some of the pupils.

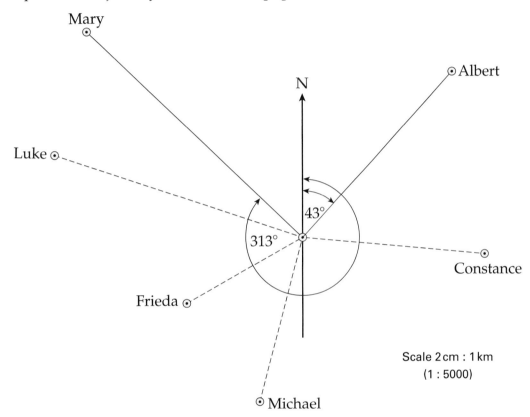

Scale 2 cm : 1 km
(1 : 5000)

4 a Give the three-figure bearings and distances for the journeys from school to home for Constance, Michael, Frieda and Luke.

  From school Albert's home is 6 km away on a bearing 043°.
  From school Mary's home is 8 km away on a bearing 313°.

  b What is the bearing from their homes to school for
    i Albert   **ii** Mary?

  c What is the distance between Mary's and Albert's homes?

  d What is the bearing of Albert's home from Mary's home?

> Work with a partner to solve these problems.

This is a draft plan of the schoolhouse. It is not drawn to scale.
The plan shows the plan view, side elevation and front elevation.

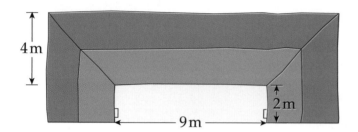

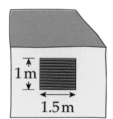

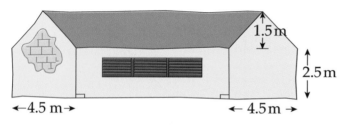

1 a Sketch a 3-D drawing of the schoolhouse.
Start like this.

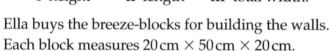

b Label the sketch to show these measurements
i height **ii** length **iii** total width.

Ella buys the breeze-blocks for building the walls.
Each block measures 20 cm × 50 cm × 20 cm.

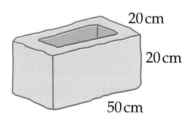

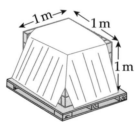

2 The blocks are sold by the pallet.
The stack of blocks measures 1 m × 1 m × 1 m.
How many blocks are there on each pallet?

3 A wooden pallet weighs 28 kg.
Each block weighs 4.8 kg.
A pick-up truck can just about carry a load of two tonnes.
Maxine thinks that it will be able to carry 8 pallets at a time.
Show that her calculations are wrong.

4 The gable walls are covered in a cement mixture.

   a Use the plans to calculate the area of a gable wall.
Round your answer to the nearest m^2.

   b The students have $0.5\,m^3$ of cement mix to coat both
gable walls.
Josh works out that they can make the coat 2 cm thick but
Imran disagrees and says the maximum thickness is less
than that.
Who is correct? Show your calculations.

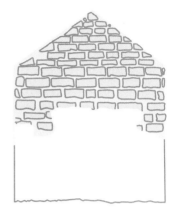

5 Maxine notices that there seem to be quite a few cracked or
broken breeze–blocks. As Imran lays the blocks Maxine records
the number of damaged blocks that they come across.
She samples every hundred blocks laid.

Sample	1	2	3	4	5	6	7	8	9	10
Cracked	3	11	3	0	21	1	12	13	0	23
Broken	6	0	3	0	5	6	1	8	0	8
Good	91	89	94	100	74	93	87	79	100	69

   a Maxine estimates that 70% of the blocks are in good condition.
Imran estimates that nearer to 90% are in good condition.
Use the table to see who is closest. Show all of your working.

   b Use the table to estimate how many blocks Imran can expect
to be damaged if they ordered 6000 blocks to build the school.

   c If they need 6000 undamaged blocks how many should
they order?

6 **a** Calculate the length of the rafters of the roof.

   b To cope with heavy rainstorms, the roof must
have a 'pitch' or angle of at least 35°.
Will the schoolhouse roof will be safe in the rain?

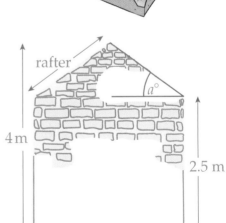

Greg and Wah Wah are laying the path.

1 A pallet of paving blocks is delivered.
The surface of each block is 10 cm by 20 cm.

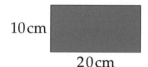

10 cm

20 cm

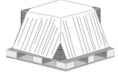

There are 75 blocks on a pallet.

a What area will one pallet cover?

b They have to cover 7 m².
How many pallets will they need to order?

They try out some different patterns for the paths.

2 This is Wah Wah's pattern.

She counts the tiles and says they have 8 yellow tiles
and 160 red tiles.

If they use all the yellow tiles, how many red tiles will
they have left over?

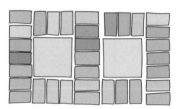

3 Greg has his own idea using red blocks and green slabs.

BLOCK

SLAB

20 cm   750 mm

a How many green slabs will need to be laid before the
pattern begins to repeat itself?

b If the path is 12 m long, how many times will the pattern
repeat?

c How many blocks and slabs will need to
be bought?

d What percentage of the path is made up of the green slabs?

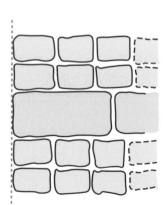

4 Greg and Wah Wah notice that this basic shape on Jacob's shirt tessellates to form this pattern.

Using isometric paper, make your own copy of the shape and show that it tessellates.

5 Wah Wah finds a catalogue containing paving stones in the shape of regular polygons.

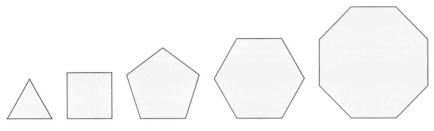

a Greg says only three of these shapes will tessellate, is he right?

b Wah Wah says she can make a tessellation using a pair of shapes. Sketch a pattern that she could use.

c Is it possible to make a tessellation using three of the shapes?

> Remember that the angles at a point must add up to 360°.

6 Maxine is planning another path made from arcs of circles with differing radii.

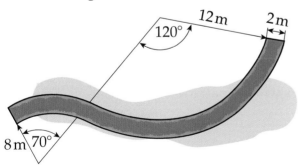

a The path is 2 m wide, so she bases her calculations on the centre line of the path. What is the length of the path?

b The cost of the path is $10.25 per metre for the first 5 m and $9.50 for the rest. To the nearest $5.00 what is the total cost?

The students are going to help make a basketball court.

1 Josh makes the basket by bending a metal strip into a circle.

22.5 cm

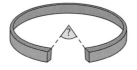
120 cm

The radius of the ring has to be 22.5 cm.
Josh makes a mistake and only cuts a 120 cm length of metal strip.

a What is the radius of the circle made by this strip?

b Calculate the percentage error in the cutting of the strip.

Use π = 3.14

Maxine straightens the strip and bends it into a ring of the correct radius.

With a radius of 22.5 cm, the strip is too short and makes only an arc, not the complete circle.

c To the nearest 5°, what angle is made by the arc of the circle?

2 Ella sinks the basket poles into wet concrete.

To support them whilst the concrete dries she anchors them to the ground with 6 m long wires. She connects the wires 3 m up the pole.

a To the nearest 10 cm calculate the distance of the anchor from the pole.

b What angle do the wires make with the ground?

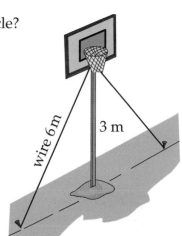
wire 6 m

3 m

When they have completed the basketball court the students organise a celebratory tournament.

They play the local school team.
Here are the records of their performances.

Number of baskets per game	Interval mid-point	Local team Frequency	Local team Cumulative frequency	Local team Estimated total	Visiting team Frequency	Visiting team Cumulative frequency	Visiting team Estimated total
0 to 4	2	0	0	0	2		
5 to 9	7	1	1	7	1		
10 to 14		1	2		3		
15 to 19		1			3		
20 to 24		2			6		
25 to 29		2			5		
30 to 34		3			5		
35 to 39		8			4		
40 to 44		9			1		
45 to 49		3			0		
	Totals						

3 a Copy and complete the above table and the accompanying cumulative frequency graph.

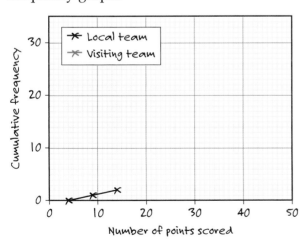

b Using the above results and graph complete the table of statistics.

c Using the three averages, which team was the stronger side?

The school helps to grow food for the village.
They fence off a plot of land 20 m × 20 m.

The head teacher says he wants to divide the
field into five sections.

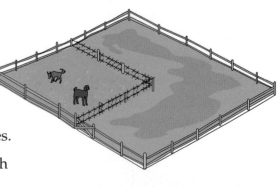

One quarter of the field is reserved for goats.
The rest is divided up into four congruent shapes.

1 a Work with a partner to find the shape which
will tessellate for the four crops.

b Make a sketch of the shape and show its
measurements.

c What is the area given to each crop?

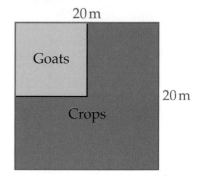

2 The field is bounded by a fence.
Greg drives posts into the ground 2 m apart and
joins them with two cross-bars.

a Greg has ordered 38 posts to fence the large field.
Is this the right number?
Show your calculations.

b Construct a formula to connect the length of fencing in
metres and the number posts needed.
Use *p* for the number of posts used and *m* for the length
of fencing.

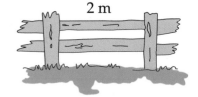

c Show that your formula works for part **a**.

3 Greg, Maxine and Josh start to construct the fence.
They estimate that it will take them ten days.
This is too long to wait; the head teacher needs the fence
completed in four days.

a How many more workers will be needed to grant the head
teacher his wish?

b What does your calculation assume?

4 Here is another rectangular plot of land which will be used for keeping hens safely.
Its area is 36 m².
One of its sides has to be 7 m shorter than the other.

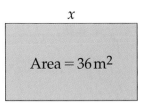

x

Area = 36 m²

   a If the longer side is x metres long, write an expression using x for the shorter side.

   b Hence construct an expression for the area of the field.

   c Solve the equation and use your answer to find the dimensions of the plot.

5 Josh and Wah Wah are preparing a planter for a flower display.
The shape of the planter is a prism with a trapezoidal cross-section.

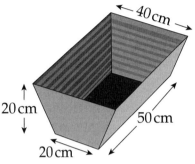

40 cm
20 cm
50 cm
20 cm

   a Find the volume of the planter.

   b The compost is delivered in a 72 litre bag.
When the planter is filled, what percentage of the compost remains?

6 Imran puts 3 bags of soil and 2 bags of compost onto the weighing scales and then sits on top of the bags.
The total weight is 146 kg.

Imran puts 4 bags of soil and 4 bags of compost onto the weighing scales and then sits on top of the bags.
The total weight is 195 kg.

Imran puts 1 bag of soil and 3 bags of compost onto the weighing scales and then sits on top of the bags.
The total weight is 123 kg.

Calculate the weights of the two types of bags and Imran.

15

Assessment criteria

- Develop and use alternative methods — Level 8

- Reflect on the approach used to solve a mathematical problem — Level 8

- Combine known results and problem solving strategies to solve complex problems — Level 8

- Use algebra to express results precisely — Level 8

- Comment constructively on results and the methods used to obtain them — Level 8

- Distinguish between a practical demonstration and a proof; recognise the importance of any assumptions that you make and the effect of changing them — Level 8

- Solve demanding problems and check solutions; explore connections between different parts of mathematics; find more general solutions — Level 7

- Explain why you chose to solve a given problems in a particular way — Level 7

- Justify generalisations, arguments and solutions — Level 7

- Recognise the difference between a mathematical explanation and experimental evidence — Level 7

Check in and Summary answers

1

Check in
1 a i Start with 3, add 3 to get the next term. **ii** 12

b i Start with 2, add 5 to get the next term. **ii** 12

c i Start with 4, add 3 to get the next term. **ii** 10, 13

d i Start with 21, subtract 4 to get the next term. **ii** 17, 13

e i Start with 5, add 8 to get the next term. **ii** 13, 29

f i Start with 50, subtract 6 to get the next term. **ii** 44, 32

2 a $y = 2$ **b** $x = 4$ **c** $y = x$
d $y = x + 2$ **e** $y = 4 - 2x$

Summary
2 a 28   **b** $-1, 0, \frac{1}{9}$

2

Check in
1 a i 10   **ii** 13.0   **iii** 12.973

b i 340   **ii** 342.9   **iii** 342.914

2 a $\frac{13}{21}$ **b** $\frac{6}{35}$ **c** $\frac{8}{15}$ **d** $\frac{5}{6}$

3 a £36   **b** 16.8 kg
c £64.80   **d** £337.75

4 a 3:4   **b** 13:5   **c** 7:30

5 a 560p   **b** 165 g

Summary
2 $\frac{2}{6} = \frac{1}{3} = 0.3333 = 33\%$ to the nearest per cent.

3

Check in
1 a $a = 54°, b = 180°$ **b** $c = 72°, d = 72°$
c $e = 106°$

2 B and C

3 A (1, 2), B (-1, 0), C (-1, -2), D (0, -2), E (2, -1)

Summary
2 No. There are three possible triangles because the 5 cm side could be opposite the 20° angle, the 60° angle or the 100° angle.

4

Check in
1 a $24x + 120$ **b** $20a + 27$
c $5x^2 - 20x$ **d** $10y - 5$

2 a 3   **b** 7

3 $3(2x + 7) = 57, x = 6$

4 $x^2 + x + 5$

Summary
2 $x = 1.5, y = 5$

5

Check in
1 1.1 cars (1 dp)

2

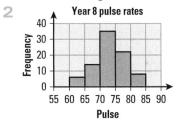

Summary
2 a Negative
b The gradient should be negative, but $y = x + 40$ has a positive gradient

6

Check in
1 a 1430   **b** 35   **c** 36.1
d 300   **e** 6000

2 a 37.68 cm   **b** 113.04 cm³

3 a 236 cm²   **b** 240 cm³

Summary
2 Area, area, volume

Check in

1 a 0.038 **b** 27.5 **c** 0.045

2 a 27 **b** 32 **c** 1 000 000 **d** 625

3 a 17 **b** 0.74

4 a 688.8 **b** 148.58

  c 23.5 **d** 45.9 (1dp)

5 a $\frac{11}{13} = 0.846...$ **b** $\frac{97}{50} = 1.94$

  c $\frac{2}{3} = 0.666...$

6 a $2^2 \times 5^2$ **b** $3^2 \times 7^2$

7 a 4.472

  b Because it is rounded and most
     square roots are irrational.

Summary

2 a Odd, because odd $\times$ odd $\times$
     odd $\times$ …….. is always odd.

  b 3^{200}

Check in

1 a

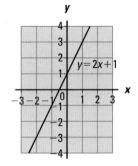

b

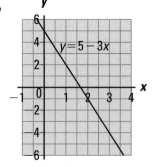

c

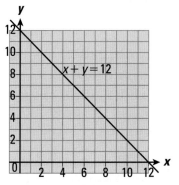

d

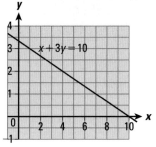

2 a $x^2 + x - 3 = 9$ $x^3 - 2x = 21$
     $3x^2 = x^3 = 27$ $(3x)^2 = 81$

  b $x^3 = -8$ $x^3 - 2x = -4$ $x^2 + x - 3 = -1$
     $3x^2 = 12$ $(3x)^2 = 36$

3 a Gradient = 2, y-axis intercept (0, 1)

  b Gradient = -3, y-axis intercept (0, 5)

  c Gradient = 3, y-axis intercept (0, 4)

  d Gradient = $-\frac{1}{3}$, y-axis intercept (0, 5)

4 a $x = 3, y = 2$ **b** $x = -1, y = 4$

Summary

2 a $\frac{6-1}{10-0} = 0.5$ **b** $y = 0.5x + 1$

  c $y = 0.5x + c$

Check in

1 a $\frac{1}{3}$ (two square numbers, 1 and 4)

  b $\frac{2}{3}$

2 $\frac{6}{78} = \frac{1}{13}$

Summary

2 $\frac{1}{36}$

10

Check in

1 a, b

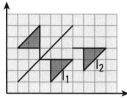

2 195 cm, 80 cm

3

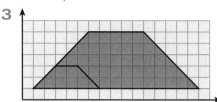

4 53 cm

Summary

2 a 8

b Any length and width such that $l = 2.5w$ or $w = 2.5l$

11

Check in

1 a $3x$ **b** $9y$ **c** $7a$

d $5b - 2$ **e** $4p$ **f** $a + 5b$

g $x^2 + 2x$ **h** $y^2 + 6y$

2 a 42 cm   **b** 46 cm

3 a $2x + 10$ **b** $7p - 21$ **c** $10k + 5$

d $12 - 3y$ **e** $x^2 + 2x$ **f** $ab - 6a$

g $4p^2 + 4pq$ **h** $15t - 6t^2$

Summary

2 a $e = \frac{P}{2} - f$ **b** $d = c - 2r$

Check in

1 Angles, 295°, 22°, 33°, 10°

Breakdown of Westminster MPs

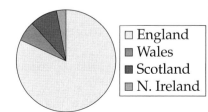

☐ England
▨ Wales
▩ Scotland
▤ N. Ireland

---

2 a

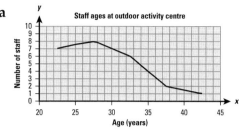

b the modal class is $25 \leq x < 30$.

Summary

2 a $28 - 22 = 6$

b $65 - 56 = 9$

c Yes. The IQR is smaller in Year 11, 18 versus 33, though the range in the same, 70.

Check in

1 a Cylinder

b Square-based pyramid

c Hexagonal prism

d Cone

2 a $a = 125°$, $b = 55°$

b $b = 40°$, $c = 140°$

3 a $a = 2.5$ cm   **b** $b = 24$ cm

Summary

2 $\sin 5.5° = 0.096$

but $5.2 \div 56 = 0.093$

Check in

1 a £235.84   **b** 43.3125 kg

2 a 8.9%   **b** 1.47

3 a 30   **b** 0.08   **c** 3000

d 4×10^2 **e** 5×10^{-2}

4 a 5 m   **b** 12.1

c 3678 kg   **d** 29.5

Summary

2 a 1920   **b** 4.5×10^4

Index